CHRISTIAN HUMANISM AND THE REFORMATION

CHRISTIAN HUMANISM AND THE REFORMATION

SELECTED WRITINGS OF
ERASMUS

WITH HIS LIFE BY BEATUS RHENANUS AND
A BIOGRAPHICAL SKETCH BY THE EDITOR

Edited by
JOHN C. OLIN

Third Edition

FORDHAM UNIVERSITY PRESS
NEW YORK
1987

First edition 1965
Second edition 1975
Third edition 1987

Printed in the United States of America

CONTENTS

ABBREVIATIONS

Allen   *Opus epistolarum Des. Erasmi Roterodami.* Edd. P. S. Allen, H. M. Allen, and H. W. Garrod. 12 vols. Oxford, 1906–1958.

CWE   *Collected Works of Erasmus.* In progress. Toronto and Buffalo, 1974—.

LB   *Erasmi Opera Omnia.* Ed. Johannes Clericus. 10 vols. Leiden, 1703–1706.

Nichols   *The Epistles of Erasmus.* Trans. and ed. Francis Morgan Nichols. 3 vols. London, 1901–1918.

PREFACE

This volume is a revised and amplified edition of a work bearing the same title that I first published as a Harper Torchbook in 1965. It was subsequently republished with slight revision (and a generous Foreword by Craig Thompson) by Fordham University Press in 1975. This present version, however, includes two major changes and additions. I have replaced my former introductory essay on "Erasmus and Reform" with a short biography of Erasmus that I originally wrote for *European Writers*,[1] and I have added as Selection X the translation of Erasmus' Letter to Carondelet, the preface to his 1523 edition of St. Hilary of Poitiers, that first appeared in my *Six Essays on Erasmus*.[2] I have also expanded the notes and updated the bibliographical references. My object, of course, remains the same: to acquaint the reader at first hand with the life and thought of a truly central figure in the religious drama of the early sixteenth century, and to clarify both the character of Erasmian reform and the role of Erasmus in the religious crisis. I hope that this new edition will more amply serve that purpose.

My biographical Introduction as well as Erasmus' own autobiographical sketch (Selection I) and the first biography of the great humanist by his friend and colleague Beatus Rhenanus (Selection II) set the stage for the selected writings that follow, and I have keyed all the Selections in this volume into my Introduction. Erasmus' *Compendium vitae* and Beatus' Life of Erasmus, it should be noted, are prime documentary sources for his life. In understanding Erasmus, the tone and thrust in Beatus' Life—Erasmus as Christian scholar and reformer—are especially interesting. The emphasis in the other eight Selections is also on his reform aims and on his position in the religious controversy that in his age disrupted the Church. They cover the years 1515 to 1523, the decisive years in the great Reformation crisis, and they accurately reveal, I believe, Erasmus' response to the problem of reform and within that context to the widespread controversy that so rapidly and dramatically developed. This is not the whole story of

Erasmus, but it is the heart of his story and the most essential part; not only is it important in terms of Reformation history, but it has a deeper and more enduring relevance. Erasmus had a message for his own times, but his Christian humanism and idealism also speak to ours. Like his close and dear friend Thomas More, his life and work offer a perennial subject for reflection and inspiration.

Nearly all the Selections were newly translated for the original edition, and for some it marked their first appearance in English. I am particularly mindful of the help rendered by the late John Bush, s.j. in the translation of the Letter to Martin Dorp. At this time also I want to thank again my close friend and colleague Professor James F. Brady for his expert collaboration in the translation of the Letter to Carondelet. Further information about texts and translations will be found in the footnotes.

I dedicated the first edition to my children. I would like to dedicate this third edition once again to them and also now to their families and especially to my grandchildren. May the *bonae literae* and the *veritas evangelica* which inspired Erasmus inspire them as well.

JOHN C. OLIN
Professor Emeritus

Fordham University
12 July 1986

NOTES

1. *European Writers: The Middle Ages and the Renaissance,* 2 vols. (New York: Scribners, 1983), II 571–93.

2. *Six Essays on Erasmus, and a Translation of Erasmus' Letter to Carondelet, 1523* (New York: Fordham University Press, 1979), pp. 93–120.

ILLUSTRATIONS

1 A page (fol. S₃ʳ) from the 1515 Froben edition of *The Praise of Folly* with a pen sketch of Erasmus by Hans Holbein. The enlarged detail shows that Erasmus is writing the *Adagia*. This and other marginal drawings by Holbein were made in a copy of the book belonging to Myconius (Oswald Geisshüssler), a schoolmaster at Basel and friend of Erasmus. See p. 22; Betty Radice, "Holbein's Marginal Illustrations to the *Praise of Folly*," *Erasmus in English*, 7 (1975), 9–17.

2 Quentin Metsys' portrait of Erasmus, in the Royal Collection at Hampton Court. It was painted at Antwerp in 1517 and was part of a diptych sent as a gift to Thomas More that September; the other portrait was of Peter Gilles (Pieter Gillis), town secretary in Antwerp. The three books on the shelves labeled on their edges are The New Testament, Lucian, and Jerome, a triad that practically comprises the main inspirations of Erasmus. There is controversy whether this portrait or the following one, which is in the Galleria Nazionale in Rome, is the original painting by Metsys. See pp. 22–23; Margaret Mann Phillips, "The Mystery of the Metsys Portrait," *Erasmus in English*, 7 (1975), 18–21; Lorne Campbell et al., "Quentin Matsys, Desiderius Erasmus, Pieter Gillis and Thomas More," *The Burlington Magazine*, 120 (November 1978), 716–24.

3 Quentin Metsys' portrait of Erasmus, in the Galleria Nazionale d'Arte Antica, Palazzo Barberini, Rome. Note especially the absence of titles on any of the books and of Erasmus' handwriting. See the above note for further comments.

4 An engraving of Erasmus by Albrecht Dürer dated 1526. The Greek inscription reads: "His writings give a better picture." See Andrée Hayum, "Dürer's Portrait of Erasmus and the *Ars Typographorum*," *Renaissance Quarterly*, 38, No. 4 (Winter 1985), 650–87.

5 The first page of the *Paraclesis* from the 1522 Froben edition of Erasmus' New Testament (from the copy at Duane Library, Fordham University). See pp. 18–19 and Selection IV.

6 The title page of Erasmus' edition of St. Hilary of Poitiers published by Froben in 1523. It was dedicated to Jean de Carondelet, and the presentation copy, which is in the Houghton Library, Harvard University, bears Erasmus' autograph inscription "To the Most Reverend lord, Lord Jean Carondelet, Archbishop of Palermo, chief counselor of the imperial court." See Selection X.

7 The portrait of Jean de Carondelet by Jan Cornelisz Vermeyen, before 1525, in The Brooklyn Museum. See Selection X.

8 The opening page of St. John's Gospel in the 1522 Froben edition of Erasmus' New Testament (the Fordham University copy). Note that Erasmus changed the beginning of the Vulgate text's *In principio erat verbum* to *In principio erat sermo*, a significant but very controversial alteration that he subsequently abandoned. On this, see Marjorie O'Rourke Boyle, *Erasmus on Language and Method in Theology* (Toronto, 1977), esp. pp. 3–31.

The Illustrations are between pages 86 and 87.

INTRODUCTION

Erasmus,
a Biographical Sketch

"He was born in Rotterdam on the vigil of Simon and Jude." So begins the short sketch of his life that Desiderius Erasmus once composed (Selection I). He then tells a sad romantic story about his parents. His mother had been left with child by a young man named Gerard, who had fled to Italy when his family blocked their marriage. After his birth, Erasmus continues, Gerard was sent word that the girl he had sought to marry was dead; and out of grief he became a priest. The deception was soon discovered when he returned home, but he remained a faithful priest and at the same time was solicitous for the education and welfare of his son.

It is a very touching tale, the precision of which, however, is open to doubt. Erasmus was deeply sensitive to the illegitimacy of his birth and may have depicted the circumstances of his origin and background in slightly fanciful terms. The memoir itself is not a fabrication. Although the liaison between his mother and Gerard may have been more commonplace (Erasmus had an older brother, Peter), the basic facts are true enough. He entered life under the bar sinister in a small country town in Holland, then an outlying and watery part of the territories of the dukes of Burgundy and soon after his birth to become part of the vast Hapsburg domain. His birthday, the vigil of the Apostles Simon and Jude, was October 27, but the exact year is uncertain. Erasmus was always vague on chronology. The year 1466 is most probable, although 1467 and 1469 are strong contenders. He was christened Erasmus, which he later expanded into the more elegant Desiderius Erasmus Roterodamus, or Desiderius Erasmus of Rotterdam. The brief autobiography speaks of large families on his mother's and especially his father's side, yet no relatives or their descendants ever appear in Erasmus' story. In view of his later renown, that feature is surprising.

The education that helped form a famous author or scholar or thinker is always important to a biographer, and in Erasmus' case much is made of an influence that soon bore upon him. After Erasmus attended elementary school at Gouda, his father sent him in his ninth year to a well-known school attached to the church of St. Lebuin in Deventer. His mother accompanied him. There he remained for several years—from about 1475 to 1484—until his mother, and a short time later his father, died of the plague. The influence, or rather influences, to which he was exposed in these formative years were the *devotio moderna* and the new humanism or classical learning that was making its way out of Renaissance Italy. Erasmus' mature thought is sometimes viewed as a fusion, an amalgam, of these two dissimilar currents. However one may interpret the evidence pertaining to this early time and place, certain facts stand firm. Deventer was the original center of that movement of simple and practical piety which we call the *devotio moderna* and which expressed itself in the work and spirit of the Brethren of the Common Life and the Augustinian monks of the Windesheim congregation. Thomas à Kempis' *Imitation of Christ* (ca. 1425) is the great masterpiece of the spiritual life that emerged from the movement. The Brethren engaged in various activities: tending the sick, copying manuscripts—their *scriptoria* are celebrated—teaching school. Some of their members staffed St. Lebuin's. Erasmus was critical of the instruction there, but two masters, he tells us, began to introduce some better literature. One was Alexander Hegius, a disciple of the first great German humanist, Rudolph Agricola, who became headmaster toward the end of Erasmus' stay; the other was Brother John Zinthius, who was much taken by Erasmus' talent and promise. The better literature they imparted was the Latin classics in their purer form. On one occasion the famous Agricola himself gave a lecture at the school, which deeply impressed Erasmus.

After his father's death, Erasmus came under the care of three guardians whom his father had designated. According to the autobiography, they abused their trust. They poorly managed the legacy his father had left, sent him to a dismal school run by the Brethren at 's Hertogenbosch where he wasted nearly three years, and then pressured him (and his brother) to enter the monastic life. This last step came to be the cause of much bitterness and regret on Erasmus' part, though at the time the attractions of a particular monastery of Augustinians at Steyn overcame his resistance. He was deceived, so he claims, but he remained at Steyn, professed his vows, and was ordained a priest by the bishop of Utrecht in 1492. Meanwhile, he continued to cultivate his now lively interest in the Latin classics and the new humanism. His letters from this period reveal a wide range of reading, a marked literary sensitivity, and warm friendships with several of his fellow monks.[1] Erasmus may never have had a genuine vocation to the religious life, but he seems to have adapted himself without great difficulty at this time and to have profited from the opportunities for study and companionship that the monastery afforded. The lineaments of the future author and scholar now began to appear, and the humanist ideal of *bonae literae*, which ever remained his guiding light, now first found expression.

Two very disparate works have their origin in this early monastic period of his life: an essay, *De contemptu mundi*, praising the monastic life, and the *Antibarbari*, a defense of classical learning for Christians against its ignorant and narrow-minded opponents. These works were not published until many years later (*De contemptu mundi* in 1522, the *Antibarbari* in 1520, when there were five editions), and by then major changes and additions had occurred. A final chapter, for instance, was attached to *De contemptu mundi* that took a very critical view of contemporary monasticism and nullified many of the arguments advanced in the earlier part of the essay. The whole work is somewhat puzzling. The *Antibarbari*, on the other hand, develops an issue and a theme ever present and foremost in the mind of Erasmus. The early version was recast into dialogue form around 1494 and later expanded still further, but the polemical purpose remained the same; from the start, the work was an affirmation of humanism, which Erasmus came more and more ardently to represent, and a defense of *bonae literae* against its enemies.

Erasmus left the monastery in 1493. He was then about twenty-seven years old, and the wider world now beckoned to his sensitive and eager spirit. He had been offered the post of secretary to Henry of Bergen, bishop of Cambrai, who wanted a good Latinist for his journey to Rome to obtain a cardinal's hat. It was a splendid opportunity for the extremely talented young monk, and Erasmus received the necessary permissions from his superiors and the bishop of Utrecht to join the entourage of this new patron. The journey to Rome unfortunately did not take place, but Erasmus was retained nevertheless, and his service with Henry of Bergen was not without its rewards. He found a new and valued friend in Jacob Batt, town clerk at Bergen and later tutor in the household of Anne of Veere, and he discovered and devoured the works of St. Augustine. This latter event should be stressed, for the patristic character of Erasmus' thought was strong and is more keenly appreciated now than it was formerly. He already knew and treasured the letters of the other great Latin Father, St. Jerome, and now the powerful Augustine came more fully within his ken. The influence of these two scholars and theologians of the early Church must be added to the fascination and force of the classical humanism that so engaged him, if we would fully appreciate his intellectual growth. His familiarity with St. Augustine's *De doctrina Christiana*, for example, is evident in the revision of the *Antibarbari* he undertook at this time.

Erasmus did not go to Rome, but in the late summer of 1495 he did go to Paris. At the urging of Batt, the bishop of Cambrai approved and promised support for Erasmus' theological studies at the University of Paris. "He thus became a Scotist in the college of Montaigu," wrote his first biographer and a close friend and colleague, Beatus Rhenanus (Selection II); but it was not for long. Erasmus found living at Montaigu, whose principal, John Standonck, was an austere reformer, too hard to bear. The bad eggs and squalid quarters, he felt, permanently injured his health. As for the arid and disputatious theology he confronted—it was the dialectical theology of the medieval schools, or scholasticism, as it is generically called—he shrank from its study with aversion and disgust. It had little in common with the learning and eloquence of the ancients, and he saw nothing of value or virtue in it. He tells us that he soon would have been branded a heretic if he had continued on that path. This antipathy to scholastic theology found constant expression in the writings of Erasmus and is one of the keys to understanding his life's work. His chief aim, very simply put, was to replace that brand of theology with what he deemed the genuine theology of the early Christian Church.[2] This goal became the most integral part of the revival of letters and learning Erasmus sought to achieve.

But meanwhile more immediate concerns prevailed during these early days in Paris. Because of illness or the plague he returned several times to the Low Countries. When funds from his bishop failed to arrive, he supported himself by tutoring private students in Latin literature and style. We know that he had two German students from Lübeck and three well-to-do Englishmen, including William Blount, Lord Mountjoy, who in 1499 invited Erasmus to visit England. From these teaching labors eventually derived some of his most popular writings. His famous *Colloquies* has its origin in conversational Latin exercises he composed at this time, and the prototype of other educational materials and manuals dates from this period: *De copia verborum ac rerum* and *De ratione studii*, both first published in 1512, and *De conscribendis epistolis*, first published in 1522. Education based on the humanities, that is, on the literature and liberal arts of antiquity, is the very essence, indeed the meaning, of Renaissance humanism. (The classical term *humanitas* is the root of our words "humanities" and "humanism"; the term implies the education and training most in keeping with our full human nature and most advantageous to our intellectual and moral growth.) Thus in his early occupation as a teacher, modest though it was, Erasmus was in his proper sphere, and the texts that came out of this experience are among his most important contributions. They were to serve schoolmasters and educators for generations.

Erasmus also entered the threshold of the Paris humanist circle during these years and, in a sense, began his career as a man of letters. He made the acquaintance of the distinguished French scholar and general of the Trinitarians, Robert Gaguin, and by a stroke of good fortune was asked to contribute a commendatory letter to Gaguin's history of France, *De origine et gestis Francorum compendium*, which was published in the fall of 1495. The printer required such a piece to fill the blank pages at the end of his edition. It was Erasmus' first published writing and his first association with the new art of printing. The appearance of his name and handiwork in the company of Gaguin's brought him suddenly to the attention of a wider public.

In May 1499 Erasmus went to England. The visit was an important event, perhaps a decisive one, in his life. The biographer Johan Huizinga calls it "a period of inward ripening" and stresses the influence of friends he met there, John Colet in particular, in sharpening his resolve and helping him set his life's goal.[3] Others have emphasized the influence of Renaissance Neoplatonism on him at this time through the mediation of his English friends; many of them had been to Italy and had absorbed elements of the Platonic revival.[4] Be that as it may, Erasmus loved England, was charmed by the pretty girls and their custom of bestowing kisses at every turn (as he jokingly wrote to a friend in Paris), and was even more impressed by the flowering of learning and the zealous scholars he found there. He stayed about eight months, until the beginning of the next year. He visited Mountjoy's estate at Greenwich, where it appears he first met the young and brilliant Thomas More, then but twenty-one or twenty-two, who would become his dearest friend. On that occasion he and More walked to nearby Eltham Palace, where the children of the royal family were residing, and Erasmus was introduced to the boy who ten years later would become Henry VIII. He also spent time in London, where he met the Greek scholars William Grocyn and Thomas Linacre, and in the fall he was at Oxford, where his close friendship with Colet began.

John Colet, the son of a former lord mayor of London, was the same age as Erasmus but his senior in point of view of serious purpose and settled aim. He had traveled and studied widely, and when Erasmus met him he was lecturing on the Epistles of St. Paul at Oxford, where he had gone in 1496, soon after his return from Italy. These were memorable lectures, and Erasmus was inspired. When he listened to Colet, so he said, he seemed to hear Plato himself. In expounding St. Paul, Colet used the method of the humanists as well as the insight of the Platonists, and he gave his presentation a moral and theological relevance that struck Erasmus deeply. He commended Colet for doing battle with the "squalid mob" of modern theologians and attempting to restore the true theology of the ancient church—the *vetus ac vera theologia*, as he called it. Colet wanted him to assist in the task and lecture on the Old Testament at Oxford, but Erasmus, conscious of his present inadequacy, declined the invitation. "As soon as I feel myself to possess the necessary stamina and strength," he declared, "I shall come personally to join your party and will give devoted, if not distinguished, service in the defense of theology."[5] And so he did.

He also had an interesting discussion with Colet regarding the nature of Christ's agony in the garden of Gethsemane, which can be followed in letters they exchanged at this time. Erasmus defended the traditional view that Christ's fear of suffering and death proceeded from his human nature, whereas Colet claimed that Christ drew back at that awesome hour out of concern about the crime that would be committed. Not long after, Erasmus published the exchange in the form of a scholarly debate. It is his first theological writing. It may also be worth noting that Thomas More's last work, written in the Tower of London shortly before his execution in 1535, was on this self-same theme of Christ's passion, though it is a profounder meditation than the Colet–Erasmus debate.

As Erasmus was leaving England on his way back to Paris in early 1500, an unfortunate incident occurred—one that he was long in forgetting because of the personal distress it caused. A customs official at the port of Dover confiscated a modest sum in gold coin he had accumulated to support himself in his studies in the immediate future. Both More and Mountjoy had assured him that he could take the money out, but his young friends were wrong in their understanding of what was permissible under the law (More was not yet a lawyer). The loss was a blow and left him in poverty. It had a bright side, however. It forced him rather hastily to bring out his first book, the *Adagiorum collectanea,* a collection of over 800 Latin proverbs drawn from the classics, which he hoped would be of interest and use to students. Greatly expanded in subsequent years, it had many editions during his lifetime and afterward.

Erasmus' return to the Continent following his English visit and the first publication of the *Adages* in 1500 is a convenient point at which to pause and signal a division in our narrative. The early and more formative phase of his life was over, and a highly active and very prolific phase now began. A period of uncertainty had ended, and a time of achievement and renown lay ahead. His books and editions started to appear in increasing numbers; his reputation and his influence grew; his fame reached a pinnacle attained by few other writers or scholars in European history.

This is not to say that suddenly all was smooth sailing and halcyon days. Far from it. The years immediately after Erasmus' return to Paris were very difficult. He was poor, unsettled, fearful of the plague, obsessed with the need to master Greek. He moved about considerably. He was in Orléans for part of 1500, and in the following spring he left Paris for the Low Countries. He again visited his native Holland and then stayed for a while at the castle of Tournehem in Artois, which belonged to Anne of Veere, a temporary patroness; at nearby St. Omer; and finally at Louvain. But though his movements were somewhat erratic, his scholarly aims were fixed. He was determined to learn Greek, and he had set himself the ambitious task of emending the corrupt text of Saint Jerome and of restoring true theology. The three goals were closely connected in his mind, for a knowledge of Greek was essential in correcting Jerome and studying Scripture, and the one was the representative par excellence and the other the very fountainhead of the true theology Erasmus hoped to restore. His efforts were now directed untiringly toward this end.

"The revival of a genuine science of theology," as Erasmus phrased it in one of his letters, was certainly his basic aim as a humanist scholar.[6] It was not, however, his only concern, nor did scholarly pursuits blind him to the more practical questions of the Christian life and the problems of personal and social reform. Scholarship for Erasmus was never an end in itself, but was intended to conduct men to a better life. Learning was to lead to virtue, scholarship to God; and thus the restoration of theology was to be the means toward the revival of a more vital Christianity. Erasmus, in short, was a moralist and reformer, and a treatise he began to write in the fall of 1501 clearly sets forth the essential elements of this aspect of his thought.

When he was at Tournehem, he was asked to write something that might have a salutary effect on a man of unruly temperament and dissolute conduct (who is said to have been a German armament maker by the name of Johann Poppenruyter), and with this incentive he composed a work that eventually became one of his most celebrated—the *Enchiridion militis Christiani*. The title means the handbook—or dagger—of the Christian soldier, the Greek word ἐγχειρίδιον having been used as a title by St. Augustine for one of his treatises. Erasmus' work was first published in Antwerp in 1503 and had numerous editions as well as translations from the original Latin thereafter. (Erasmus, it must be remembered, wrote in Latin, but translations of many of his works were made into the vernaculars. William Tyndale made an early English translation of the *Enchiridion* that was published in 1533, and St. Ignatius Loyola read a Spanish version at Alcalá in 1526. Even the Aztecs had it available in their tongue.)

The work is a guide to Christian attitudes and behavior as Erasmus perceived them. It embodies what we may call his spirituality as well as his reformist thought, for, as Huizinga points out, he "had for the first time said the things which he had most at heart."[7] Developing the theme that life is a constant warfare against sin, he explains the weapons that the Christian must employ and the rules and precepts that must govern his unending struggle. Two fundamental and related ideas run throughout the book: one is that the great weapon of the Christian is the knowledge of Holy Scripture (the first weapon is prayer); the other is that religion is not primarily a matter of outward signs and devotions but rather of interior disposition and the inward love of God and neighbor. These views became Erasmus' master thoughts, and we shall see them reflected in all his work. The second concept, which has been interpreted as excessively spiritualizing and even Platonizing the Christian religion to the detriment of more formal observances, is especially prominent. Its implications as well as its source are the subject of some debate. Erasmus derives it from Scripture—"It is the spirit that gives life"—and he urges the Christian soldier to the zealous study of the word of God. As preliminary training, he suggests that reading the ancient pagan authors may be helpful. He views the Platonists as very close to the Gospel pattern, but "any truth you come upon at any place is Christ's," he says, reiterating a not uncommon patristic maxim that Étienne Gilson has called "the perpetual charter of Christian humanism."[8] And in interpreting Scripture, he commends St. Paul and the ancient Fathers, not the modern theologians who stick to the letter and miss the deeper meaning of the sacred text.

When Erasmus was composing or about to compose the *Enchiridion*, he met at St. Omer a Franciscan friar, Jehan Vitrier, who greatly influenced the work. In fact, Vitrier ranks with Colet in the impact he had on Erasmus, and many years later Erasmus gave impressive testimony to this in a letter he wrote to one of Martin Luther's disciples (Selection IX). He sent him a sketch of both men's lives—"two men of our era whom I consider to have been true and sincere Christians"—as examples to consider and imitate. Vitrier loved Scripture and the early Fathers. He knew the letters of St. Paul by heart, and he admired above all the ancient Greek Father Origen. Though in a monastery, he was very critical of a religion consisting of rites and ordinances of human invention. He stood, in short, for much of what we read in the *Enchiridion*, and Erasmus tells us how thoroughly he approved of the little book. The imprint of Origen, who became one of Erasmus' great favorites, is likewise very marked in the *Enchiridion*.[9]

During these years of residence in the Low Countries, Erasmus made an important discovery. In the summer of 1504, while browsing in the library of a Premonstratensian monastery near Louvain, he found the manuscript of Lorenzo Valla's *Annotationes* on the New Testament, a collection of grammatical and philological notes wherein the Latin Vulgate text is collated with and corrected by the Greek. Valla was a famous Italian humanist with whose work Erasmus had long been acquainted, though not with this specific one. When he was a young monk at Steyn he had read and been inspired by Valla's *Elegantiae linguae Latinae*, a treatise on the pure Latin tongue and a work that perhaps more than any other helped spread the classical humanism of the Renaissance outside Italy. The discovery of this new manuscript led Erasmus to turn his attention to the task of emending the New Testament itself—a task that became a major part of his program to restore theology. As a first step, so to speak, he arranged for the printing of the *Annotationes* by Josse Badius in Paris in March 1505. It foreshadowed the great edition of the New Testament he brought out in 1516.

In the autumn of 1505, Erasmus made his second trip to England. He was drawn by the promise or hope of a benefice, and, of course, he had many friends there—Mountjoy; Colet, who was now dean of Saint Paul's in London; Grocyn; More. He visited them all, and he made several new friends in the course of his travels—John Fisher, bishop of Rochester; and, most impressively, William Warham, archbishop of Canterbury and lord chancellor of the realm. Erasmus presented the latter with his Latin translations of two of Euripides' plays, *Hecuba* and *Iphigenia in Aulis* (they were published the following year by Badius in Paris). He had attained his command of Greek. He saw a good deal of More, who was now an active young lawyer in London and very recently married. More delighted in the Greek satirist Lucian, Erasmus tells us, and together he and More translated into Latin several of Lucian's dialogues (which Badius also published in 1506). Erasmus himself was enamored of Lucian. "How he mixes the serious with banter, how laughingly he speaks the truth," he exclaimed. "No comedy, no satire can be compared with his."[10] Erasmus' own *Praise of Folly* was to become its peer.

His stay in England was suddenly interrupted in June 1506 when an opportunity to go to Italy was offered. The Italian court physician of Henry VII was looking for someone to accompany his two sons there and supervise their university studies. Erasmus took the post, and he soon found himself back in Paris and, a while later, on the road through the pass at Mt. Cenis to the land he had long desired to see. He was then nearly forty. His years weighed heavily upon him, and as he crossed the Alps, he composed a very touching poem on the passage of time and his approaching old age.

At Turin, where he arrived in early September, he received the degree of doctor of theology. "Thus he carried into Italy dignity and erudition," writes Beatus Rhenanus, "which others have been accustomed to bring back from that country." He then proceeded to Bologna with his wards, but they all withdrew to Florence temporarily because of fighting in the area. He was back in November to witness the triumphal entry of Pope Julius II, who had wrested the city from the Bentivogli tyrant. Bologna was part of the papal state, and Julius was restoring papal control, but Erasmus was aghast at the sight of a warrior pope. He spent most of 1507 in Bologna, and in December he moved to Venice, where he had already made contact with the great Venetian scholar–printer Aldus Manutius. Aldus headed the most prestigious press of his day. His aim was to make good texts of the Latin and Greek classics available in small, attractive volumes, and

Erasmus was greatly impressed with his scholarly undertaking as well as his technical skill. He stayed in Venice nine months, working closely with Aldus and living in the home of his father-in-law, Andrea Torresani, who housed a lively community of scholars, many of them Greek, sometimes known as the Aldine (New) Academy.[11] Erasmus shared a room there with the young Jerome Aleander, a future cardinal and papal official of considerable prominence. Their paths crossed again many years later when the Lutheran controversy was dividing Europe, and hostile suspicions disrupted their friendship.

The chief fruit of this year in Venice was a new and enlarged edition of the *Adages*, which Aldus published in his beautiful type and format in September. Called the *Adagiorum chiliades*—literally, "Thousands of adages"—the book now contained over 3,000 proverbs culled from Greek as well as Latin authors. Erasmus learnedly indicated their origin and use and added his own interesting comments and digressions. With the proverb *Festina lente* ("Make haste slowly"), for example, which described the trademark of the Aldine press—an anchor with a dolphin entwined about its shaft—he gives a glowing account of Aldus' "tireless efforts" to restore good literature.[12] "Aldus is building up a library which has no other limits than the world itself," he declares. The new edition of the *Adages* was a huge success, and Erasmus' claim to scholarship and brilliant erudition was now firmly established.

At the end of 1508 he went to Padua, where, as a tutor, he joined the household of Alexander Stuart, the illegitimate son of James IV of Scotland. He traveled to Siena and later to Rome with the young nobleman, for whom he had high hopes and warm affection. When the youth was summoned home to Scotland by his father, he gave Erasmus as a souvenir an antique ring with the Roman god Terminus—a god whose stone statue marked boundaries—engraved on it. Erasmus thereafter used this ring, with its motto, *Concedo nulli*—"I yield to no one" —as his seal and device, interpreting it, as he once explained, not in an arrogant sense but as a reminder of mortality, death being the ultimate boundary. The young Stuart was tragically slain a few years later, together with his father, when the Scots invading England were defeated at Flodden Field. It was a dreadful loss in Erasmus' eyes and further evidence for him of the stupidity and waste of war.

In early 1509 Erasmus was in Rome, where, as he himself reports in the brief autobiography, "a distinguished and favorable reputation preceded him." He was cordially received by the most eminent cardinals and prelates—Giovanni de' Medici, who would soon succeed Julius II as Pope Leo X; Raffaele Riario; Domenico Grimani; and Egidio da Viterbo, then general of the Augustinians and a distinguished scholar himself. He was pressed to remain in the Eternal City, and it was tempting, but in June a letter from Mountjoy arrived urging his return to England. The old king had died, and his son, whom Erasmus had met at Eltham back in 1499, had succeeded as Henry VIII. A new day had dawned; an enlightened prince had come to power. Erasmus was bidden to enjoy these blessings. Without great delay he left Rome and headed north. He decided to spend the rest of his days in that favored isle.

As he rode back across the Alps, this time by the Splügen pass into Switzerland at Chur, meditating on the world that he had seen and its vanity and folly, and anticipating his reunion with the wise and witty Thomas More, the idea for his most famous book arose in his mind. This became the masterpiece of humor, irony, and biting satire that he entitled *Moriae encomium* or *The Praise of Folly*. He dashed it off soon after he arrived at More's house in London, as he recuperated from the long journey back from Italy and from an attack of kidney stone, and he dedicated it to More, punning on his family name in the title and the theme, the Greek word for folly being μωρία. It was not published until two years later, when Erasmus saw it through the press of Gilles Gourmont in Paris. It was then quickly reprinted and republished in many other cities and became what we can truly call a best seller. About forty editions appeared in Erasmus' lifetime. "It delighted the whole of Europe," so it has been said with a degree of exaggeration perhaps, for its banter and its critical thrust were viewed amiss at least by some. It is nevertheless Erasmus' most popular and enduring work. Huizinga calls it his best. In this little book, he says, "Erasmus gave something that no one else could have given to the world."[13]

The form of the work is a declamation, a discourse in praise of folly delivered by a garrulous woman—actually a goddess—who is the personification of folly itself. The imagery is whimsical and paradoxical. Folly praises herself, yet her encomium is not altogether foolish. It is often ironic and in places straightforwardly and severely critical of the self-deceptions and harmful stupidities of this life. The tone and meaning of Folly's address thus frequently vary, and one of the problems in reading the essay, one of its challenges, is interpreting correctly what Folly has to say. Is she speaking foolishly and amusing us—or is she telling us the truth and instructing us? The ambiguity is not always resolved.

Aside from this ambiguity and the book's playful quality, and aside from the final section, where Erasmus eulogizes Christian folly—"the folly of the cross"—as St. Paul did in his First Letter to the Corinthians, the most striking and best-remembered parts of *The Praise of Folly* are its criticism of religious superstition and its indictment of theologians, monks, and prelates who disfigure religion with their conceits and un-Christian lives. (These parts were greatly expanded in the 1514 and 1515 editions.) The scholastic theologians wrapped up in their syllogisms and irrelevant speculations are given rough treatment, as we might expect. Nor are the popes with their pomp and their wealth and their triumphs spared. It is clear that Erasmus at this point had in mind Julius II, whom he had seen in action in strife-torn Italy, and there follows a ringing condemnation of war as "something so monstrous that it befits wild beasts rather than men" and as completely alien to Christ and His teaching. These critical and satirical parts occupy a fair portion of the book and give it its cutting edge. Its impact on its times should be measured here; and in evaluating it, the historical context of the work as well as Erasmus' deeper purpose should be kept in mind. It was written and published in a Europe still Catholic though urgently in need of religious renewal and reform. This Erasmus grasped and devoted his energies to achieve. He is not playing the mocker or cynic or skeptic in this book, as some have mistakenly believed, but the sincere reformer. In a response to the critic Martin Dorp, he said that his intentions in *The Praise of Folly* were the same as in his other works, though his method differed. "The same thing was done there under the semblance of a jest," he wrote, "as was done in the *Enchiridion*" (Selection III).

From the summer of 1509, when Erasmus wrote *The Praise of Folly* in More's house in London, to the summer of 1511, when he published the work in Paris, we know practically nothing of his life. (The lack of extant correspondence from this period is an enigma.) Most probably these two "lost years" were spent congenially with his English friends and in productive scholarly work. Finally, we find him at Cambridge, where he had gone in August 1511 to teach Greek. Bishop Fisher of Rochester was also chancellor of the university and extended the invitation that led to Erasmus' tenure as a professor. He stayed at Cambridge nearly two-and-a-half years, residing in Queen's College, occasionally riding his horse for exercise and recreation, and working very hard on projects for new books and editions. One of these was a recension of St. Jerome's letters (he also lectured on Jerome). Another was a fresh Latin translation of the New Testament directly from the Greek. Still another was the preparation of two educational works, *De copia verborum ac rerum* and *De ratione studii*, for publication by Josse Badius in Paris in July 1512. He dedicated the *De copia* to John Colet, and it was intended as a text on Latin composition and style (the word *copia* signifies "richness" or "fullness" of expression) for use in St. Paul's school in London, which Colet had recently founded. He also worked on a new revision of the *Adages* and on several classical texts and translations, and during this time very probably he wrote a short satiric dialogue entitled *Julius exclusus*. The latter is a lampoon in the Lucianic vein of Julius II, who had died in February 1513. In it the warrior pope has a long wrangle with Saint Peter at the gate of heaven and is refused entrance. The contrast between the haughty papal prince and a true Christian pastor is sharply drawn. Erasmus denied authorship of this invective (which was very likely never meant for publication), but there are indications that the work is his, and we know that Julius was a particular scandal to him.

He left Cambridge in early 1514, went to London, and in the summer departed for the Continent. The high hopes that had brought him to England in 1509 had not been realized (he had many complaints about life at Cambridge), and he decided now to try his fortune elsewhere. Back in the Low Countries, he soon made his way up the Rhine to Basel, which for the time being was the object of his travels. In that bustling city in the heart of Europe, Johann Froben, partner and successor of the late Johann Amerbach, had his printing office, and it was Erasmus' intention to join forces with him and see some of the projects he had long been working on through the press. He had heard too that the Basel firm was preparing an edition of St. Jerome, and this in particular was strong motivation for him to go there. He was generally impressed with Froben's work and not entirely satisfied with Badius' labors in Paris. Also, a not-too-trustworthy printer's agent, Franz Birckmann, had diverted certain manuscripts, including the revised *Adages*, which had been promised to Badius, to the Basel enterprise. Erasmus may not have connived at this transaction, but it probably did not distress him. The switch inaugurated his contact with Froben and marked the beginning of a long and famous association.

We come now to the climactic point in Erasmus' career—a period of culmination when he made many of his most important contributions, when his full program of reform found its most effective expression, and when his fame too reached its peak. Margaret Mann Phillips, in her excellent biography of Erasmus, epitomizes the great humanist's state of mind as well as his actual status in the world of his time during this period:

> Erasmus was attempting the complete reorganization of his world, partly through comparison with the ideas of the maturer minds of the past, and partly through the inspired common sense of his own mind, having before him the ideals of the Gospel. This immense vision had grown upon him slowly, and was coming to fruition now in the years 1514–18 at Basel. Those years placed him in the central and supreme position at the very heart of the Renaissance.[14]

This busy and vital period of his life opened with an amusing scene —a circumstance not entirely out of character for the author of *The Praise of Folly*. The trip up the Rhine in the midsummer of 1514 had been a triumphal one, and Erasmus was exhilarated by the enthusiastic reception given him at Strasburg by the German humanists. He was in high good spirits when he reached Froben in Basel. The two men had never met, and Erasmus seized the opportunity to play a joke. He introduced himself as a friend of Erasmus with whom Froben could talk and negotiate as with Erasmus himself. "We are so alike," he said, "that if you have seen one, you have seen the other." Froben soon caught on, however, and welcomed the renowned scholar warmly. Erasmus promptly moved into Froben's household, and their close collaboration began.

The situation repeated to a certain extent Erasmus' experience in Venice in 1508, save that his ties with Froben were more intimate and enduring than his affiliation with the Aldine press. Froben had a coterie of scholarly associates and friends, and Erasmus joined their number. Beatus Rhenanus, his future biographer, was an editor there, and active too were the sons of Johann Amerbach, who was recently deceased. The youngest son, Boniface, became a very close friend of Erasmus. New editions of *The Praise of Folly*, *De copia*, and the *Enchiridion* were brought out in 1515, as were an edition of Seneca and a still further expanded edition of the *Adages*. This last work, which had originally been intended for Badius, is a notable revision of the popular anthology. It contains two celebrated essays: a forceful anti-war tract entitled *Dulce bellum inexpertis*—"War is sweet to those who have not tried it"—and an incisive statement aimed at the reform of the Church entitled *Sileni Alcibiadis*. ("The Sileni of Alcibiades": Sileni are statuettes that are ugly in appearance but can be opened to reveal a beautiful carved figure inside. The image or reference comes from Plato's *Symposium*, and its use was proverbial. Erasmus was very fond of it, and we find it in the *Enchiridion* and *The Praise of Folly*. In this instance he compares Christ and the Apostles to Sileni, and he compares prelates of his own day with their fraudulent outward show to Sileni in reverse.) More important than any of these works, however, were two larger projects that Froben published in 1516 and with which Erasmus had been occupied since his arrival in Basel: a huge edition of the works of St. Jerome and an annotated Greek and Latin New Testament. The appearance of these together with other circumstances in that year, which we shall consider, make 1516 the *annus mirabilis* in the story of Erasmus and Erasmian humanism.

The Jerome edition had been in preparation both by Erasmus and quite independently by the Amerbach–Froben press.[15] Erasmus knew Jerome's works from his earliest years and had undertaken to emend and comment on his letters as early as 1500. Johann Amerbach, whose ambition it was to publish good editions of the major Western Fathers (he had brought out an edition of St. Ambrose in 1492 and of St. Augustine in 1506), had long planned an edition of Jerome and had gathered manuscripts and employed some excellent scholars in collating and restoring his writings. Froben and Amerbach's sons continued the effort after his death, and it was at this point that Erasmus entered the scene. He now worked assiduously to bring the project to completion. "I have thrown myself into this task so zealously," he wrote to Cardinal Riario, "that one could almost say that I had worked myself to death that Jerome might live again."[16] Finally, the editing and printing were completed in nine folio volumes in the summer of 1516, and the book was on the market in September.

Erasmus' part in this enormous undertaking was confined chiefly to the letters and treatises in the first four volumes, though he assisted in the whole work. He contributed extensive notes, or *scholia*, to the letters, and he composed a long dedication to Archbishop Warham of Canterbury, to serve as a general preface, and a remarkable life of St. Jerome that has been called his biographical masterpiece. It is the first critical life of the saint, and one of Erasmus' modern editors, Wallace K. Ferguson, has described it as "a labor of love, an act of filial piety by one who considered himself Jerome's spiritual descendant."[17]

The importance of St. Jerome for Erasmus cannot be overestimated. He identified with this most literary and erudite of the Latin Fathers. His very style resembles the saint's. And he saw Jerome as the model Christian scholar and the embodiment of true theology. From the start, as we have seen, the restoration of Jerome's works was closely linked to Erasmus' program of theological reform. This linkage is crystal clear from the life Erasmus wrote. Jerome's status as a theologian is staunchly defended against those scholastics who follow an entirely different tack: "Who had a more thorough knowledge of the philosophy of Christ? Who expressed it more vigorously either in literature or in life? Are not these the qualities of the theologian?"[18] They were, indeed, in the purview of Erasmus, who saw theology not as a speculative or academic science but as the living and transforming "philosophy of Christ"—an understanding rooted in Scripture and expressing itself in the moral life.

"The philosophy of Christ" is a famous Erasmian term, actually patristic in origin, which gained currency in 1516. It is first used and defined in the *Paraclesis*, or introduction to the New Testament, which Erasmus published earlier that year (Selection IV). The expression simply means "what Christ taught," and it includes the notion of a doctrine that easily penetrates our minds and transforms our lives. "What else is the philosophy of Christ, which He himself calls a rebirth," Erasmus asks in a striking passage in the *Paraclesis* (he uses the Latin *renascentia* for "rebirth"), "than the restoration of human nature originally well formed?" The source of that philosophy, of course, is the New Testament, and thus the publication of Erasmus' New Testament in March 1516 is an extremely important event.[19]

This edition is unique because it marks the first publication in print of the Greek New Testament, the original language of the Gospels and Epistles. Erasmus accompanied it with an emended Latin version in a parallel column, and he annotated the entire work extensively. The edition is prefaced by a dedication to the reigning pope, Leo X, wherein Erasmus calls a return to Scripture "our chiefest hope for the restoration and rebuilding of the Christian religion," and by the aforementioned *Paraclesis*, as well as by a short essay on theological method. The latter was expanded and published separately as the *Ratio verae theologiae* in 1518. The New Testament edition, like practically all of Erasmus' works and editions, was revised and republished several times—in 1519, 1522, 1527, and 1535.

It is by no means a modern critical edition of Holy Scripture (it has been often faulted on this score), and it was hastily printed in 1516, but it is nevertheless a landmark book, and it was widely acclaimed. Colet expressed the view of many when, receiving and examining his copy, he exclaimed: "The name of Erasmus shall never perish." The Greek was now readily available to scholars for the first time. (Cardinal Ximénes' even more scholarly polyglot New Testament, which also had the Greek text with an interlinear translation, had already been printed at Alcalá in Spain, but its publication was held up until 1522.) Above all, it focused renewed attention on the sacred writings—the source of Christian faith. The book "struck its perfect hour," in the words of Margaret Mann Phillips, and "stood for the New Learning."[20]

Despite Leo X's full approval (his commendatory letter was published in the second edition), there were many who were shocked at Erasmus' temerity in correcting the Vulgate text and giving priority to the Greek, and who criticized specific changes or comments that he made. Several controversial exchanges took place on these various points. One was with Martin Dorp, a Louvain theologian, who launched his criticism of Erasmus' audacity in altering the Vulgate together with his disapproval of *The Praise of Folly* even before the publication of the New Testament. Erasmus replied in an important apologia, which was published by Froben in 1515 in the first collection of Erasmus' letters to appear (Selection III). Thomas More also wrote to Dorp in 1515 in Erasmus' defense and is said to have won over the critic, or won him back (for Dorp had been a friend and fellow humanist), to the humanist cause. Another very lengthy and very sharp exchange occurred with the French humanist Jacques Lefèvre over a disagreement about the translation of a Hebrew word in the eighth Psalm that was quoted in Hebrews 2:7. The most interesting criticism of all, perhaps—and one fraught with historical consequence and meaning—came from an obscure Augustinian monk in the Saxon town of Wittenberg, who was lecturing on Scripture at the university there. He had obtained the new publication and found that he disagreed with Erasmus' interpretation of St. Paul on the matter of justification by works. He conveyed that information to a friend, George Spalatin, secretary to the Elector Frederick of Saxony, and the latter relayed the criticism to Erasmus in a letter of 11 December 1516.[21] "His view," wrote Spalatin, "is that we do not become just by performing just actions . . . but that we become just first and then act justly." The Augustinian monk was Martin Luther, and his criticism of Erasmus is one of the early expressions of his basic notion of justification by faith alone. Spalatin's letter marks Luther's first contact, albeit indirect, with the famous humanist, and foretokens the radical divergence between them that later emerged. (Shortly after this Luther wrote to another friend the following: "My opinion of Erasmus decreases from day to day. . . . I fear that he does not promote the cause of Christ and God's grace sufficiently. For him human considerations have an absolute preponderance over divine."[22]) The controversy that was to rend the Church and overshadow the reforms of Erasmus was near at hand.

Erasmus published another noteworthy book in 1516—a moralistic political treatise entitled *Institutio principis Christiani.* Addressed and dedicated to young Prince Charles of Burgundy, who became king of Spain in 1516 and was soon to become Holy Roman Emperor Charles V, it is a book of devout maxims in which he who is destined for the highest office may, to quote Beatus Rhenanus, "learn the conduct worthy of a Christian as in a mirror." Erasmus had been named a councilor to Prince Charles in 1516, and the work was an act of homage as well as instruction for him. In his same capacity as councilor to Charles and at the behest of Jean Le Sauvage, the chancellor of Burgundy, he also wrote another significant condemnation of war and plea for peace—an essay in the form of a declamation, entitled *Querela pacis*. We must emphasize that Erasmus was a pacifist and that his pacifism was an essential aspect of his Christian humanism and his reform program; we must also stress that his pacifism was not simply the dream of a scholar in an ivory tower.[23] It was conceived and developed as relevant advice and advanced as practical counsel to the rulers and other important figures of his day. And Erasmus indeed was influential. In 1516–1517, with a new and more promising group of princes at the helm—the Medici pope and the kings of England, France, and Spain—all of whom he knew and corresponded with, he was especially hopeful that Europe would have peace and that a better day was dawning.

It will not be amiss to recall at this point that 1516 was also the year of Thomas More's *Utopia*. That fascinating book, a true Renaissance masterpiece, might almost be called the joint work of More and Erasmus. They shared the attitudes and ideas it expressed. In fact, the dialogue between Raphael Hythloday and More that constitutes book 1 of *Utopia* seems in many ways a discussion between Erasmus and More, with Hythloday voicing characteristic views of Erasmus, particularly with respect to war. Erasmus was actually in England in the summer of 1516, when More was working on this portion of the book. And book 2 of *Utopia*, which consists of the description of the ideal commonwealth, where all goods and wealth are held in common and private property does not exist, is actually a highly imaginative rendition of the first proverb in all the editions of the *Adages*—*Amicorum omnia communia*: that is, "Among friends all things are shared in common." More sent Erasmus the manuscript of the book in September, and Erasmus arranged for its initial printing that fall by Dirck Maertensz in Louvain. It was an immediate success. It too reflected the buoyant and confident spirit of the humanists at this period.

From the late summer of 1516 to November 1521, Erasmus lived in the Low Countries, chiefly at Antwerp and Louvain and finally, for several months, at Anderlecht. At the end of 1521 he returned to Basel, where he took up residence once again at Froben's. Meanwhile, other travels interrupted his sojourn in Brabant. He visited England briefly in April 1517 to receive the full dispensations he had sought from Rome that would permit him to forgo wearing his religious habit, allow him to remain outside his monastery, and, most importantly, enable him to hold Church benefices despite the illegitimacy of his birth. These had come through the good offices of a close friend, Andrea Ammonio, a papal representative in London. The summer of 1518 found him once more back in Basel, where he published a new edition of the *Enchiridion* (Selection V) and worked on a revision of his New Testament, replacing, in general, the Vulgate text with his own Latin translation. In the summer and fall of 1520, he was for a time in the entourage of the new emperor, Charles V, and attended his coronation at Aachen in October (Selection VII). His travels would have been even more extensive had he answered the many invitations and appeals that came to him from all sides. He tended nevertheless to be restless wherever he was, like Petrarch "a pilgrim everywhere," truly Erasmus of Christendom, as Roland Bainton appropriately entitled his study of the great humanist.

Shortly after Erasmus' return from his visit to England in 1517—it was his last voyage there—the Antwerp painter Quentin Metsys did an imposing portrait of him as a scholar of serious mien in a black habit and cap writing in a large book. It was Erasmus' first portrait. Others by Albrecht Dürer and Hans Holbein followed. Two years before the Metsys portrait, the youthful Holbein, who had just come to Basel, had done two small ink drawings of Erasmus in the margin of a copy of the 1515 Froben edition of *The Praise of Folly*. One of these depicts Erasmus as a handsome young man seated at a small desk and writing in a book. When Erasmus saw this miniature sketch he is reported to have exclaimed: "Ah! If Erasmus still looked like that, he would quickly find himself a wife!" The Metsys painting was accompanied by a similar portrait of Peter Gilles, town clerk of Antwerp and a good friend of Erasmus as well as of Thomas More. The two portraits formed a diptych and were sent that year as a gift to More from the sitters. (Two copies of each portrait survive today. One Erasmus portrait is in the Galleria Nazionale in Rome; the other is at Hampton Court Palace in England.) In the Metsys painting of Erasmus, the book he is working on is his paraphrase of St. Paul's Epistle to the Romans, the first of a series of *Paraphrases* of the Gospels and Epistles, which he was actually writing at this time. (In the Hampton Court portrait, but not in the one in Rome, the opening lines of the paraphrase in a hand very similar to Erasmus' are clearly legible.)[24] In Holbein's famous portrait of Erasmus (today in the Louvre), which was painted in Basel several years later, Erasmus is also pictured writing in a book. This time the opening lines of his paraphrase of St. Mark's Gospel, which he dedicated to Francis I of France and published in 1523, are represented. The depiction of Erasmus busily writing at a desk recalls Renaissance representations of his great favorite, St. Jerome, and the similarity, for example, between the Metsys portrait and Antonio da Fabriano's *Saint Jerome in His Study* (dated 1451),[25] even to facial expression, is striking. St. Jerome is usually shown with a cardinal's hat hanging on the wall behind him. Erasmus had not yet been offered that high dignity.

In 1517 a wealthy friend, Jerome Busleiden, died. At Erasmus' urging he had left a bequest in his will for the establishment of a college at Louvain where the three learned languages—Latin, Greek, and Hebrew—would be taught. Beatus Rhenanus, in his life of Erasmus, lays great emphasis on the importance of this trilingual college and on Erasmus' role in its acceptance. Its example, he tells us, influenced the king of France to set up a similar college in Paris and to invite Erasmus to preside over it. The latter declined, but the steps taken at this time led to the later Collège de France. "And so," Beatus comments, "it is generally acknowledged that the growth of learning in these countries is due most of all to Erasmus."

At the same time that Busleiden's trilingual college was being organized, Erasmus published at Louvain (at Maertensz' press in November 1518) his extended treatise on theological method, the *Ratio verae theologiae*, wherein he stressed the necessity for the theologian of the knowledge of ancient languages in comprehending and expounding Scripture. This publication increased tension between Erasmus and the more academic or conservative theologians at Louvain. The dispute actually was between two very different conceptions of theology—the humanist and the scholastic—the roots of which go back to Erasmus' early days and the reality of which was ever-present in his program and writings. In early 1519, it found significant expression in an exchange between Erasmus and the most eminent of the Louvain theologians, Jacob Latomus. Latomus wrote a *Dialogue* defending theology as a dialectical science and taking issue with the whole literary or humanist approach of Erasmus' *Ratio*. Erasmus replied in an *Apologia* focusing on the importance for the theologian of studying the learned languages and the literature of antiquity. It was a high-level debate, but Erasmus was very upset by the opposition he now confronted. The "barbarians" were unrelenting, so it seemed to him, in their efforts to suppress good learning.

It is at this point that Martin Luther and the Reformation impinge on our story, and they do so, it must be noted, in the context of the dispute we have just described. Luther, to be sure, had entered the scene before this. On 31 October 1517 he had posted his famous Ninety-five Theses concerning indulgences on the door of the castle church in Wittenberg, and these, widely circulated, gave rise to the controversy that began the Protestant Reformation. The theses criticized the traffic in papal indulgences, a practice that was a scandal to many, including Erasmus; but there was more to Luther and the controversy that developed than the criticism of this abuse alone. Out of his personal experience as a monk and his exegetical probing as a professor of Holy Scripture, Luther had come to the conviction that it was faith in Christ's merits alone that justified and saved Christians and not works or efforts on the part of sinful man. The implications of this belief as Luther elaborated them were to be very radical in terms of many traditional doctrines and devotions. Luther arrived at this realization, he tells us, as he pondered the message in Romans 1:16–17 that "the just shall live by faith." It was what had inspired his disagreement with Erasmus' interpretation of St. Paul and his reservations about the humanist, and it came more and more to the foreground in his preaching and polemics as the religious controversy expanded after 1517. Differences of scriptural interpretation, then, separated Erasmus and Luther from the beginning, though superficially at first it appeared that Luther was engaging in the same reform efforts as Erasmus and was contending with the same opposition.[26] Young Luther had broken with scholasticism and seemed to be in the humanist camp of good literature and biblical theology. Indeed, as professor at Wittenberg he was using Jacques Lefèvre's new editions of the Psalms and St. Paul's Epistles, and he had obtained Erasmus' New Testament.

In March 1519, Luther, the center now of great contention, addressed his first letter to Erasmus.[27] He wrote deferentially, seeking the acknowledgment and, implicitly, the support of Christendom's most renowned scholar. Erasmus answered somewhat reservedly in May, reporting chiefly on the agitation among the theologians at Louvain.[28] They thought that he had helped write Luther's tracts, he said, and was the standard-bearer of his party. The view is the forerunner of the notion that "Erasmus laid the egg Luther hatched." He told Luther, however, that important people there as well as in England thought highly of his writings, and he added: "As for me I keep myself as far as possible neutral, the better to assist the new flowering of good learning; and it seems to me that more can be done by unassuming courtesy than by violence." He concluded on this note: "We must everywhere take care never to speak or act arrogantly or in a party spirit." Not that Luther needed this advice, Erasmus politely assumed, but he gave it clearly—and farsightedly—nevertheless.

Later that year, in October, Erasmus wrote a longer and more incisive letter regarding the controversy over Luther to Albert of Brandenburg, archbishop of Mainz, the man whose appointment to that see in 1514 had occasioned the papal indulgence Luther had attacked (Selection VI). There is an unusual fitness in Erasmus' forthright remarks to this prelate. The gist of what he has to say is that Luther is being defamed and abused by shameless men who are troublemakers and enemies of learning, and that he deserves a fair hearing: "If he is innocent I do not want him crushed by a faction of rogues, and if he is in error I wish him to be corrected not destroyed." Though he dissociates himself from the actual case of Luther, there is no mistaking his sympathies. And in the midst of his appeal for fairness and moderation in dealing with Luther, he gives a remarkably outspoken analysis of where the real trouble lies:

> The world is weighed down with human ordinances, burdened with scholastic opinions and dogmas, oppressed by the tyranny of the mendicant friars. . . . They preached indulgences in such a way that even the ignorant could not bear it. Due to this and many other similar causes the vigor of the Gospel teaching was gradually disappearing. And it looked as if, with things ever heading for the worse, the spark of Christian piety, whence an extinct charity could be rekindled, would at last be totally put out. The sum of religion was tending toward a more than Jewish ceremonial. . . . Pious minds were troubled when they heard in the universities scarcely any discussion of evangelical doctrine and observed that the sacred writers approved of old by the Church were now regarded as obsolete. . . . This must be blamed, in my opinion, even if Luther has written somewhat intemperately.

The causes of the Reformation crisis are not simply explained, and different perspectives on the event can give quite different appraisals. Erasmus' analysis, given in the fall of 1519, however, touches on some key issues and in terms of his reform goals is highly consistent.

We do not have the space here to trace in detail the evolution of Erasmus' attitude toward Luther and the Reformation or describe his reaction to all its developments. We will confine our account to a more general description of his involvement and role. As the controversy became more vehement and widespread, as it certainly did after 1520, he became alarmed about its eventual outcome. It took on for him the proportions of a "tragedy," a great disaster. He sought to moderate the quarrel and prevent a serious breach within the Church. This was the natural bent of his mind and the natural direction of his efforts. He stood for renewal and reform but also for unity and peace. "What else is our religion than peace in the Holy Spirit?" he wrote to Jodocus Jonas, one of Luther's followers, in May 1521 (Selection VIII). It was a profound sentiment on Erasmus' part and one he often repeated. He thus occupied a middle ground in the controversy that raged, and he maintained this position as the schism deepened. But his mediatory efforts were of no avail. The Church was seriously rent, and the changes and reforms that were introduced were not exactly those Erasmus had in mind. He ran afoul too of both extremes—of both factions, as he viewed the warring parties—for neither side could see him as its own, and both came to regard him as faithless and disloyal. He became more and more an anomaly in an age of increasing Protestant–Catholic polarization. Even in recent times there has been puzzlement and suspicion among some biographers over the "ambiguity" of his position, though few scholars today question either the sincerity of his Catholic faith or the quality and firmness of his convictions.

At the end of 1521, Erasmus left the Low Countries and his hostile critics at Louvain for Basel. Restless and unsettled though he was, he never again journeyed far from that busy city. Luther, meanwhile, had been excommunicated by Rome in 1521 and placed under the ban of the empire following his defiant stand at the Diet of Worms, and Erasmus was now being pressed to write authoritatively against him. This was probably part of the reason he withdrew to Basel, where the atmosphere was less charged and more congenial. He also wanted closer contact with Froben, and an extremely productive period now followed. Whatever else it did, "the Lutheran tragedy" did not sap Erasmus' energies or becloud his own reform purpose. A further revision of his New Testament appeared in 1522, and Froben that year brought out two major editions of his *Colloquies*, the work that after *The Praise of Folly* remained his most famous and enduring. In September, Erasmus also published an edition of Arnobius' *Commentaries on the Psalms* that he dedicated to the new pope, Adrian VI, a Hollander like himself and a former Louvain professor whom he knew well. Adrian responded by asking Erasmus to write against the heresies of Luther and by inviting him to come to Rome. Others also urged that he take up his pen against the rebellious Wittenberg monk, and finally, one might say reluctantly, he did so in 1524 in a treatise entitled *De libero arbitrio*.[29]

In this essay Erasmus took issue with Luther's basic teaching that man is totally corrupt and therefore unable and unfree to do anything that might aid in his own salvation, and he upbraided Luther for being so intemperate and for disputing so dogmatically against the consensus of the Church. He argued strictly from Scripture against Luther's point of view, affirming man's obligation to lead a moral life and defending his ability to respond to God's grace and thereby do so. Erasmus' theology was essentially that of Saint Thomas Aquinas; it rested on the principle that grace restores man's fallen nature and liberates and strengthens his will. It was the view that we might expect from a humanist conscious of the need to uphold the dignity and freedom of man. Luther was enraged, and after some delay responded in a lengthy diatribe entitled *De servo arbitrio*. He attacked Erasmus mercilessly as a godless skeptic "oozing Lucian from every pore," and he asserted in the most extreme terms his theological determinism and his view of man's helplessness and enslavement to sin. Erasmus subsequently replied to the attack in his two-fold *Hyperaspistes*—the word is Greek and means "one who protects with a shield"—of 1526 and 1527, defending himself against Luther's vituperation and further explaining his theology of man's freedom and grace.

Although Erasmus went to the heart of the matter in his dispute with Luther, not all his Catholic critics were satisfied or reassured. For some, *De libero arbitrio* was too moderate in tone and too circumspect, and other writings of his continued to rankle and upset. This was particularly true of the *Colloquies*, which came under the formal censure of the Sorbonne, the theological faculty at Paris, in May 1526, a few months after Luther's angry onslaught in *De servo arbitrio*. Erasmus was truly a man caught in the middle. He was now near sixty, and these later years were far from offering that tranquillity and leisure he undoubtedly desired.

The *Colloquies*, as we have already noted, is one of Erasmus' most celebrated works. Its origin goes back to his early days in Paris, when he composed short exercises in Latin conversation for pupils he was tutoring. Some of these *formulae* were first printed in 1518 and 1519, but it was not until Froben's editions in 1522 that the work was greatly expanded and took on the character we recognize today. After that, like the *Adages*, it was enlarged, republished, and reprinted many times. Over a hundred such editions and reprintings appeared in Erasmus' lifetime. By the final edition of 1533, it came to contain more than fifty of the lively sketches or dramatic dialogues called colloquies.

In the Erasmian corpus—in fact, in the literature of the Renaissance—the *Colloquies* occupies a very special place. It harks back to the dialogues of Lucian and in some instances to the dialogues of Plato. It has much of the wit and satire we find in *The Praise of Folly*, and it sets forth those characteristic themes Erasmus expressed as early as 1501 in the *Enchiridion*. At the same time, it is full of lively scenes and stories and is replete with pungent comment and personal observation. Not the least of its features are the satiric jabs at the abuses of religion that Erasmus had so long criticized—at ignorance and superstition and at the monks and friars whose practices he abhorred. The book is comparable to *The Praise of Folly* in this regard. And it was this aspect that raised the hackles of the Sorbonne and other Catholic opponents. (We might note that Luther also denounced the *Colloquies* and its Lucianic author, albeit for different reasons.) Whatever else may be said about the work, it clearly shows that Erasmus had no intention of softening his criticism of abuses or curtailing his efforts toward reform because of his theological disagreement with Luther or because of the schism that had come.

There is a great variety of scenes and topics in the *Colloquies*. The following will give some idea of their character and scope. In an edition of 1522, one of the greatest appeared—the "Convivium religiosum" or "The Godly Feast." The setting is a garden where a group of friends are idyllically conversing. Their conversation is very elevated, and one important theme touched on is how Christians can learn and profit from many of the works of the ancient pagans. "Perhaps the spirit of Christ is more widespread than we understand," remarks one of the speakers. Another, a little later, moved by the attitude of Socrates in the face of death, and his resignation and hope, so proper to the Christian, says that he could hardly help exclaiming, "Saint Socrates, pray for us!"—memorable words that go to the heart of Erasmian humanism. The next year the colloquy "The Shipwreck" made its debut. It tells the story of a ship caught and destroyed in a terrible storm. All on board, panic-stricken, scream to the saints for help and make extravagant vows. A young mother with a child in her arms alone retains her calm and dignity and prays in silence. When the ship breaks up, she is the first to reach shore and one of the very few who is saved. The dialogue-narrative is humorous and fast-paced, and the description of the storm at sea is masterly.

Early in 1524, a few months prior to *De libero arbitrio,* Erasmus published a colloquy bearing on the religious controversy—the "Inquisitio de fide" or "An Inquiry Concerning Faith." It stands in rather sharp contrast to the tone and argument of the later treatise on free will. In it, two speakers, one a Lutheran (or Luther), the other a Catholic (or Erasmus), review the articles of the Creed and discover that they agree on all these fundamental beliefs. The point seems to be that their disagreement involves not the basic articles of the Christian faith but rather other matters that are of lesser importance, and that they should keep talking and work out their differences. It seems a plea for continuing dialogue, the idea of which is unquestionably an Erasmian motif, but the fruitfulness of which was belied by the actual Erasmus–Luther exchange that soon took place. The differences that then emerged seemed fundamental.

A surprising number of colloquies feature women, who are depicted with sympathy and affection, and who present views on their education and on courtship and marriage that are refreshing and enlightened. The More family, and particularly More's eldest daughter, Margaret, who married William Roper, come to mind in this connection. Erasmus dedicated to her a commentary on two hymns of Prudentius in 1524, and she in turn translated into English Erasmus' meditation on the Lord's Prayer—the first of his works to be published in English. She was also very likely the model for the intelligent young lady in the delightful colloquy "The Abbot and the Learned Lady." The lady in this work, with her love of books and good learning, offers quite a contrast to the witless and unconscionable abbot, who attempts to lure her from her scholarly pursuits. In the *Colloquies* and other writings, too, Erasmus frequently praised marriage and family life, often upholding the ideal as preferable to celibacy—a view that did not sit at all well with his clerical opponents. He wrote a devotional treatise on Christian marriage in 1526 that he dedicated to Catherine of Aragon, wife of Henry VIII of England—whose husband, ironically, was soon to seek a divorce. Again one thinks of Thomas More and his family, whom Erasmus knew so well and whom he once so fondly described in a famous letter to the German knight Ulrich von Hutten.[30] He had not seen them for a number of years, but the painter Hans Holbein did a marvelous pen sketch of the entire More family in their house in Chelsea in 1527 and brought it back to Erasmus in Basel as a memento from his dearest friend. "I should scarcely be able to see you better if I were with you," Erasmus wrote to More in reply.

Comparable to the *Colloquies* and also related to the controversies that engaged Erasmus in the 1520s is a satiric dialogue entitled *Ciceronianus*, which he first published in 1528. In it, Erasmus responds to certain Italian humanists who pedantically measured everything by the structure and vocabulary of Cicero and in turn were critical of Erasmus' Latin style and literary abilities. Erasmus, like all the humanists, held Cicero in high regard and indeed viewed him as the great exemplar of Latin prose. Erasmus' humanism, however, far transcended a narrow classicism or Ciceronianism; language or style for him was not the servile imitation of any author but the product of an assimilation more living and more personal. "He himself always loved an open, extemporaneous, pure, fluent and lively style," Beatus Rhenanus tells us in his biography of Erasmus, "and he made certain terms serve the Christian subjects that he treated." The language of Cicero, who lived before Christ, was limited in that last regard, and Erasmus objected to the neopaganism as well as the pedantry of the Ciceronians. In his life of St. Jerome, defending the Father against criticisms of his eloquence and style, he had launched an attack on Ciceronianism, and now in the *Ciceronianus* he used the same arguments in his own defense, though the satiric mode and the witty banter of the dialogue are different. Erasmus had entered the lists against a new band of foes with banners flying. To his old critics among the scholastic theologians and the friars and to Luther and his militant adherents were added a third contingent—the more purely or puristically classical Italian humanists. Julius Caesar Scaliger was the most vehement respondent. "Indeed I war on three fronts," Erasmus had written as early as 1524 to his friend John Fisher in England.

Erasmus had ridiculed an excessive classicism in the *Ciceronianus*, but it must be remembered that he was one of the great classical scholars of his day and that no one did more in fostering the New Learning, as it is called, than he.[31] In the service of this cultural renewal such works as the *Adages* and the *De copia* were of prime importance, and he also produced many editions of the classical authors. These range from an edition of Cicero's *De officiis* in 1500 to an important edition of Seneca that Froben published in 1515, editions of Pliny's *Natural History* in 1525, and Livy's *History* in 1531, and they include many others, Greek and Latin, as well as translations from the Greek authors into Latin. Here the Greek satirist Lucian must again be mentioned. It is, however, Erasmus' editions of the early Church Fathers that should be given pride of place in any account of his textual scholarship and editorial achievements.[32] These form the largest and one of the most important segments of his life's work, and they contribute directly to the chief aim of Erasmus as a humanist scholar—the reform of theology through a return to the earliest theological tradition: that is, to the old and true theology of the first Christian centuries.

The first and foremost of these editions is that of St. Jerome, which appeared in 1516. (Jerome and Lucian, as we have noted, were Erasmus' favorite authors—an interesting combination revealing among other things the creatively synthetic quality of Erasmus' mind.) Next came an edition of St. Cyprian in 1520, and then the Arnobius *Commentaries* in 1522 along with an edition of St. Augustine's *City of God*, which Erasmus had persuaded the Spanish humanist Juan Luis Vives to edit and annotate. Erasmus wrote a preface to the last-named work in which he tells of the preparation of a multi-volume edition of the works of St. Augustine—a project that was finally completed in 1529 and published by the Froben press in ten folio volumes. Erasmus dedicated this massive set to Archbishop Alfonso Fonseca of Toledo, the primate of Spain and a friend sympathetic to humanist studies and reform. It was in part at least a gesture of gratitude for Fonseca's support at a time when Erasmus was under severe attack in Spain. Meanwhile, other patristic editions appeared: an edition of St. Hilary of Poitiers in 1523 with a memorable and controversial dedicatory preface addressed to Jean de Carondelet, a high official at the Hapsburg court in the Low Countries (Selection X); a revised edition of Jerome's letters in 1524; various works of St. John Chrysostom, the first Greek Father Erasmus would edit, publish, and in part translate during the next few years, climaxed by a five-volume *opera omnia* in Latin translation in 1530; a first edition of St. Irenaeus' *Adversus haereses* (*Against Heresies*) in 1526; and a four-volume edition of St. Ambrose in early 1529.

What is the significance of Erasmus' achievement here? He produced more accurate and more complete editions of the Fathers than had hitherto been available. Theologians must know the ancient Christian writers, Beatus Rhenanus stressed, and "it is to this knowledge that Erasmus has so greatly encouraged students." In most cases the prefaces to these editions are notable essays containing incisive comments on each Father as well as observations relevant to Erasmus' own aims and times. Outstanding in this regard is the St. Hilary preface of 1523. Erasmus used the example of Hilary confronting the Arians of the fourth century to clarify his point of view in the Lutheran controversy, and the preface contains some of his most pungent comments on the nature of theology and the baleful consequences of theological argument and contention. His recurrent theme is that excessive theologizing and dogmatic pronouncement destroy the peace and unanimity that should exist among Christians, for Christianity is a matter more of how we live than of the articles we profess. The preface gave rise to further accusations against him. Several passages were condemned by the Sorbonne in 1526, and still other passages were vehemently assailed at a conference of theologians in 1527 at Valladolid, in Spain, where Erasmus was charged with denying the Trinity. He had powerful friends in Spain, however, including the grand inquisitor, Alfonso Manrique, and Archbishop Fonseca, and he was spared formal condemnation.

Erasmus replied vigorously to his Spanish critics in 1528, but difficulties close to home were now causing even greater discomfort. In the course of the 1520s, Basel began to feel the impact of radical reform preaching, and the winds of change began to blow there. The leader of the movement was a scholarly priest, "learned in the three languages," Joannes Oecolampadius, who had assisted with the publication of Erasmus' New Testament in 1516 and had also made an extensive index for the Jerome edition that had been published separately by Froben in 1520. By 1523 Oecolampadius had become a professor of Scripture at the University of Basel and a staunch follower of Ulrich Zwingli, the reformer in nearby Zürich. These reformers preached a cleaner break with tradition than Luther and were particularly opposed to the Mass, the cult of the saints, and the doctrine of the Real Presence of Christ in the Eucharist. They were called Sacramentarians, and from them stems a more Puritanical version of Protestant reform. By early 1529 they had gained ascendancy in the city. In January and February there was much agitation and disorder capped by raids on the churches and the smashing and removal of all images. On the heels of these iconoclastic riots the Catholic members of the town council were expelled, the university was closed, the Mass was suppressed, and the reformers came into full control. Erasmus observed all of this with sadness and dismay and determined at once to leave the city. He departed by boat on 13 April and traveled a short way down the Rhine to the not-too-distant German city of Freiburg im Breisgau. A close friend, Ludwig Baer, once the rector of the University of Basel, moved to Freiburg with him. Another intimate friend of these later years, Boniface Amerbach, accompanied him on the journey. Freiburg was a pleasant town, strongly Catholic and firmly in the orbit of the Hapsburgs. It was a logical refuge, and Erasmus was given a cordial reception there.

He remained in Freiburg for the next six years. Age was now beginning to exact its toll, and Erasmus was ill with kidney stone, arthritis, gout, and other maladies a good deal of the time. He was increasingly weary, and disheartened, too, at the loss of friends and the sad deterioration of the world about him. Nevertheless, he kept at work pursuing his scholarly interests and his publishing projects. He brought out revised editions of many earlier works and produced some important new ones. The huge Chrysostom edition appeared in 1530, and in 1532 he published—with Froben in Basel as usual—an edition of St. Basil in Greek, the first to be printed in that language. He followed this with his own Latin translations of two treatises of St. Basil. During these years, he also wrote and published commentaries on several Psalms, the most important being an essay on Psalm 84 (83 in the Vulgate and Erasmus' enumeration) entitled *De sarcienda ecclesiae concordia*.[33] True to his convictions, he pleaded for religious reform in what under the circumstances can be called the moderate spirit of the *Enchiridion* and for tolerance and accommodation in the face of extremism and deep division. Psalm 84 itself was an appropriate prayer for the unity of the Church.

The major work that Erasmus completed in these final years was his *Ecclesiastes*, a lengthy, comprehensive treatise on the art of preaching.[34] It had been long in preparation, and it is the most voluminous of all of Erasmus' writings. The mold of his thought was essentially rhetorical: that is, he was ever concerned with the effective communication of virtue and truth, and he viewed rhetoric or eloquence—the true *ars humanitatis*—as basic to everything else. Indeed, this is a characteristic of humanism in general. *Ecclesiastes* is not simply a specialized treatise and sacred oratory but a summing-up of all his thought and work—an extended colophon, so to speak, to a long and very productive life. He intended the work for John Fisher, but that saintly man was beheaded on 22 June 1535 just as Erasmus was finishing the treatise, and he dedicated it to the bishop of Augsburg. Fisher, like Thomas More, had run afoul of Henry VIII, who had declared himself supreme head of the Church in England, and both were executed as traitors for refusing to acknowledge that title; More followed Fisher to the block two weeks later. England would never see their like again, said Erasmus.

A month prior to Fisher's execution, Erasmus had returned to Basel. Boniface Amerbach had urged him to come back, and besides he wanted to see his *Ecclesiastes* through the press. He hoped also that the change of scene might improve his health, but that was not to be. Crippling arthritis now beset him, and he remained bedridden most of the time in Jerome Froben's home, Zum Luft, where he stayed. (The house still stands in the Bäumleingasse, no. 18. Jerome, together with his brother-in-law Nicholas Episcopius, continued the famous press after the death of his father, Johann, in 1527.) In failing health, Erasmus still managed to work; his last undertaking was an edition of the works of the early Greek Father Origen in Latin translation. Erasmus considered him one of the greatest scriptural exegetes. The end came before the edition was complete, and it was finished by his old colleague Beatus Rhenanus and published posthumously.

Erasmus died at Zum Luft on 12 July 1536, in his seventieth year. In the preface to the Origen edition, Beatus gives a moving account of his final hours. Worn and exhausted but at peace, he implored Christ's mercy with his dying breath. "Jesu misericordia! Domine miserere mei!" he prayed, and then at last in his native Dutch, "Lieve God!" He was buried in the old cathedral of Basel, where his red marble gravestone remains.

What appraisal can we make of Erasmus' message, of Erasmus' career? I am inclined to say that his writings and his work, prolific as they are, speak for themselves. Over and over again he declared his intentions and his ideals. There really does not seem to be any mystery about them. In a letter of October 1527, he gave this description of his endeavors:

> I have vigorously raised my voice against the wars which we see for so many years now agitating all of Christendom. I have attempted to call back theology, sunk too far in sophistical quibbling, to the sources and to ancient simplicity. I have sought to restore to their own splendor the sacred doctors of the Church. . . . I have taught good literature, previously nearly pagan, to celebrate Christ. I have supported to the best of my ability the blossoming of languages once again.[35]

He tirelessly pursued these goals, and he flooded literate Europe in his day with his own works and with his editions of the ancient authors. No one before him had used the new medium of print so fully and so effectively. His learning was prodigious; his style, albeit Latin, was most fluent and engaging; his purpose was lofty and true. From the humblest beginnings he won world renown. His influence penetrated everywhere.

He had, as we have also seen, his critics on every side. "The Lutheran tragedy," he himself tells us, "had burdened him with unbearable ill will." Both extremes attacked him, and by virtue of what he stood for as well as of the schisms that rent Europe he became highly controversial. And he has, unfortunately, continued to be seen in partisan and prejudicial terms ever since. "That great injur'd Name, / the glory of the Priesthood and the shame," wrote the poet Alexander Pope, and Roland Bainton in his study has reminded us that "Erasmus has never had his due."

Have we succeeded in giving an objective account, an authentic portrait? It is our hope, of course, that in some measure at least we have done so. But Erasmus is a complex and many-faceted individual. His true face is difficult to delineate. And there is also the tendency to picture him in one's own mold or to interpret him in the light of one's own convictions and preconceptions. A study of the studies about him and of the various judgments that have been passed reveals this quite clearly.[36] We strive for the historical truth, however, and I venture to say that with care and caution we can approach it. And I think today that we begin to understand more clearly what it was he sought to achieve, and to appreciate more justly the ideals that inspired his work. The distance from his own times may be one of the reasons, and, paradoxically, the relevance of what he had to say for our own times may be another.

NOTES

1. CWE 1: *Epp.* 17–30.
2. See John C. Olin, *Six Essays on Erasmus* (New York, 1979), pp. 33ff.
3. J. Huizinga, *Erasmus of Rotterdam* (London, 1952), pp. 29–30.
4. Roland H. Bainton, *Erasmus of Christendom* (New York, 1969), chap. 3.
5. CWE 1: *Ep.* 108.
6. Ibid., *Ep.* 139.
7. Huizinga, p. 53.
8. *The* ENCHIRIDION *of Erasmus*, trans. Raymond Himelick (Bloomington, 1963), p. 56, and E. Gilson, *The Spirit of Medieval Philosophy*, trans. A. H. C. Downes (New York, 1940), pp. 27–28.
9. André Godin, "The *Enchiridion Militis Christiani*: The Modes of an Origenian Appropriation," *Erasmus of Rotterdam Society Yearbook Two* (*1982*), pp. 47–79.
10. CWE 2: *Ep.* 193.
11. Deno John Geanakoplos, *Greek Scholars in Venice* (Cambridge, Mass., 1962), chap. 9.
12. Margaret Mann Phillips, *Erasmus on His Times* (Cambridge, 1967), pp. 3–17.
13. Huizinga, p. 78. See also Olin, *Six Essays*, essay 4: *"The Praise of Folly"* (pp. 49–56).
14. Margaret Mann Phillips, *Erasmus and the Northern Renaissance* (London, 1949), p. 72.
15. Olin, *Six Essays*, pp. 35–38.
16. CWE 3: *Ep.* 333.
17. *Erasmi Opuscula*, ed. Wallace K. Ferguson (The Hague, 1933), p. 125. See also John C. Olin, *"Eloquentia, Eruditio, Fides*: Erasmus's *Life of Jerome,"*

in *Acta Conventus Neo-Latini Sanctandreani*, ed. I. D. McFarlane (Binghamton, N.Y., 1986), pp. 269–74.

18. *Erasmi Opuscula*, p. 179.

19. On this landmark work see Jerry H. Bentley, *Humanists and Holy Writ* (Princeton, 1983), chap. 4, and CWE 3: *Epp.* 373 and 384 (including headnotes).

20. Phillips, *Erasmus and the Northern Renaissance*, pp. 76–77.

21. CWE 4: *Ep.* 501.

22. Quoted in Heinrich Boehmer, *Martin Luther: Road to Reformation* (New York, 1957), p. 160.

23. Olin, *Six Essays*, essay 2: "The Pacifism of Erasmus" (pp. 17–31).

24. See Plates 2 and 3; Illustrations, p. ix, notes 2 and 3.

25. Fabriano's painting is in the Walters Art Gallery, Baltimore, and will be reproduced in the *Erasmus of Rotterdam Society Yearbook Seven (1987)*, with my discussion of it and its similarity to the Metsys portrait: "Erasmus and Saint Jerome: The Close Bond and Its Significance." Note the prominent HIERONYMVS inscribed on the edge of the bottom book on the bottom shelf in the Hampton Court version (Plate 2).

26. On this relationship and their divergent theologies see John W. O'Malley, "Erasmus and Luther, Continuity and Discontinuity as Key to Their Conflict," *Sixteenth Century Journal*, 5 No. 2 (October 1974), 47–65.

27. CWE 6: *Ep.* 933.

28. Ibid., *Ep.* 980.

29. On the exchange that followed see Marjorie O'Rourke Boyle, *Rhetoric and Reform: Erasmus' Civil Dispute with Luther* (Cambridge, Mass., 1983).

30. CWE 7: *Ep.* 999.

31. Margaret Mann Phillips, "Erasmus and the Classics," in *Erasmus*, ed. T. A. Dorey (Albuquerque, 1970), pp. 1–30.

32. Olin, *Six Essays*, essay 3: "Erasmus and the Church Fathers" (pp. 33–47).

33. Trans. Raymond Himelick in *Erasmus and the Seamless Coat of Jesus* (Lafayette, 1971).

34. See John W. O'Malley, "Erasmus and the History of Sacred Rhetoric: The *Ecclesiastes* of 1535," *Erasmus of Rotterdam Society Yearbook Five (1985)*, pp. 1–29.

35. Allen, VII *Ep.* 1891 (184–91).

36. Olin, *Six Essays*, essay 5: "Interpreting Erasmus" (pp. 57–73).

I

The *Compendium vitae* of Erasmus of Rotterdam

The *Compendium vitae* is a short autobiographical sketch composed by Erasmus in early 1524.[1] It was sent from Basel as a confidential memorandum to a very close friend, Conrad Goclenius, a professor of Latin at Louvain.[2] When Erasmus wrote this sketch, he was ill, depressed, and fearful of impending death, and he wanted to leave some sketch of his early years for the guidance of future biographers. He was entrusting these details about his private life to Goclenius, but he enjoined strict secrecy on him. This sketch (along with his letter to Grunnius in 1516 and a few other references) is the chief source for our knowledge of Erasmus' early life.

The *Compendium vitae* apparently was not known until its publication by a Professor Paul Merula in Leyden in 1607. This circumstance, as well as the quality of the narrative, has caused its authenticity to be challenged. It is accepted, however, by the best authorities, and there seems little reason to doubt its genuine character.[3] Huizinga and other biographers have nevertheless questioned certain facts in the narrative, especially the "romantic" story of Erasmus' star-crossed parents.[4] This part of the account perhaps should be read with caution. Deeply sensitive to the illegitimacy of his birth, Erasmus in his later years may have depicted his origin and family background in somewhat imaginative terms. But even this is revealing, and it would be wrong to dismiss the memoir as a fabrication. It is a moving and extremely valuable document affording a unique

1. The Latin text is in Allen, I 46–52. There is an English translation in Nichols, I 5–13 and in CWE 4: 400–10. The present translation was made by the editor from Allen with reference to Nichols' translation.

2. Erasmus' covering letter to Goclenius is in Allen, V 431–38. On Goclenius (1489–1539), see Allen, IV 504–5. Erasmus' last surviving letter, of 28 June 1536, is addressed to him.

3. Both Allen and Nichols accept it as genuine. See Allen, I, App. I, and Nichols, I xlvii–li, 1–4. For a criticism of its authenticity, see Roland Crahay, "Recherches sur le *Compendium Vitae* attribué à Erasme," *Humanisme et Renaissance*, 6 (1939), 7–19, 135–53.

4. Huizinga, p. 5, and Albert Hyma, *The Youth of Erasmus* (Ann Arbor, 1930), pp. 52ff. Charles Reade's novel *The Cloister and the Hearth* is based on the story Erasmus gives of his parents and birth.

insight into Erasmus' life and personality, and so great an Erasmian scholar as P. S. Allen judges its facts to be "correct even in small points."[5]

The narrative begins with short, jerky sentences, but it becomes more fluent, more like Erasmus' usual style, as it progresses. The third person is used except at the very end when Erasmus speaks directly to Goclenius in the first person. These concluding remarks are not, strictly speaking, a part of the autobiographical sketch, and they should be read as a kind of postscript to it. The vigil of SS. Simon and Jude is 27 October, and if the reference in the opening lines to his present age is understood exactly, the year of Erasmus' birth is 1466.

He was born in Rotterdam on the vigil of Simon and Jude. His age is about fifty-seven years. His mother was named Margaret, and the daughter of a certain physician Peter. She was from Zevenbergen. He saw two brothers of hers at Dordrecht, nearly ninety years of age. His father was named Gerard. The latter secretly had an affair with Margaret, in the expectation of marriage. And some say that they exchanged words of betrothal. The parents and brothers of Gerard were indignant about this. His father was Elias, his mother Catherine: both lived to a ripe old age, Catherine to nearly ninety-five. There were ten brothers, no sisters, of the same father and mother; all were married. Gerard was the youngest save one. It seemed to all that from so large a number one should be consecrated to God. You know the feelings of the old. And the brothers wished to hold on to the property and to have a hospitable retreat for themselves. Gerard, seeing himself completely barred from marriage by the solid opposition of all, did what the desperate do; he secretly fled, and on his journey he sent his parents and brothers a letter inscribed with clasped hands and with the sentence, "Farewell, I shall never see you again."

Meanwhile, his intended wife was left with child. The boy was raised at his grandmother's. Gerard went to Rome. There he supported himself adequately as a scribe, for the art of printing was not yet in use. Moreover, he had a very fine hand. And he lived like a young man. He soon applied himself to liberal studies. He gained an excellent knowledge of Greek and Latin. And he even made unusual progress in the study of law. For Rome then bloomed marvelously with learned men. He heard Guarino. He copied all the authors with his own hand. When his parents learned that he was at Rome, they

5. Allen, I 577–78.

wrote him that the girl he had sought to marry was dead. Believing this, out of grief he became a priest, and he applied his whole mind to religion. When he returned home he discovered the deception. However, she never afterward wished to marry, nor did he ever touch her again.

He provided a liberal education for the boy and sent him to elementary school when he was scarcely four years old. In his first years the boy made little progress in those disagreeable studies, for which he had no native aptitude. When he was in his ninth year, he was sent to Deventer; his mother followed to watch over and care for him in his tender age. That school was still barbarous (the *pater meus* was studied, tenses were required, Ebrardus and Johannes de Garlandia were read).[6] But Alexander Hegius and Zinthius had begun to introduce some better literature.[7] At last, from schoolmates who, being older, were in Zinthius' class, he first got the scent of better learning; later he heard Hegius several times, but only on feast days when he lectured to all. Here he reached the third class. Then a plague raging there carried off his mother, and the son, now in his thirteenth year, was left behind. When the plague daily became worse and worse and ravaged the whole house in which he lived, he returned to his home. Gerard, on receiving the sad news, became ill and died soon after. Both parents were not much more than forty years old when they died. Gerard appointed three guardians in whom he had the fullest confidence. The principal one was Peter Winckel, then a schoolmaster at Gouda. He left a modest legacy, if the guardians had administered it in good faith. And so the boy was sent away to 's Hertogenbosch, although he was ready enough for a university. In fact, they feared a university, for they had decided to rear the boy for the religious life.

He lived there—that is, he lost—nearly three years in the Brothers' House, as it is called, in which Romboldus then taught. This kind of man is now widely spread through the world, although the type is the

6. The *pater meus* was probably a Latin declension exercise; Ebrardus was the author of an elementary Latin text; Johannes de Garlandia was a thirteenth-century poet studied in school.

7. Alexander Hegius (1433–1498), German scholar and teacher, and one time student of Rudolph Agricola, became headmaster of the Deventer school in 1483, during Erasmus' last year there. John Zinthius (d. 1498) was one of the Brothers of the Common Life who taught at Deventer. See Beatus Rhenanus' reference to him in Selection II.

ruin of good natural talent and the seedbed of monasticism. Romboldus, who was greatly attracted by the ability of the boy, began to urge him to join his flock. The boy pleaded the inexperience of youth. When the plague arose there, although he had been ill for a long time with a quartan fever, he returned to the guardians; and he possessed by this time a sufficiently fluent style developed from several good authors. One guardian had died of the plague; the other two, not having managed the legacy very well, began to promote a monastery. The young man, weak with a fever which had gripped him for over a year, was not disinclined to piety; however, he did shrink from a monastery. Therefore they gave him time to consider. Meanwhile one of the guardians induced others to entice, to threaten, to influence the unsteady mind. And he had in the meantime found a place in a monastery of canons, commonly called regulars, at a college near Delft named Sion, the principal house of its chapter. When the day came for the reply, the young man answered prudently: he did not yet know what the world was, nor what the monastery was, nor what he himself was; accordingly, it seemed wiser that he should spend some years in the schools until he knew himself better. When he saw the young man firmly stating this, Peter immediately roared: "I have labored in vain then to prepare such a place for you through many entreaties. You are a good-for-nothing, you have a bad disposition. I give up my guardianship of you. Find your own living." The young man replied that he accepted the resignation and that he was old enough not to need guardians. When Peter saw that he made no progress, he induced his brother, who was himself a guardian, to conduct the business. This one used flattery. Others seeking to influence the youth approached on every side. He had a companion who betrayed his friend.[8] And the fever pressed upon him. Nevertheless, the monastery was not acceptable, until quite by chance he visited a monastery of the same order at Emmaus, or Steyn, near Gouda. There he found Cornelius, who had been a roommate of his at Deventer. He had not yet accepted the religious habit; he had seen Italy, but he had returned without having learned much. For reasons of his own he

8. Nichols, I 9, explains this allusion as applying to Erasmus' older brother Peter, who yielded to the guardians and entered a monastery.

began to depict with marvelous fluency the holy life, the abundance of books, the leisure, the peace, the angelic companionship. Why not? Childish affection drew him [Erasmus] toward his old companion. Some enticed him, some pushed him on. The fever weighed upon him. He chose this place, having no taste for the other. He was duped, however, until he took his religious habit. Meanwhile, although a young man, he sensed the absence of true piety there. Nevertheless, he encouraged the whole flock to study. Preparing to leave before his profession, he was restrained partly by human shame, partly by threats, partly by necessity.

He was professed. Finally, by chance he became known to the bishop of Cambrai, Henry of Bergen. The latter was hoping for a cardinal's hat, and he would have had it but for his lack of ready cash. For this journey he wished to have a man skilled in Latin. Thus, he [Erasmus] was summoned by him with the permission of the bishop of Utrecht, which by itself was sufficient. Nevertheless, he also secured the permission of the prior and the general. He joined the retinue of the bishop, retaining his habit, however. When the bishop lost all hope of a cardinal's hat, and he [Erasmus] perceived that the bishop was not very steadfast in his affection toward others, he arranged to go to Paris for the purpose of study. An annual stipend was promised; nothing was sent. Such is the way of princes. There at the college of Montaigu he took ill from the bad eggs and the unhealthy quarters, an illness in a hitherto most healthy constitution. And so he returned to the bishop. He was received honorably. He recovered from his illness at Bergen. He visited Holland with the thought in mind that he would remain with his brothers. But at their spontaneous urging he returned to Paris. There without the help of a Maecenas he lived rather than studied; and because of the plague which continued there for many years, he had to return each year to his own country. He shrank from the study of theology because he felt that his mind was not well disposed with the result that he might upset all of their fundamental principles and thereafter be branded a heretic. Finally, when the plague raged all the year, he was forced to move to Louvain.

Before that he had visited England at the invitation of Mountjoy, then his pupil, now his Maecenas, but more friendly than generous.

At that time he won the good will of all worthy men in England, especially because, when he was robbed at the port of Dover,[9] he not only took no revenge for the injury but soon published a little book in praise of the king and of all England. Later he was called back to England from France by great promises, at which time he gained the friendship of the archbishop of Canterbury. When the promises did not materialize, he went to Italy, where he had always ardently longed to go. Now on in years, that is, about forty, he stayed a little more than a year in Bologna. Then he went to Venice and published the *Adagia*; after that to Padua, where he spent the winter; a short time later to Rome, where already a distinguished and favorable reputation had preceded him. Raffaele, cardinal of San Giorgio, especially was kind.[10] Great good fortune would not have failed him, except that he was called back to England at the death of Henry VII and the succession of Henry VIII by the letters of friends promising the richest rewards. There he had decided to spend the rest of his days; but when even then the promises were not fulfilled, he betook himself to Brabant, invited to the court of Charles, now emperor, to whom he was made a councilor through the efforts of Jean Le Sauvage, the great chancellor.[11] The rest is known to you.

He has given the reason for changing his attire in the first tract wherein he replied to the calumnies of Lee.[12] You yourself can describe his appearance. His health was always delicate; thus he was frequently beset by fever, especially during Lent because of the fish diet, the mere smell of which was offensive to him. His nature was straightforward; and he was so averse to lying that even as a child he hated boys who lied and as an old man even shuddered at the sight of such persons. Among his friends his language was rather free, sometimes

---

9. See Beatus Rhenanus' account of the Dover incident in Selection II.

10. This was Cardinal Riario, a nephew of former Pope Sixtus IV, and during the time of Erasmus' sojourn in Italy (1506–1509) one of the most prominent prelates in Rome.

11. Jean Le Sauvage (1455–1518) was an important Netherlandish noble and a high official at the court of the youthful Charles V. He became chancellor of Burgundy in 1515 and chancellor of Castile in 1516.

12. Edward Lee was an English student at Louvain who in 1518 launched a sharp attack on Erasmus. Erasmus conducted bitter polemics with him for a number of years. The reference here is to Erasmus' abandoning his Augustinian canon's dress. See Beatus Rhenanus' explanation for this in Selection II. Lee later succeeded Wolsey as archbishop of York (1531–1544).

too much so; and though often deceived, he could not, however, mistrust his friends. He was somewhat fastidious, nor did he ever write anything that pleased him. He was not even pleased with his own face, and it was only with effort that his friends forced him to agree to sit for a painting. He had lasting contempt for honors and wealth, nor did he hold anything before his leisure and freedom. He was an honest judge of the learning of others and would have been a unique patron of talent, had his means been adequate. In promoting scholarship no one accomplished more, and because of this he incurred the oppressive envy of the barbarians and monks. Up to his fiftieth year he had not attacked anyone, nor was he attacked by anyone's pen. He had determined to keep his pen altogether free from blood. Faber was the first to attack him, for Dorp's undertaking was checked.[13] He was always polite in his reply. The Lutheran tragedy had burdened him with unbearable ill will; he was torn apart by each faction, while he sought to serve the best interests of each.

I will enlarge the catalogue of my works;[14] from this also much may be obtained. Gerard Noviomagus has written me that some men are considering a life of Erasmus, part in verse, part in prose.[15] He himself desired to be provided with information privately, but I have not ventured to send it. If you happen to talk with him, you can share this with him. But it is not expedient to attempt anything with respect to a life unless circumstances themselves demand it. But about this perhaps at another time, or even when we meet.

When I had written this, Birckmann came, burdened with lies.[16]

13. Faber is Jacques Lefèvre d'Etaples (Faber Stapulensis), the famous French scholar, who took issue with one of Erasmus' annotations on the Epistle to the Hebrews in his 1516 edition of the New Testament. A long controversy developed over this in 1517–1518; see CWE 5: 11, 121–24, 135, 310*n.* Martin Dorp, a Louvain theologian, criticized Erasmus' *Praise of Folly* and his projected New Testament in a letter of September 1514. Erasmus' reply to Dorp appears in this volume (Selection III).

14. This is the Botzheim Catalogue (Allen, I 1–46), first published by Froben in 1523 and greatly enlarged for a second edition in September 1524.

15. Noviomagus is Gerard Geldenhauer (ca. 1482–1542), who at this time was secretary to the bishop of Utrecht. He was a scholar and a close friend of Erasmus. He went over to Protestantism after 1525 and in his later years served as a professor at Marburg.

16. Franz Birckmann was a bookseller at Antwerp and a printer's agent. Through him in 1513 Erasmus arranged his first publication with the Froben press, a transaction discussed by Beatus Rhenanus in Selection II.

I know how difficult it is to keep a secret; nevertheless I entrust everything to you alone. I have celebrated our Viandalus; Levinus will show you the little book.[17] Urge Ceratinus whenever he reads an author to take some notes.[18] Favor must be shown to Froben; I cannot always be with him. And on account of him I am burdened with great ill will. You know how craftsmen are. Again farewell.

17. Erasmus dedicated his *Paraphrasis in tertium Psalmum* to Melchior Viandalus, a teacher at Tournai, in early 1524. Levinus was evidently the bearer of the letter and the *Compendium vitae* to Goclenius.

18. Jacob Ceratinus, a scholar apparently at Louvain at this time, collaborated on a Greek lexicon which Froben published in the summer of 1524.

II

The Life of Erasmus
by Beatus Rhenanus

This short biography of Erasmus was written by a close friend and colleague, Beatus Rhenanus, in 1540.[1] It was commissioned by the Froben firm in Basel as a preface to the nine-volume edition of Erasmus' complete works which the famous printing house published in 1538–1540. It introduces volume I of this first authorized *Opera omnia* and is in the form of a dedicatory letter to Emperor Charles V.

Beatus Rhenanus (1485–1547), the son of a butcher of Schlettstadt (Sélestat) in Alsace, was a noted scholar and editor in his own right. Along with Jacob Wimpfeling (1450–1528), he was one of the most prominent members of the Strasburg–Schlettstadt literary circle. He knew Erasmus very well and had worked for many years with him at the Froben press in Basel. His biography is the first extended account of the life of the great humanist, and as such it is a prime source for his life and the predecessor of all subsequent biographies of Erasmus. In writing this life Beatus enlarged an earlier sketch which he had composed in 1536, shortly after Erasmus' death, as a preface to Erasmus' last work, an edition of Origen.

Beatus' life is an interesting complement to the *Compendium vitae*, and in several instances it elucidates references made in this latter work. It is particularly valuable on Erasmus' stay in Italy, about which not too much more is known, and on Erasmus' scholarly labors. Beatus is speaking throughout as one who had long known and worked with Erasmus.

Erasmus was born in the early years of the reign of your great-grandfather Frederick III on the twenty-eighth of October at Rotterdam in Holland, your province in lower Germany, which the Batavi once held but which now is more famous to all students as the birthplace of one native son, Erasmus, than for the memory of its former inhabitants,

---

1. The Latin text is in Allen, I 56–71. There is an English abridgment in Nichols, I 25–37. The present translation was made by the editor from Allen with reference to Nichols' translation. On Beatus Rhenanus, see P. Adam, *L'Humanisme à Sélestat* (Sélestat, 1962), pp. 51–67; on this Life, see Bruce Mansfield, *Phoenix of His Age* (Toronto, 1979), pp. 17–21.

however pre-eminent they were in feats of war. Because of this son Rotterdam will always boast and be esteemed by the learned. The next praise is claimed by Deventer, which undertook to educate the boy, who previously had been a chorister in Utrecht cathedral, where, accustomed to take part in the musical presentations, he had served because of his small, high-pitched voice, after the fashion of cathedral churches. Alexander Hegius of Westphalia was then in charge of the school in Deventer, a man by no means deficient in scholarship and with some skill in Greek, which he acquired from Rudolph Agricola, whose close friendship he enjoyed after the latter returned from Italy, where he had attended the lectures of Guarino of Verona, teaching at Ferrara, and several other famous scholars. The talent of Erasmus soon shone forth, when immediately he grasped what was taught him and faithfully retained it, surpassing all his classmates. At that time there was among those who were called Brothers there—they were not monks, but lived and dressed like monks—John Zinthius, a man very well educated for that time; the grammatical commentaries which he published testify to this, and they brought him a great name in this period in the German schools. Delighted by the progress of Erasmus (for these long-robed cenobites preside over certain classes of students and teach publicly), Zinthius on one occasion embraced the boy and said, "Well done, Erasmus, some day you will reach the very summit of learning," and he kissed and dismissed him. This prophecy was not mistaken, as all are aware. But deprived of both parents soon after this, Erasmus was thrust from the school of Deventer, a most fertile seedbed for every kind of monk, into a monastery of canons, called in addition regulars in the Latin term, by the evil design of a guardian who wished to be rid of his responsibility. There he had for several years as a companion in his studies William Herman, of Gouda, a youth most devoted to letters and the author of the *Odarum sylva*. Aided and encouraged by this companion, there was no volume of the Latin authors he did not examine. By day and night, they engaged in study. The time which others of the same age slothfully wasted in jesting, sleep, and feasting, these two spent in perusing their books and exercising their pens.

Having heard of the fame of Erasmus, Henry, bishop of Cambrai and descendant of the princes of Bergen, invited the young man, now ordained a priest, to join him as he prepared to go to Italy and petition Rome [for a cardinal's hat]. For he saw that Erasmus had ability in letters and eloquence and that he was endowed with cultivated manners, as his gracefully written letters showed; and thus he could be useful as well as ornamental to his entourage if he had to transact business with the Roman pontiff or with the cardinals. It is not clear to me what prevented the bishop from undertaking this journey. William Herman was certainly much grieved that Erasmus had been taken from him, for thus he wrote in one of his odes:

> Now fate divides us,
> To you a boon, to me a bitter lot.
> Without me you go,
> Without me you gain the Rhineland glens, the Alpine peaks.
> Pleasant Italy will your happy haven be. Etc.

Although the bishop of Cambrai changed his mind about going to Rome, he nevertheless kept Erasmus at his court, delighted with his natural charm and with the distinction and candor of his youth. Here, truly amiable, he gained the friendship of many, especially of Anthony, abbot of St. Bertin, who was of the same family of Bergen, and of Jacob Batt, who was secretary to the council of the town of Bergen, to whom so many of his epistles are addressed and who later held a high position for a long time in the household of Anne of Borsselen, mother of Adolf, prince of Veere. Moreover, the bishop of Cambrai, considering the rich talent of his son Erasmus, willingly provided him with the means of going to Paris and of undertaking there the study of scholastic theology. He thus became a Scotist in the college of Montaigu; for among the theological disputants Duns Scotus was especially proclaimed because of his sharpness of intellect. And when he found the college life too hard, he gladly moved to the house of a certain English noble, who had two young English noblemen living with him; Mountjoy, I gather, was one of them. For the English saw that among the professors of literature in the entire university of Paris there was no one more learned or more faithful in teaching. For Faustus Andrelinus, otherwise intent upon writing his poems with great care, taught in a perfunctory way, seeking the applause of an ignorant audience by certain jokes more amusing than scholarly. Gaguin had been employed on missions to foreign princes and was not quite so accomplished in these studies, nor did he publicly teach.[2]

And from this time on Erasmus began to be known in England, which he himself visited shortly afterward at the invitation of his pupils, who had returned home. After he had stayed there a while, at the time of his departure he was deprived of nearly all his fortune by the customs collector at the port of Dover, and, not yet aboard ship, he met shipwreck because he attempted to take out some gold pieces beyond the prescribed amount and without royal permission (Mountjoy and More, unaware of English law, persuaded him that there was danger only in the case of English money). This wrong, however, had to be endured in silence, for with the law opposing, there was no remedy. It did not, however, estrange the injured spirit of Erasmus, nor did it deter him from returning to England frequently afterward. That region had then begun to abound in learned men: William Grocyn, Thomas Linacre, William Latimer, who had undertaken the study of literature in Italy and were renowned for their skill in both languages, and also John Colet, Thomas More, Richard Pace, and Cuthbert Tunstall, by all of whom he was eagerly loved. And as for the bishops, those who were more acquainted with literature did more for Erasmus and treated him more kindly. He taught for some time at the university of Cambridge; he also taught at Louvain, when he stayed with John Paludanus, the orator of that school. At last persuaded by friends, he traveled to Bologna with John and Bernard, the sons of Battista Boerio of Genoa, the physician of the English king; and he saw at length Italy, which he always had a great desire to see (this was not unmerited, because no place in all the world is more cultured in every way than this region). He accompanied them not as an attendant, for he had not undertaken the care of their conduct, nor as a teacher, but as one who would direct and supervise their studies, as his letter to Botzheim states. There, among the professors he gained the friendship of Paulus Bombasius, a learned man of stainless charac-

2. Robert Gaguin (1433–1501) was a leading scholar and author in Paris. When Erasmus first arrived there in 1495, he made his acquaintance. Soon after this Erasmus wrote a commendatory letter to fill the blank space at the end of Gaguin's *De origine et gestis Francorum compendium*, published in September 1495. This was Erasmus' first published writing. Thus his career, in a sense, begins with his association with Gaguin.

ter, who in turn was greatly delighted with the genius and learning of Erasmus. For Beroaldus, the Achilles among professors of his time, had already died, and Baptista Pius, an unfortunate imitator of antiquity, dreamed of Oscans and Volscians. On the journey Erasmus, along with an English companion, was made a doctor of theology at Turin in the Cottian Alps. Thus he carried into Italy dignity and erudition, which others have been accustomed to bring back from that country.

While he completed at Bologna the volume of *Adagia* begun long before (for he had published at Paris many years previously a brief and rough specimen of his future work), he was forced by the following circumstance to change his monastic garb as a canon regular, which up to that time he had worn. There is a laudable practice in that city that if anyone is suspected of having the plague, a surgeon appointed for the purpose is summoned at once. In order that he can more easily be avoided by all who meet or pass him, because of the deadly infection, he is accustomed to wear a white napkin over one of his shoulders and to carry a rod in his hand. By chance one day Erasmus was walking alone through an unfrequented street in the town in his customary canon's dress. Two or three inexperienced youths met him there, and catching sight of his white scapular, they thought him to be the plague investigator; and as Erasmus proceeded along his way suspecting nothing, they threatened violence with stones they had gathered and pursued him with loud shouts, not, however, going beyond words. Surprised, Erasmus sought to know the reason for the indignation. Some people who had heard the brawling and were looking on from their houses told him that his scapular, tied in a knot at his side, had alarmed the youths, and that mistaken by the similarity in dress, they thought he was returning from some plague victim and had no intention of getting out of their way. Therefore, lest he incur a similar danger again, Erasmus sent a petition to Pope Julius II that he grant him permission either to wear or not wear his religious habit. Because of his singular merits this concession was made without difficulty, provided that he wear the dress of a priest; and this Leo X for other good reasons, not so much to lay down a rule of life as to show his esteem of Erasmus, later confirmed in the fullest form (as they say): specially and expressly overruling each and every objection, and holding their contents to have been sufficiently expressed and enumerated.[3] And who can doubt that the Popes have full power in human constitutions of this kind, when the interpreters of the law concede them no little authority in the interpretation and regulation of matters pertaining to divine law and the law of nations, and indeed hand down that they have the power of freely disposing and dispensing, to use their own phrase, except in articles of faith?

When work on the *Adagia* was completed, he wrote to Aldus Manutius to ask if he wished to undertake the printing of the book. The latter replied that he would do so with pleasure. Erasmus then moved to Venice. When he came to the printing shop, he was forced to wait a long time before he was received because Aldus was busy correcting proofs and thought that he was one of those ordinary visitors, who more out of curiosity than for the sake of offering their help or counsel constantly descend on a man busy with other affairs and are always annoying. When he found out that it was Erasmus, he begged his forgiveness and embraced him with great delight; and he received him as his guest in the home of his father-in-law, Andrea of Asola, the proprietor of that famed establishment, where he shared a room with Jerome Aleander of Motta, renowned for his knowledge of the three languages, now a cardinal. Among others he also enjoyed the intimate friendship of the noble Paulo Canale, of Ambrosio of Nola, an eminent physician, and of Giovan Battista Egnazio. Nor was his stay in Venice a brief one, for he revised and published again two tragedies of Euripides, *Hecuba* and *Iphigenia in Aulis*, and he corrected the comedies of Terence and Plautus with special reference to their poetry. During that time Alexander, son of James, king of Scots, and already archbishop of St. Andrews in Scotland, was studying at Padua and attending the lectures of Raffaele Reggio. Erasmus became his teacher of rhetoric, and he later moved with him to Siena. For he had sometime before parted with his Boerio pupils because of the ill-humor of their father, after spending a year with them. At Padua he was in the company of the most learned Marcus Musurus of Crete and Scipio Carteromachus of Pistoia, whose kindness I have often heard him extol. He had proof of their sincerity many times when he sought

3. These lines quote and refer to Leo X's letter of 26 January 1517 (Allen, II 433–35), which dispensed Erasmus from wearing his canon's dress, permitted him to live in the world, and granted him the power to hold Church benefices, despite the illegitimacy of his birth.

their advice while he was working on the corrupt manuscripts of such Greek authors as Pausanias, Eustathius, the interpreter of Lycophron, and commentaries on Euripides, Pindar, Sophocles, Theocritus, and similar authors, most of which were in the Aldine library. There was nothing so abstruse which Musurus could not explain, nor so involved which he could not disentangle: Musurus, truly the guardian and high priest of the Muses. He had read everything, he had weighed everything. He knew perfectly the forms of expression, the myths, the histories, the ancient rites. A remarkable dutifulness even enhanced this consummate erudition, for he had an aged Greek father whom he tended with loving and constant care. Scipio was endowed with a many-sided learning and with an upright character. Both died at Rome, Musurus having been made archbishop of Monemvasia by Pope Leo.

While Erasmus lived in Siena in the house of the archbishop of St. Andrews, whom he taught and whose ability he often praised—the truth of his appraisal would have been more apparent if that most illustrious youth had not been killed shortly after, together with his royal father as he closed his flank in the battle in which the army of King Henry of England, whose sister was the wife of the king of Scots, clashed with the invading Scots, who were allied with the French[4] (Henry at that time being in Belgium and besieging Tournai at the instigation of Pope Julius II)—while there in Tuscany, I repeat, Erasmus obtained leave to visit nearby Rome. It is impossible to describe with what great applause and with what great joy he was received there among the cultured, not only among those of ordinary status but also among those resplendent in the rank of cardinal, especially Giovanni de' Medici, who chosen in the place of the dead Julius II took the name of Leo X, Domenico Grimani of Venice, and Egidio da Viterbo, most learned in the three languages, all distinguished men born and devoted to the encouragement of studies, in which they so uncommonly excelled. He also saw, as I recall hearing, that illustrious Tommaso Phaedra, incomparably eloquent in extemporaneous speech, who evoked venerable antiquity by his recounting of plays and comedies. And he saw other professors. If he wished to re-

---

4. This is the battle of Flodden Field, 9 September 1513, in which James IV of Scotland and his son were killed.

main in Rome, he was offered the office of a penitentiary, which would lead in the future to higher dignities; certainly the gain could not thereafter be considered of small account. But he had to return to the archbishop, with whom he afterward went again to Rome, which that most noble youth wished to see before he returned to his native Scotland; and they visited not only Rome (though with the archbishop incognito, lest he trouble anyone) but Italy farther south as far as Cumae, and they stole into the cave of the sibyl, which is still exhibited by the natives there.

After the departure of the archbishop of St. Andrews, the memory of old friends whom he had left in England prompted the hurried return of Erasmus to his homeland. And thus he traveled through the Rhaetian Alps first to Chur, then to Constance on the lake of Bregenz; and after he crossed the district of the Lentienses, who are at the beginning of the Martian forest, which in ancient times was Orcynium, he came through the Breisgau to Strasburg, whence he was carried down the Rhine into Holland. Then, after greeting his friends at Antwerp and Louvain, he left for England. He was gripped by the longing to see the theologian John Colet, who was dean of St Paul's in London, Grocyn, Latimer, Linacre, mentioned above, and especially Thomas More. His old Maecenas was William Warham, archbishop of Canterbury, primate of all England and chancellor of that realm, that is, the highest judge, who surpassed all the bishops of that island by his generosity. He gave him money and, in addition, the Aldington benefice in the diocese of Canterbury; and when Erasmus was hindered by a scruple from accepting this immediately because the whole income belonged rather to the pastor, who, at hand day and night, instructed the people under his care—that which no one can deny—the archbishop said to him hesitating, "Who lives more justly than you from an ecclesiastical income, the one who by your most useful writings instruct, teach, and help all the priests themselves who are in charge of the churches? and not only these, but also all the churches everywhere in the world, which they individually govern and serve." I well remember Erasmus more than once saying that princes have the duty of helping students by their own generosity; but that they, with the intention of sparing their own expense, took recourse in conferring priestly benefices, which the followers of learning are forced to accept so that they may be able to have the leisure for scholarship. He honored others, as, for example, Mountjoy with the dedication of the *Adagia*, and John Colet, the founder of a new school in London, with the twofold *De copia verborum et rerum*, to whom he once jokingly said that the publication of both *Copia* clearly made him a poor man. Thus he decided to make immortal his most distinguished Maecenas, William Warham, with the dedication especially of the works of Jerome.

Emulating Aldus, Johann Froben had printed quite handsomely the *Adagia* for eager students. Erasmus was moved by this pleasing edition and also by the renown of the more diligent firm, and since he knew that another, enlarged copy of the *Adagia*, formerly promised and intended for Badius,[5] together with several books of Plutarch recently translated, had gone astray to Basel in line with the plan of Franz Birckmann, and that there all the works of St. Jerome were in the Froben press, he betook himself there also, pretending a journey to Rome in fulfillment of a vow. Nor had the report been groundless. For a long time ago Johann Amerbach, having completed the works of Ambrose and Augustine, had wholly devoted himself to the correction of the volumes of Jerome.[6] He had collected the old manuscripts from everywhere and had employed learned men to restore the Greek passages scattered throughout. One of these was Johann Reuchlin, the lawyer, who tried to fill in the empty gaps with the aid of dictionaries.[7] He was succeeded by a more successful corrector, Johann Kuno of Nuremberg, a Dominican who, having followed a better method, diligently replaced what had been either missing or corrupt from traces in the old documents. And this he could do as a man nearly more learned in Greek than in Latin, trained certainly in the best authors, and for several years one of the most attentive students of the best professors in Italy, Musurus and Scipio, whom we have mentioned

5. Josse Badius, scholar and proprietor of the Ascencian Press in Paris, had printed a great many of Erasmus' works. On this episode, see Huizinga, pp. 82–83.

6. Johann Amerbach (ca. 1430–1513) had founded the famous press in Basel which is generally associated with the name of his partner Johann Froben (ca. 1460–1527). One of Amerbach's great ambitions was to publish good texts of the Doctors of the Church. His edition of Ambrose had appeared in 1492 and that of Augustine in 1506. The great edition of Jerome was brought to completion by Erasmus, who long had an interest in such a project, and it appeared in 1516, three years after Amerbach's death. On Erasmus and the Jerome edition, see Allen, II 210–11.

7. Johann Reuchlin (1455–1522), the famous German scholar and champion of the study of Hebrew literature, had law degrees from Orléans, Poitiers, and Tübingen. He was employed by Amerbach in this task in the summer of 1510.

above, and John of Crete. And now with Amerbach dead, his sons Bruno and Basil together with Johann Froben had begun the printing of Jerome and had advanced as far as the commentary on the Prophets. The elegance of the edition, and especially the extraordinary zeal and diligence of the Amerbach brothers in their correcting, pleased Erasmus, who as a new guest had been received immediately into the Froben house. Therefore if he himself was ever consulted when there was need for judgment because of variant readings in the manuscripts, he was there to help. But he particularly claimed the volumes of letters for himself and occupied himself in part in completing the marginal notes, which he had already begun a long time before, and in part in adding new annotations and arguments. This task was considerable. A greater one by far was added. Students in France and Germany separately desired an edition of the New Testament in Greek which they might add to the Old from Venice. Erasmus had formerly written annotations on it, following Lorenzo Valla.[8] When he found these among his papers, he hastily revised and enlarged them amid the din of the presses. Nor were they lacking who thought that the New Testament itself should be polished, having been written, or rather translated, it appeared, for the mass of Christians. And by virtue of his own willingness he complied with those advising this. In fact, he dedicated this work to Pope Leo X, who as the highest guardian of the same indeed deserved the dedication of the principal document of our religion. On the other hand he dedicated the revision of the works of Jerome to Archbishop Warham of Canterbury, a lasting monument of singular respect.

He returned then to lower Germany on account of business, and having come back to us a short time later, he went thither again at the time when Your Majesty was consecrated at Aachen with the symbols of the Roman Empire, whose antiquity [has been preserved] for us by the Goths themselves, Theodoric of Verona and others. Then he was at Cologne prior to the Diet of Worms, notable among those who were

8. Lorenzo Valla (1405–1457), the Italian humanist, had written *Annotationes* on the New Testament, which Erasmus discovered in a monastery near Louvain in 1504 and whose publication he arranged for by Badius in Paris in 1505. On Valla and Erasmus, see Jerry H. Bentley, *Humanists and Holy Writ* (Princeton, 1983), chaps. 2 and 4.

your councilors;[9] for you had most wisely taken him into this body a long time before, when Jean Le Sauvage was still alive and held the post of great chancellor. After the meetings at Worms were over and the city of Tournai had been regained, when Your Majesty had again left Brabant for Spain, Erasmus returned to Basel intending to re-edit the *Adagiorum chiliades* and to complete the *Paraphrases* of St. Paul and the Gospels. It is doubtful whether he undertook these more because of the applause of students everywhere or whether he himself wrote them more out of the joy [in doing so]. "Here I am on my own field of action," he said. And so he was. He examined especially the old commentators, Ambrose, Jerome, Augustine, Hilary among the Latins, Chrysostom and his imitator Theophylactus among the Greeks. He himself merely adapted the style. One of these, namely the first *Paraphrase* on the Gospel of Matthew, he dedicated to Your Majesty, and the last he dedicated to your brother, King Ferdinand. Who, devoted to your court and bound by the most honorable office, has honored you more greatly as a youth and as the heir of so many kingdoms, who esteemed you more when you were raised to the summit of the Roman Empire by the unanimous vote of the princes? He prepared for you, still a young man, the *Institutio principis Christiani*, expressed in devout but short aphorisms, a little book (may God so love me as this is true!) in which he who has been destined for the administration of the highest affairs may either himself learn the conduct worthy of a Christian as in a mirror, or a teacher working with him may see with what kind of first principles pertaining to a youthful education the mind of rulers should be imbued while yet still tender. Indeed Erasmus has always sought by every kind of deference, proper to a man of letters, to give honor to the most noble House of Austria, cradle of so many Caesars, whose empire is scarcely limited by the Julian and Rhaetian Alps and by the northern ocean. The panegyric to your father, Philip, presented at the time of his return from Spain and regarded by him with very great affection, demonstrates this; and Philip deemed that this service should be followed by extraordinary munificence, first

---

9. It was at this time (November 1520) that Erasmus, in the train of Charles V, had the interview with Elector Frederick of Saxony, out of which came the *Axiomata*. See Selection VII.

showing as if by some fortunate omen, what great value the writings of this man would have one day, and all but establishing a model which other great men might emulate. Nor did it happen otherwise.

And indeed Erasmus knew a similar benevolence on the part of many kings and popes, as yours in the first place, august Emperor, as that of your brother Ferdinand, now King, as that of King Henry VIII of England, by whom he was addressed in letters from that prince's own hand when his father Henry VII was still alive, and as that of Pope Clement VII. Nor was Pope Adrian of another mind, if Erasmus had wished to accept the benefice offered him or an honorary post. Moreover, what might Erasmus not have expected from Francis of Valois, king of France, if we consider his disposition and what he wished to bestow upon him? He did not disdain to write in his own hand at the end of at least one letter that Erasmus' arrival would be most pleasing. That Pope Paul III, as much because of his opinion and inclination for Erasmian virtue and learning as for the result [it would have], was in fact prepared to favor him at every opportunity, this henceforth is clear because not only had the proposal been made that Erasmus be admitted into the college of cardinals, but the Pope himself also offered Erasmus the provostship at Deventer in the diocese of Utrecht, which is said to grant an income of six hundred gulden. He offered it, did I say? On the contrary, he bestowed it, not only dispatching an apostolic letter concerning it, lest the weariness and expense of the undertaking diminish the value of the benefice, but also in an affectionate letter addressing your sister Mary, the most illustrious queen of Hungary and your regent in Flanders, that in consideration of her filial devotion toward the Roman See and of her royal generosity toward deserving men, she take care that the occupancy of the aforementioned provostship be kept free from intruders for Erasmus. However, Erasmus, an autarch because he had determined to refuse a benefice, remained his own master, saying that he, who was about to die in a short time, had sufficient resources. Truly it would be a very lengthy affair to draw up a list of princes and bishops who were munificent to Erasmus.

Erasmus was not only honored by the princes, but also by the cities of Germany; and if he passed through them and the magistrates knew it, he was presented with wine, an honor shown to magnates and the ambassadors of cities according to the custom of the nation. This happened at Basel in my presence, at Constance on the lake of Bregenz, where the jurist and consul Bartholomew Blaurer of his own accord deigned to attend the banquet, at Schaffhausen under the auspices of the abbot and magistrate, at Freiburg im Breisgau, at Breisach, at Schlettstadt, at Strasburg, and also at other places. For many had known that he was in the council of your Majesty. Indeed, on account of the excellence of his learning, which was more clearly displayed in all his published books from day to day, he was deemed worthy besides that all should respectfully desire to honor him eagerly with the gifts they sent, none of which he sought, and to favor him with every kind of distinction. And if we commonly see those men who, if ever necessity demands, are prepared to defend their country at the peril of their lives distinguished by titles of military glory, how much more justly is he honored who of his own accord consumed, not any brief time, but his whole life in the service of letters, employing his talents to the public advantage, unmindful of his own enjoyment? He could have been great and daily have become greater at Your Majesty's court. Was not your former teacher, Adrian of Utrecht, raised to the highest pinnacle of ecclesiastical authority? He could have lived in splendor at the courts of whatever kings he wished; for who of the highest princes has not sought him? He could have dwelt in leisure and enjoyment, but he preferred the public usefulness of his studies to all honors and to the crass pleasures of this life.

It is probable that in addition to other motives the happy issue of a scholarly revival also greatly fired the man to pierce through no matter what. In Germany and France letters lay cold and lifeless; hardly anyone knew Latin, no one Greek. And behold, immediately when the *Adagiorum chiliades* and the *De copia verborum et rerum* were published, the knowledge of languages began to come forth, like the sun breaking through the clouds. Other books useful for this purpose appeared: Theodorus' *Grammaticae institutiones*, translated into Latin, and the texts in both languages of many Greek authors, fully suitable for those wishing to learn without the help of an instructor. For in this way even Hermolaus Barbarus, the immortal glory of Venice, is said formerly to have made progress in private study, by comparing versions of the most learned Gaza. And then, as if by a given signal, the best men were promoting the cause of letters in those countries.

But the greatest aid of all was given by the Trilingual College established at the University of Louvain on the recommendation of Erasmus.[10] Jerome Busleiden, provost of Aire and brother of Francis, at one time archbishop of Besançon, who died while abroad in Spain, had left at his death great wealth; and as he had intended that this be used for students, Erasmus proposed to those who drew up the will that they found an athenaeum at Louvain where the three languages would be publicly taught by virtue of appointments to salaried posts. And from this institution, as if from a Trojan horse, innumerable men provided with a knowledge of languages have up to now come forth, and in turn they are going to hand this knowledge over to those favoring higher things. Your universal sway, mighty Caesar, has nothing more illustrious than this. This example also moved Francis, king of France, to give thought to the establishment of a similar college in Paris and by letter to summon Erasmus, on whose advice everything would be arranged. And he had already received a royal diploma for the security of the journey, but reasons intervened to prevent his departure. Nevertheless, professors were also appointed there. And so it is generally acknowledged that the growth of learning in these countries is due most of all to Erasmus. For what stone did he not move, as they say, that studies might advance? With what great openness did he hand over everything, wishing to be understood by all, although many explain obscure matters far more obscurely? When he was about to publish the *Adagia*, certain scholars said to him, "Erasmus, you are divulging our secrets." But he was desirous that these be accessible to all so that they might attain to complete scholarship. Because of this candor that scholar was abandoned who once said to Aldus Manutius in Venice as he was preparing to publish Greek commentaries on Euripides and Sophocles, "Take care in doing this lest the barbarians, aided by these studies, remain at home and fewer of them come to Italy." Now nothing was so insignificant that it did not engage this great man for the sake of students. He even deigned to correct and explain the song of Cato itself, together with its title, so that neither in great matters

10. There is an extensive history of this famous college in its early period: Henry de Vocht, *History of the Foundation and the Rise of the Collegium Trilingue Lovaniense, 1517–1550* (4 vols; Louvain, 1951–1955).

nor in small ones would his work be lacking. Indeed, anyone can hardly be mentioned who has done more for general studies.

France indeed has Budaeus, a prince of letters, with whom he is happily compared.[11] This scholar was not only the first to explain in a most learned and thorough fashion the very abstruse subject of ancient money, but he also analyzed most elegantly the ancient forms of speech of the jurists when he published his annotations on the Pandects, to the great glory of his nation (it cannot be denied); finally he composed commentaries on the Greek language, than which nothing more useful can be near the student of Greek. But our scholar has expended more labor on theological studies. And these studies he treated with somewhat greater freedom because he saw (I use his own words from a letter to a certain friend) too much deference being given to the prattler of theology, the old theology being utterly effaced and the theologians so absorbed in the subtleties of the Scotists that they do not approach the springs of divine wisdom. Moreover, he saw that ecclesiastical discipline had declined far from the purity of the Gospels, that the Christian people were weighed down with many practices, and that the consciences of men were ensnared by various tricks. And on account of this state of affairs, he attacked the arrogance, the ambition, the greed, and the superstition of certain men wherever they may be with a rather free pen, flattering no one however powerful he may be, though today, however, many do this excessively. Nothing is more injurious to princes, especially ecclesiastical princes, as not pointing out clearly what they should do, while we praise what they do. In this regard he is never remiss. Although I do remember him often saying while he was alive that if he had foreseen such an age arising as ours, he would not have written many things or he would not have written them in the way he did.[12] But, thank God, we see some fruit from these admonitions. The body of theologians in his own time study

11. Budaeus, or Guillaume Budé (1467–1540), was one of the greatest of the French classical scholars. There is considerable correspondence between him and Erasmus, some of it in Greek. Budaeus' very learned and extensive treatise on ancient coinage and its value, De asse, was published in Paris in 1515. His important work on the Pandects (the digest of Roman judicial opinions compiled for Justinian) had been published by Badius in 1508. He also published a Greek lexicon in 1529.

12. Erasmus expresses the same thought in his letter to Jonas of 10 May 1521 (Selection VIII).

Cyprian, Augustine, Ambrose, and Jerome in place of Alexander of Hales and Robert of Holcot.[13] Peter Lombard attempted to reduce diffuse theological study to a system in the collected books of the *Sentences*, as they are called. But his method is looked for in vain in the commentaries of modern authors. John of Damascus tried to do a similar thing among the Greeks. From the ancients one may learn of the most simple beginnings of the early Church, which little by little has grown to its present majesty. And without reading these authors, he who has been occupied only with the modern writers will discuss many topics injudiciously, [and he will have] a white rule, as the proverb says, for measuring sacred things.[14] Therefore a knowledge of the ancient writers is very necessary for the future theologian; and it is to this knowledge that Erasmus has so greatly encouraged students, correcting their lucubrations and comparing them with the ancient models.

His books are extant, nor is it necessary to recount them by name. In a great number of passages he has added severe judgments, which as an outstanding quality and clear proof of the most resolute and discerning character I admire more than anything else. For I think that there has been no one for many generations now who has been more influential on judgment, a fact which is wont to affect the highest scholarship ultimately of all. To some, measuring everything severely by the structure and vocabulary of Cicero, it appeared that it was enough to be Ciceronian. But he himself always loved an open, extemporaneous, pure, fluent, and lively style; and he made certain terms serve the Christian subjects that he treated. For he did not approve the superstition of those who restore certain empty ancient models rather than maxims that are concise and distinguished. Indeed, we admit that the age of Cicero was most pure and worthy of imitation, and that therefore it is a great felicity if anyone attains the genuine diction of that time during which the Latin language especially flourished. And

13. Alexander of Hales is a thirteenth-century English Franciscan theologian, and Robert of Holcot is a fourteenth-century English Dominican theologian. The two men mentioned in the next sentences are Peter Lombard, a twelfth-century theologian whose chief work, the *Sentences*, was a basic theological text in the Middle Ages, and John of Damascus, an important eighth-century Greek theologian.

14. This apparently is a reference to the Lesbian measuring rule of soft lead (Aristotle, *Eth. Nic.* 5.10.7). In this context it would seem to mean no fixed principle or standard of judgment.

we perceive that some men elegantly advance this cause, nor are we envious. But let them produce for our benefit as many useful, holy, and wise writings as the Christian world received from Erasmus, and we will agree with them and even praise the Ciceronians for piety and virtue.

He wrote a great part of these books at Basel in Froben's home situated on St. Peter's hill and part also at Freiburg im Breisgau. For he was forced to migrate with his baggage to that town, under the jurisdiction of your brother, King Ferdinand, at the warning of Bernard à Gles, cardinal of Trent, who feared lest anything happen to him at Basel after the religious change took place. This change, however, occurred far more peacefully than many foresaw because of the prudence of the magistrates, and none of the clergy suffered injury. At Freiburg he first lived in that magnificent house which your grandfather Maximilian had formerly ordered prepared for himself by Jacob Willinger of his Majesty's treasury as a nest in his old age. Afterward he bought a house of his own. But when he was invited to Brabant by your most illustrious sister Mary, queen of Hungary, whom you had made regent in the Low Countries at the death of your aunt Margaret, and when his *Ecclesiastes* was first about to be published, in order that he might be present while it was going through the press and might add the colophon to the work, as they say (for I do not know what remained to bring it to a conclusion), and at the same time in order that he might dispel the more tenacious vestiges of illness by a change of sky, he sold his house and returned after seven years to Basel with all his belongings, the greatest part of which were books, staying as a most welcome guest with his old friend Jerome Froben; and he had this in mind, that when he had regained his health and had completed those affairs which he had at hand, he would go by ship down the Rhine to lower Germany. Meanwhile arthritis, which for some time had been quiescent, again seized the man and sorely distressed him so that he could not be moved from the place, the change of sky having been in vain. As the torments abated, he passed from a biped first to a quadruped, then to a triped, supporting himself with the help of crutches and gradually creeping forward. Whenever he unfolded one by one the letters which he had received in former years from various friends, on account of I know not what new publication—and very many came into his hands from those who had departed from this earthly scene—he repeatedly said, "And this one is dead"; and finally, "Nor do I wish to live any longer, if it please Christ the Lord." And so dysentery, the fatal misfortune, tormented him, feeble and destitute of strength though entirely sound of mind; and having gradually exhausted him, it at last brought his death with the greatest calm and acceptance as he implored Christ's mercy in his final, oft repeated words. He who, when he lived, treated the teaching of Christ with such sincerity, in death received without a doubt a full reward from the highest Judge.

Relying on the authority of your Majesty, he had made a will, in which he provided in a threefold way for the needs of the poor out of his resources left at the time of death, that is, for helping the ill and aged, for aiding virgins who lacked marriage dowries, and for assisting students. Boniface Amerbach, professor of law, having been designated heir, together with his associates executed the will in good faith according to the mind of the testator with regard to the payment of annual stipends and incomes, and he took care to do everything which Erasmus wished to be done with exactness. He himself placed on a pillar in the cathedral of Basel, adjacent to the tombstone bearing the sculptured device "Terminus," a memorial engraved in Siebengebirge marble to the excellent patron.

Your Majesty knew that in stature he was, as he himself describes More in one of his letters, neither tall nor noticeably short. His body was compact enough and well proportioned, but because it was of a very delicate constitution and was easily disturbed by even the least change, as, for example, in the matter of wine or food or air, it was subject in later years to frequent ills, including the stone, not to mention rheum, in itself the constant and common ailment of all students. He had a fair complexion, light blond hair in his youth, bluish-gray eyes, a pleasant expression; his voice was thin, though his language was admirably straightforward; his dress was dignified and grave, as befits an imperial councilor, theologian, and priest. He was most constant in retaining friendship, and whatever the cause, he never changed a dedication. He had a most excellent memory, for as a child he memorized all of Terence and Horace. He was generous to those in need, to whom, as elsewhere, he was always accustomed to give alms through a servant as he returned home from mass; but he was especially kind and generous to young students of promise and talent, if any should come to him in need of money for study abroad. In social intercourse he was courteous and pleasant, without a trace of arrogance, in every respect surely ἐράσμιος, that is, amiable; and he was sorry that he had not taken that name when he first began to write and to be known for his published books. "For who," he said, "has heard any mortal called Love?" That is what ἐρασμός means in Greek.

On the other hand, with regard to the publication in a single edition of the numerous books which he had written throughout his life, both sacred as well as secular, this most modest man at the time of his death made no provision, having been of the opinion that in the future these writings of his would certainly be disregarded by the more educated daily arising. But since the printers Jerome Froben and Nicholas Episcopius felt that students desired these writings brought together at the same time in that order which he himself, when alive, made known to Johann Botzheim and later to Hector Boece in the catalogue of his works[15]—namely, first those which pertain either to literary instruction or to piety, then those of a moral character, then the *apologiae*, and in the last place the authors he had revised and completed—they resolved to gratify the students, and they undertook a project as magnificent as it is worthy of the approval of all. They were deterred neither by the magnitude of the expense nor by the greatness of the labor, whatever the final outcome might be, provided that they might complete the volumes of Erasmus' works, having followed principally the author's catalogue to Hector Boece as the more recent. They even added all of those by Amerbach, on which afterward Erasmus also labored, having omitted, however, a tenth volume only by excluding other authors which he had revised. The same printers promise to bring out separately in the course of time also this work of his for students, if they will find a comparable audience. And this edition must be made not only for other reasons of importance but also because it protects the reputation of so great a master of letters,

15. Erasmus drew up a catalogue of his works in 1523 at the request of his friend Johann Botzheim, canon of Constance. It was published by Froben and greatly enlarged for a second edition in 1524 (Allen, I 1–46). He compiled another catalogue in 1530 for Hector Boece, principal of King's College, Aberdeen (Allen, VIII 372–77).

lest anyone, either with the intention of doing harm or with a desire for gain, seeking the favor that comes from the genius evidently Erasmian, constantly attribute to him something which he has not written (we know that this happened when he was alive), or which he has not acknowledged as his own, or which, though acknowledged, he thought scarcely worthy of publication.

Schlettstadt
1 June 1540

III

Letter to Martin Dorp
May 1515

This lengthy epistle is a defense by Erasmus of his *The Praise of Folly* and of the Greek and Latin edition of the New Testament which he was about to publish.[1] It is addressed to Martin Dorp, a professor of philosophy at the University of Louvain, who had written Erasmus in September 1514 criticizing his famous satire and his temerity in correcting the Vulgate text of Holy Scripture.[2] A controversy ensued, in which Dorp replied in August 1515 and Thomas More wrote a long letter to Dorp in Erasmus' behalf in October.[3] Chambers tells us that More "converted his antagonist."[4] At any rate, the attack was checked, as Erasmus states in the *Compendium vitae*, and cordial relations continued between Erasmus and Dorp.

Dorp (1485–1525) was a scholar in the humanist tradition and an old friend of Erasmus. He had studied at the Collège du Lis in Louvain, and after completing his own course of studies in 1504, he taught philosophy there. He received a doctorate of theology in 1515 and was subsequently admitted to the University's theological faculty—facts which cast some light, it would seem, on the nature and timing of Dorp's criticisms. Erasmus viewed Dorp's letter as inspired by others, that is, by certain Louvain theologians who were opposed to the new scholarship and who were using Dorp in this instance as their mouthpiece. Whatever the situation, the crisis passed. Dorp went on to become rector at Louvain in 1523, and long before that he had renewed his interest in and approval of humanist studies. When he died in 1525, Erasmus wrote his epitaph.

1. The Latin text is in Allen, II 90–114. The present translation was made from Allen by John W. Bush, S.J., and Martin Feeney, S.J. *The Praise of Folly* was first published in 1511, and Erasmus' New Testament was brought out by Froben in February 1516.

2. Dorp's letter of September 1514 is in Allen, II 10–16.

3. Dorp's second letter is in Allen, II 126–36. More's letter to Dorp can be read in English translation in St. *Thomas More: Selected Letters*, ed. E. F. Rogers (New Haven, 1961), pp. 8–64. There is a good account of the controversy in Henry de Vocht, *Monumenta Humanistica Lovaniensia: Texts and Studies about Louvain Humanists of the First Half of the XVIth Century* (Louvain, 1934), pp. 139ff.

4. R. W. Chambers, *Thomas More* (London, 1938), p. 253. See Allen's note (IV 124–25) on Dorp's later attitude and relations with Erasmus.

The letter to Dorp is perhaps Erasmus' most important apologia and is extremely valuable in understanding *The Praise of Folly* within the context of Erasmus' aims and lifework. It was also one of Erasmus' first letters to be published, appearing in a volume by Froben in August 1515. It was subsequently reprinted in early editions of *The Praise of Folly.* The version translated here is the printed version and is an enlargement of the letter actually sent to Dorp.

TO MARTIN DORP, DISTINGUISHED THEOLOGIAN, GREETINGS FROM ERASMUS OF ROTTERDAM:

Your letter did not reach me, but a friend at Antwerp somehow or other obtained a copy and showed it to me. You lament the unfortunate publication of the *Folly*; you greatly approve of my work on the restoration of Jerome's text; you discourage me from editing the New Testament. Far from offending me, my dear Dorp, this letter of yours endears you even more, although you have always been a very dear friend. You have counseled me with such sincerity; you have admonished in such a friendly way; you have reproached me in such cordial fashion. Christian charity indeed has the ability to retain its own true sweetness even when it is exceedingly angry. I receive many letters daily from learned men, which hail me as the glory of Germany, which call me a great light—a sun, a moon—and heap upon me most brilliant titles which burden rather than adorn me. May I perish if I enjoyed any of them as much as that scolding letter from my friend Dorp. Paul rightly said that charity does not sin; it means to be of service, whether it flatters or whether it finds fault. Would that I had the leisure to answer your letter in a way that would satisfy so devoted a friend. I am most anxious to have your approval upon my work, because I prize so highly your magnificent talents, outstanding erudition, and keen judgment that I prefer to have the blessing of Dorp alone than that of a thousand others. And although I have until now been ill from my sea voyage, exhausted from traveling on horseback, and busy assembling my luggage, I thought it better to make some reply than to leave a friend in such an opinion of me, whether this be the result of your own evaluation or suggested by others who incited you to write this letter that they might act out their playlet behind another's mask.

First of all, to speak frankly, I almost regret publishing the *Folly*. That book won me no small amount of fame, or you might say, notoriety. Yet I care nought for fame if it is accompanied by envy. Heavens above! What is this whole thing called fame but an empty title bequeathed to us by pagan antiquity? Not a few words of this kind have lingered on among Christians until they call immortality the good name left to posterity and label as virtue any sort of devotion to letters. What I have aimed at in publishing all of my books was to serve some useful purpose through my efforts and, if I fell short of this, at least to avoid doing any harm to anyone. In like manner, although we see even great men misuse their writings to vent their own feelings, boasting of their silly love affairs, seducing people by flattery, using the pen to retaliate after an injury, blowing their own horns, outdoing a Thraso or a Purgopolinices,[5] I, though short in talent and with quite meager learning, have always striven to do some good if possible; and when this were not possible, at least I took care to injure no one. Homer indulged his anger against Thersites, painting a vicious portrait of him in his poetry. Plato took a great many people to task by name in his dialogues. Aristotle spared no one, not even Plato or Socrates. Demosthenes had his Aeschines against whom he raged. Cicero had his Piso, his Vatinius, his Sallust, his Antony. Seneca ridiculed quite a few people by name. And if you consider more recent examples, the pen was used as a weapon by Petrarch against a certain physician, by Valla against Poggio, by Poliziano against Scala.[6] Where will you show me an author so moderate as not to have written satirically against someone? Even Jerome, as pious and serious a man as he was, sometimes was carried away in anger at Vigilantius, is rather immoderate in his insults to Jovinianus, inveighs against Rufinus with much bitterness. It has always been the custom here for learned men to commit to paper whatever they lament or take delight in, as if to trusted companions, and on this bosom to pour out all their turbulent feelings. You even find some who take up writing books with no other purpose save to fill them with the passions of their own souls, which they thereby pass on to posterity.

---

5. Thraso is a braggart in Terence's *Eunuchus*, and Purgopolinices the boastful hero of Plautus' *Miles gloriosus*.

6. Lorenzo Valla, Poggio Bracciolini, Angelo Poliziano, and Bartolomeo Scala are all fifteenth-century Italian humanists.

As for me, in the many books I published, I very openly praised many a man but I never tarnished the reputation of anyone. I never spilled the slightest stain on anyone. No race of mankind, no profession, no individual did I ever censure by name. If you only knew, my dear Dorp, how many times I was really provoked to do this by such abuse as no one should have tolerated! But I always overcame the temptation and considered that the impression left on posterity was more important than giving these depraved men what they deserved. If the facts were known to others just as they were to me, men would think me not bitter but just, dispassionate, yes, moderate. Also, I thought to myself: what interest will people have in my private feelings? or how will these affairs of mine be sufficiently familiar to readers far away or to posterity? I shall have dealt with my enemies in a manner worthy of myself, not in the manner they deserve. Besides, no one is so great an enemy that I would not want to turn him, if possible, into a friend. Why close the door on such a person? Why write against an enemy something which in some future time I might regret because that man has become my friend? Why should I ruin someone's reputation which I could not possibly restore even though he later on deserved it? I would rather err in this direction, namely, in giving praise to those who merit it not rather than in castigating those who are worthy. Whenever you praise someone mistakenly, it is attributed to simplicity, but if you even begin to paint in his true colors a man deserving ignominy, it is attributed not to his misdeeds but to your prejudice. Moreover, let us not forget that as a great war sometimes comes out of the avenging of injuries, so out of curses in turn hurled back and forth most perilous passions frequently are stirred. Just as it is hardly Christian to weigh injury against injury, so it is scarcely worthy of a stout heart to avenge hurts by shrieking like a woman.

For reasons such as this I have persuaded myself to guard my writings from any harm-doing or vengeance and to avoid contaminating them with so much as a mention of evil. Nor did I have any intentions in the *Folly* different from those in my other works, although the method may have differed. In the *Enchiridion* I simply set down a design for Christian living. In the pamphlet *The Education of a Prince* I publicly advised in what subjects a prince ought to be instructed. In the *Panegyric*, using the form of a eulogy of the prince, I did in an oblique manner the very same thing that in the other book I did openly and directly. So for the *Folly*: the same thing was done there under the semblance of a jest as was done in the *Enchiridion*. I wanted to admonish, not to cause pain; to be of benefit, not to vex; to reform the morals of men, not to oppose them. Plato the philosopher, grave as he is, approves of rather lavish drinking bouts among companions because he is of the opinion that certain vices can be dispelled by wine's laughter which cannot be corrected by severity. And Horace also thinks that an admonition that is jocose serves no less the purpose than one that is serious. "What is the matter," he says, "with saying the truth with a smile?"[7] The wise heads of old who preferred to present the salutary precepts of life in humorous and seemingly puerile fables had insight into a good principle, namely, that a truth of itself somewhat harsh, if presented in an entertaining fashion, more easily finds its way to men's hearts. Yes, this is the honey which in Lucretius the doctors smeared on the inside of the cup of absinthe for the treatment of children. It was for the same reason that the kings of old brought fools into their courts, that in the license given to such creatures certain little vices would be disclosed and corrected without offense to anyone. Perhaps it is not proper to put Christ in such a category. Yet if we can use certain comparisons between the divine and the human, did not His parables have something in common with the fables of the ancients? Evangelical truth sinks in more pleasingly and takes firmer hold in souls when dressed up in these little enticements than if it is simply stated as naked truth, an effect Augustine certainly strives for in his work on Christian doctrine. I observed continually how the common mass of humanity in every walk of life was being seduced by the most stupid opinions, and that the desire of a remedy was more genuine than the hope thereof. So it seemed to me justifiable to use a little deceit, as it were, on these pleasure-loving souls and give them their medicine disguised as pleasure. Again and again I had already seen this lively and playful kind of thing go a long way with many people. Now if you reply that the personage whom I invented for this purpose was too frivolous to serve as a spokesman in a discussion of serious matters, that fault I would perhaps admit. I do not object

7. *Satires* 1.1.24–25.

to the charge of a lapse of judgment, but I do object to the charge of having been bitter. Yet I could answer soundly even that first charge, if by no other means than citing the example of the very many important writers whom I listed in the preface of my book.

But how did I come to do this thing? I was staying for a while with my friend More after my return from Italy, and my kidney pains were confining me to the house for a few days. My collection of books was not yet delivered to me. And even if they had been brought, the illness did not permit the strain of any serious study anyway. So I began during my inactivity to play around with the idea of an encomium of Folly, not, of course, with the intention of publishing anything but rather to relieve the discomfort of my illness with this sort of relaxation.[8] I showed a little bit of the work I had begun to some friends, just to share the fun with someone and make it more amusing. Since they found great pleasure in it, they insisted that I continue. I yielded, and in this task I spent seven days, more or less, an expenditure of time which indeed seemed to exceed the value of the theme. Then, by the efforts of the very people under whose prompting I wrote it, the book was brought into France and set up in type, but from a copy that was not only faulty but even mutilated. As if this were not enough to make me unhappy about it, within a few months it was reprinted many times and in many different places. I wondered myself why it had such popularity.

If you call this a lapse of judgment, my dear Dorp, the defendant pleads guilty or at least does not protest loudly. It was under these circumstances of my enforced leisure and in the desire to humor my friends that I committed a little indiscretion, and that once in a lifetime. But who is wise all the time? You yourself admit that my other writings are proper enough to be hailed by all pious and learned men. What censor, other than an Areopagite, is so strict that he is unwilling to pardon one single lapse of judgment in a writer? It is the last word in narrow-mindedness to forget the many times a writer was proper and circumspect and then, out of offense at one ridiculous little pamphlet, strip him of all honor. How many absurdities in other writers

8. In his dedication to Thomas More of *The Praise of Folly*, Erasmus says that the idea came to him on the journey from Italy to England. Thinking of his good friend More, he was prompted to entertain himself with a eulogy of folly, More's name being very close to the Greek word for folly (μωρία). CWE 2: *Ep.* 222.

could I not mention, in many ways more absurd than this, even among great theologians, as they contrive quarrelsome and insipid questions and fight each other over the smallest trifles, as if defending house and home? These people without using masks put on performances more absurd than the Atellan farces. Certainly I am more worthy of respect in that, meaning deliberately to be a bit silly, I donned the mask of Foolishness, and, just as in Plato's home Socrates spoke the praises of love behind a veiled countenance, I acted out that little skit of mine using an appropriate mask.

You say that these men whom my work displeases praise my talent, erudition, and eloquence but are offended by my reckless wit. Indeed, these admonitors give me more credit than I would want. I certainly do not savor praise such as this, especially coming from men whom I consider to have neither talent nor erudition nor eloquence. If they had these qualities, my dear Dorp, believe me, they would not be so greatly offended by jokes that are more wholesome than they are erudite and ingenious. I beseech you by the Muses, what eyes, what ears, what palate do they have who have been offended by the sting in this little book? First of all, where is the sting when no one's name save my own has been damaged? They ought to bear in mind what Jerome frequently teaches: that when a discussion of vices is kept general, injury is done to no one, and if someone does take offense, he has no claim against the writer. If he wants to prefer charges, let him do so against himself, for he has betrayed himself by publicly applying to himself an assertion which was made in such general terms that it referred to no man in particular, unless someone chose to apply it to himself. You can observe that in the whole book I so restrained myself from mentioning names of individuals that I was unwilling to treat of a particular nation with more than a mild criticism. There is a place in the work where I single out a particular point of pride in each of the national groups. I attribute, for instance, to the Spanish an esteem for military prowess, to the Italians a love of letters and eloquence, to the English pride in a sumptuous table and in bodily beauty, and to other nations similar qualities which each could graciously acknowledge or at least hear with a smile. Then although in accordance with the plan of my work I treated of all social classes and dwelt on the vices of each and reprehended them, I never said anything that was foul or venomous. I never uncovered the cesspool of scandal. I never stirred up the secret Camarina of human life.[9] Anyone knows how much could have been said about bad pontiffs, unworthy bishops and priests, vicious princes, or for that matter about any rank or station in life, if only, like Juvenal, one did not blush from writing about the crimes many people do not blush from committing. They were pleasant things and laughable, not loathsome, deeds that I treated of, and I did it in such a way that I could slip in here and there a word of advice, sometimes on very serious matters. It is very important that my critics realize this.

I am sure you yourself do not have the time to engage in frivolities such as these. Nevertheless, if sometime you have the leisure, give a little thought to those anecdotes in the *Folly*; surely you will find that they are more in the spirit of the teaching of the Evangelists and Apostles than are the so-called brilliant and masterful disputations conducted by certain people. Why, you yourself admit in your letter that many a truth is conveyed this way. Yet you think it was not expedient "to offend tender ears with the raw truth." If you think one ought under no circumstances to speak freely or that truth should never be proclaimed unless it offends no one, why do doctors treat patients with disagreeable medicines and rank the sacred bitters among the most praiseworthy remedies? Now if they do this in curing the diseases of the body, how much more seemly is it for us to do the same thing in healing the ills of the soul? "Reprove," says St. Paul, "entreat, rebuke, in and out of season."[10] The Apostle wants vice to be extirpated by every means possible, and you do not want so much as a sore to be touched, even when it is done with such moderation that no man could possibly be harmed unless he bring the harm upon himself. Actually, if there is any method at all of treating the ills of men without offending, this one, if I am not mistaken, is above all the best, namely, when not so much as a name of anyone appears and when caution is taken to refrain from anything that would offend pious ears. This point is well made because just as in tragedies there are certain things too atrocious to be exhibited before the eyes of the audience and

9. Camarina was a town in Sicily in ancient times, which had a stagnant and noisome pool near its walls.
10. 2 Timothy 4:2.

it is found sufficient to narrate them, so in the habits of men there are some things more obscene than can be modestly portrayed. Finally, it is helpful to have the narration spoken by some kind of a ridiculous character with cracks and jokes, so that the good humor of the situation simply rules out any offense. Do we not see how even in the courts of cruel tyrants a joke is valued if it is suitable and spoken at the right moment? I ask you, what entreaty, what serious rejoinder could have soothed the soul of the king in that famous story better than the jest of the soldier? "We were on the point," said the soldier, "of saying much more insulting things about you when the wine ran out." The king laughed and overlooked the offense. Nor was it without reason that the two rhetoricians, Cicero and Quintilian, gave such attention to the subject of laughter. Charm and an agreeable way of presenting things have such power that even when the apt phrase is turned against ourselves, we are delighted; witness the stories written about Julius Caesar. Wherefore, if you admit truth in what I wrote, if what I wrote is playful rather than offensive, what method more suitable could be devised for the treating of the common ills of mankind? Pleasure first invites the reader, and once he is caught up in the book, it makes him linger. Some seek this satisfaction, others that. Pleasure is bait for anyone and everyone, with the possible exception of one so dull-witted as to lack any taste for literature.

Those who are offended even though no one's name appears seem to me to be acting like touchy women who, if something is said against ladies of ill-repute, are disturbed as if such a reproach applied to all women. In like manner, if something praiseworthy is attributed to good women, they flatter themselves that what virtue one or other has redounds to the praise of all of them. Let this kind of absurdity be beneath men, and much more, learned men, and above all, theologians. If in this way I am charged with a fault of which I am innocent, I am not offended in the least; rather I congratulate myself if I am free of the faults of which I see many men guilty. But if the accusation has touched a sore spot and I see the mirror held up to myself, there still is no reason why I ought to take offense. If I am wise, I will hide my feelings and not betray myself. If I am without blemish, I will take caution at the admonition, lest at some time an attack like this should be directed at me personally which I see now made without the mention of my name. Why do we not make the same concessions to this little book which even the ignorant *hoi polloi* make at popular plays? How much abuse, and with what abandon, do they hurl at monarchs, at priests, at monks, at wives, at husbands, and at God-knows-whom? And yet because no one is attacked by name, all laugh and each either candidly admits or prudently dissimulates his own foibles. Even the most irascible tyrants bear with their jesters and fools when at times they are smitten by them with an open insult. The Emperor Flavius Vespasian did not take vengeance upon the fellow who said he had the face of a person in the act of evacuating. Just who are these people of such delicate ear that they cannot bear to hear Lady Folly poke gentle fun at our common human condition without at the same time touching anyone in particular? The old-style comedy would never have been driven off the stage had it abstained from mentioning illustrious people by name.

But you, good Dorp, write almost as if the book *Folly* has alienated from me the whole theological profession. "What was the need," you ask, "for lashing out so fiercely at the theological profession?" And then you lament my unhappy position. "There was a time," you go on, "when all read your writing with eagerness and hankered to meet you in person. Now *Folly* like some Davus upsets all this." I realize you write this in good faith, nor would I use a subterfuge with you. I want to ask you if you really think the whole theological profession has been attacked, if something was said against stupid and incompetent theologians who were in fact unworthy of such a title? If such a rule holds, the whole human race would consider itself offended if anything were said against wicked men. What king was ever so shameless as not to admit that some kings are bad kings and not worthy of the title? What bishop was ever so arrogant as not to admit the same for those in his state of life? Are the theologians the only group which has not in its vast ranks a stupid, an ignorant, or a troublesome member, but has only Pauls, Basils, and Jeromes to show us? Indeed, the contrary is the case; the more exalted any profession is, the fewer are the members who really measure up to it. You will find more good skippers than you will find good princes, more good physicians than good bishops. And this is nothing against the particular profession, but it is to the greater credit of those who in a brilliant profession perform brilliantly. I ask you now, tell me, why do theologians take greater offense (supposing there are some who are offended) than kings, than nobles, than magistrates, than bishops, than cardinals, than supreme pontiffs, or for that matter, than merchants, than husbands, than wives, than lawyers, than poets—for no species of the human race did Folly neglect—unless it is because these latter are not silly enough to take as said against themselves what was spoken against unworthy people in general. St. Jerome wrote to Eustochium on virginity and in this book exposed the morals of bad virgins as no Apelles could depict them. Was Eustochium offended? Was she enraged at Jerome because he cast disgrace upon virgins as a group? Not a bit of it! And why, in the last analysis? Because as a prudent virgin she would not consider it to refer to herself if something were said about bad virgins; on the contrary, she was glad to have the good virgins warned lest they degenerate into bad ones; she was glad also that bad ones were admonished to amend their ways. He wrote to Nepotian on the life of clerics. He wrote to Rusticus on the life of monks and painted them in vivid colors, but with equally marvelous acuteness he appraised the vices of both these states of life. Those to whom he wrote in no wise took offense because they knew none of these criticisms applied to them. Why was not William Mountjoy alienated, since he is prominent among the courtly aristocrats and *Folly* made great fun of the nobles of the court? I'll tell you why. Being an excellent and intelligent man, he thinks rightly that what is said against evil and ignorant nobles is not applicable to himself. *Folly* poked fun at bad and worldly bishops, too. Why was not the archbishop of Canterbury offended by this? Simply because as a man full of every virtue, he judged none of this applicable to himself.

Why should I go on recalling to you the names of the noblest princes, of other bishops, of abbots, of cardinals, of men renowned for their learning, among whom I feel no one has been alienated in the least bit from me because of my *Folly?* I cannot even be convinced that any of the theologians were irritated by this book, save perhaps some few who either are of little understanding or are envious or are of such critical disposition that they find no good in anything. As is well known, men of this high calling have in their ranks a certain few who have such poor talent and judgment that they are not capable of any kind of learning, much less theological learning. They learned by heart a few little rules from Alexander of Gaul;[11] in addition they mastered a little bit of silly sophistry; next they memorized ten propositions from Aristotle, I dare say without understanding them; then, from Scotus or Occam[12] they learned a like number of chapters; and whatever else they need know they rest content to draw it from the *Catholicon* or *Mammotrepton* or a similar dictionary, as if from some horn of plenty. Yet how they toss their heads in pride! Nothing is more arrogant than ignorance! These are the ones who condemn St. Jerome as a grammarian obviously because they do not understand him. Such men deride Greek, Hebrew, even Latin; and even though they are more stupid than any pig and lack common sense, they think they themselves occupy the whole citadel of learning. They bring everyone to task; they condemn; they pontificate; they are never in doubt; they have no hesitations; they know everything. And yet few in number as they are, these people are causing tremendous commotion. What is more impudent, more obstinate than ignorance! Such people are in one great conspiracy against genuine learning. What they are doing is campaigning for high rank among the theologians, and they are afraid lest, if genuine learning should be born again and if the world should return to its senses, they would appear to know nothing, whereas up to now people consider them omniscient. From such as these come the complaints, from them all the commotion, from them the conspiracy against men following the better scholarship. They do not like *Folly* because they do not understand either Greek or Latin. If it is against such theologians—I should rather say men who masquerade as theologians—that something was said a bit critically, what is it to that magnificent class of good theologians? If these latter are motivated by a zeal for piety, why the prejudice against *Folly*? What impious, what foul, what pernicious stuff did Poggio write? But he is everywhere accepted as a Christian author and translated into almost every tongue.[13] With what abuse, with what imprecations did

11. Alexander of Gaul is a thirteenth-century writer who composed a Latin grammar for young students, the *Doctrinale puerorum*.

12. Duns Scotus (d. 1308?) and William of Occam (d. 1349?) are two important scholastic philosophers and theologians. Erasmus had a particular dislike for the Scotist school. Occam is prominent in the development of medieval nominalism.

13. The reference is to Poggio's obscene *Facetiae*, which had been translated into English, French, Italian, and Spanish.

Pontano attack the clergy?[14] But he is read as charming and amusing. What downright obscenity is there in Juvenal? But some think him good to use in sermons. How offensively did Tacitus write against the Christians, with what hostility Suetonius? How impiously did Pliny and Lucian scoff at the doctrine of the immortality of the soul? Yet all read them for their erudition, and rightly so. The one thing they cannot stand is Lady Folly, just because she makes a few witty remarks, not about theologians who are good and deserving of that title, but against the frivolous quibblings of ignorant men and against the ridiculous title of *our master.*

Thus it is that two or three miserable fellows posing as theologians are trying to throw the weight of this odium on me, that I offended and made enemies of the whole theological profession. I have done this, I who give such a place to theological learning that I consider it the only true learning! Why, I so look up to and venerate the theologians that to their science alone, now or in the past, do I associate the name learning. Although modesty restrains me from assuming such an exalted title myself, I am nevertheless aware of what qualifications in learning and piety must accompany the name. I know of no greater profession for a man than that of theologian. The title is an adornment worthy of bishops, not of men like me. It is enough for me to have learned that saying of Socrates that we really do not know anything, and to have consequently devoted my efforts as far as possible to assisting the inquiries of other men. At all events, I am at a loss to know just who or where they are, those two or three gods among the theologians who, as you say, do not show themselves propitious to me. I have been around a bit since publishing the *Folly*; I have been at a lot of learned gatherings and in many a metropolis. Never did I sense that any theologian felt any wrath against me, except for one or other of their number who are hostile to all good scholarship. Nor did these latter ever remonstrate with me personally. What might be muttered behind my back I do not take much notice of, trusting as I do in the judgment of many good men. I am afraid I might seem more arrogant than honest in saying this, my dear Dorp, but really I can name for you many theologians, known for the sanctity of their lives, outstanding in

14. Gian Gioviano Pontano (1426–1503) was an Italian humanist, diplomat, and poet.

learning, pre-eminent in dignity, some of them even bishops, who never treated me with greater affection than after the publication of the *Folly*, and who liked the book better than I did myself. I would mention each one of them here by name and title were I not afraid that those three particular theologians would turn their hostility against even such great men on account of the *Folly*. I will go further and say that I suspect there is but one author of all this disturbance—I can almost put the story together by conjectures—and if I wanted to identify him, no one would be surprised that the *Folly* displeased such a man;[15] indeed, it would bother me if the book did not find disfavor with such as he; I too am dissatisfied with the *Folly*. But on the other hand, the fact that it does not sit well with such characters makes me a little less displeased with it. What carries more weight with me is the judgment of wise and learned theologians who not only refrain from beating me black and blue for my alleged bitterness, but praise me to the skies for my moderation, even my candor, because, although I am an impudent fellow by nature, I stop short of impudence in my writing, and when I tease, I do so without inflicting injury. And now, in direct answer to those alone whom I am supposed to have offended, look at how much has been said even in public about the bad morals of some theologians. The *Folly* does not engage in anything like that. All it does is poke fun at their silly quibblings. It does not even condemn the quibblings outright. It merely condemns those men who see in these quibblings the beginning and end, the stem and stern, as it were, of the ship of theology, and who in their verbal wars, as St. Paul calls them, are so engrossed that they have no time to read the Gospels, or the Prophets, or the writings of the early Fathers. There are all too many, my dear Dorp, guilty of this offense. I can name you some past their eightieth birthday who wasted so much of their time in this nonsense that they never read the Gospel text, something they reluctantly admitted when it was pointed out by me.

Not even through the guise of my creature Folly did I dare to mention a complaint that I often hear people repeating, yes, people who are themselves theologians, and I mean real theologians, men of in-

---

15. Allen suggests (II 100.373*n*) that this may be John Briard of Ath, but it is possible that it is Jacob Latomus, a sharp critic of Erasmus at this time and later. Both were prominent Louvain theologians.

tegrity, gravity, and learning and who drink deeply of the doctrine of Christ from its very fonts. These men, whenever they are among those to whom they can speak their minds freely, deplore this more recent brand of theology which has crept into the world, and long for the ancient one. What is holier, what more venerable, what can get right to the flavor and spirit of Christ's heavenly doctrine than the ancient theology? But this other type of theology, not to mention the base and monstrous nature of its crude, artificial style, its ignorance of good scholarship, and its ineptitude of expression, has been so adulterated by Aristotle, by trifling human inventions, and even by secular laws that I can hardly say it savors of the genuine and pure Christ. For it happens that when we fix too steadily on human traditions, we lose sight of the archetype. Hence, when the more prudent theologians are speaking in public, they are often forced to give a different account from what they would hold privately or would say to their friends. And often they may have no answer for those who question them when they realize that Christ taught one thing while petty human traditions demand another. What connection is there, I ask, between Christ and Aristotle? between the petty fallacies of logic and the mysteries of eternal wisdom? What is the purpose of this maze of disputations? How much of it is deadening and destructive by the very fact that it breeds contention and disagreement! Some problems, of course, should be investigated and others definitely settled; I quite agree. But on the other hand, there are many problems which it would be better to pass over than examine. Indeed, it is the part of wisdom to be ignorant of some things. There are many questions on which it is healthier to be in doubt than to be decided. Finally, if any decision has to be made, I would prefer that it be made with reverence and not arrogance, from the divine writings and not from the petty syllogisms fabricated by men. Now there is no end of these little questions, and yet how much discord there is on these very points among the sects and parties. Every day gives birth to a new decree. In brief, the result has been that matters of the greatest importance depend not on the law of Christ but on the definitions of scholastics and the power of some bishop. And the situation has been so hopelessly muddled that there is not even a hope of recalling the world to authentic Christianity. Men of the greatest piety and learning recognize and deplore these and many other conditions, and throw the principal blame for all of them on this bold and irreverent class of modern theologians.

Oh, dear Dorp, if you could read my innermost thoughts, you would clearly see how much I prudently conceal at this point. Of such the *Folly* makes no mention, or only a passing one, since I did not wish to offend anyone; and I have taken pains to preserve this same caution in all matters—not to write anything offensive, anything liable to destroy morality, anything seditious, or anything that could be construed as injurious to any class of society. Wherever I spoke about the cult of the saints, you will find in the passage an open assertion that nothing is being censured except the superstition of those who do not revere the saints properly. Similarly, if we say anything against princes, bishops, or monks, we always add the declaration that this was not written to injure the order itself, but against those who are corrupt and not worthy of their order, since I do not want to harm the good while I censure the vices of the wicked. And incidentally, while I am on the subject, I made it a point to mention no names, as far as possible, in order to avoid offending even the guilty. In short, in having the whole story told with wit and humor by a fictitious, amusing character, I was careful that even sad and sober people would find it agreeable.

Now you write that what I said is censured not for being satirical but for being impious. For, you say, how will pious ears take your calling the joys of the life to come a form of madness? My good Dorp, I beg you, tell me who taught a man of your openness to use this subtle sort of attack, or (as I tend to believe) what cunning person took advantage of your simplicity to spread this attack against me? This is the way those destructive critics usually work: they take a few words out of context, sometimes even changing them a little, omitting the facts which somehow soften and explain a harsh discourse. Quintilian in his *Institutes of Oratory* advocates this sort of tactic for presenting one's case in the best possible light: first give arguments, then add mitigating circumstances, extenuating circumstances, or whatever in any way helps the cause, but represent the arguments of the adversary unadorned by these devices and in the most offensive terms possible. These men of whom I speak did not learn their art from the precepts of Quintilian but from their own maliciousness. And that is why it often happens that words which would be quite agreeable if quoted as they were written, cause serious offense when they are repeated in another manner. Reread that section, I ask you, and consider carefully by what steps and what process of argumentation I arrived at the conclusion that this joy was a sort of madness. Further, look at the words I use to explain it. You will see there something which might even please pious ears, so far is it from being at all offensive. If there is any offense, it lies not in my book but in your rendering of it.

Indeed, while Folly was attempting to fix upon every class of being the label of foolishness and was teaching that the greatest human happiness depended on foolishness, every class of being was touched upon, right up to kings and supreme pontiffs. From these we came to the Apostles themselves and even to Christ, to whom we find attributed a folly of a sort in Sacred Scripture. But there is no danger at this point that anyone should imagine that Christ or the Apostles were really foolish; the point is that even they possessed some weakness and some likeness to our own passions which might make them appear lacking in wisdom when compared with that eternal and pure wisdom. But this very foolishness conquers all worldly wisdom, just as the Prophet compares the justice of all men to the wrappings of a woman soiled by the menstrual flow.[16] It is not that the justice of good men would be contaminated, but that whatever is purest in human eyes is in some ways impure when it is compared to the ineffable purity of God. And just as I declared foolishness wise, I consider madness sane and insanity prudent. In order to soften what I then said about the joy of holy people, I preface it with Plato's three forms of madness, the happiest being the madness of lovers, which is nothing else than a sort of ecstasy.[17] But the ecstasy of the pious is nothing but a foretaste of the happiness to come, by which we will be completely absorbed in God, destined to exist more in Him than in our very selves. Plato called it madness whenever anyone is swept outside himself, exists in what he loves, and enjoys it. Do you not see how carefully I distinguished shortly afterward between the types of folly and insanity, so that no man, however simple, would be led astray by my words?

"But apart from the content," you say, "the very words will offend

16. Isaiah 64:6.
17. *Phaedrus* 244–45. See M. A. Screech, *Ecstasy and The Praise of Folly* (London, 1980).

pious ears." Then why are those same pious ears not offended when they hear St. Paul saying "the folly of God" and "the folly of the cross"?[18] Why don't they call St. Thomas to account, since he wrote these words on St. Peter's ecstasy: "When, in a fit of pious foolishness, he began to talk about tents"?[19] He calls that holy and blessed rapture foolishness, and yet these very words are sung in the churches. Why didn't they call me to account in the past when once in a prayer I called Christ a magician and a charmer? St. Jerome calls Christ a Samaritan, even though He was a Jew. Paul calls the same Christ "sin," as if to say something worse than "sinner." He calls Christ accursed. What an irreverent insult, if anyone wanted to take it in the wrong sense; and what pious praise, if one takes it as Paul intended! For a similar example, if one calls Christ a thief, an adulterer, a drunkard, or a heretic, would not all good men refuse to listen? But if someone expresses this in appropriate words and gradually leads the reader by the hand through the course of his talk to the consideration of how Christ, triumphant on the cross, brought back to His Father a spoil redeemed from hell, how He took to Himself the synagogue of Moses like the wife of Uriah so that a peaceable people was born of it, how as one drunk with the new wine of charity He expended Himself for us, how He introduced a new doctrine, far removed from the commonplace utterances of both philosopher and ordinary man—who, I ask, could be offended, especially since we sometimes find in the sacred writings instances of these terms used in a good sense? In the *Chiliades* (since this happens to come to mind) I spoke of the Apostles as Sileni; indeed, I even called Christ a Silenus.[20] What would be more intolerable than if some hostile interpreter should come forward and superficially explain this in an offensive way? But let a pious and impartial person read what I wrote, and he will approve the allegory.

I am amazed, however, that these men have not noticed how cautiously I put these words and how eager I was to soften them by a correction. For I put it this way: "While I have on the lion skin, I will proceed to show that the happiness of Christians, which they seek with

18. 1 Corinthians 1:25, 23.
19. Perhaps *Commentarium in Mattheum* 17:5.
20. Erasmus is referring to the essay *Sileni Alcibiadis* first published in the enlarged edition of the *Adagia* entitled *Proverbiorum chiliades* which Froben brought out in 1515. See M. M. Phillips, *The "Adages" of Erasmus* (Cambridge, 1964), pp. 271–73.

so much toil, is nothing but a kind of madness and folly. Do not take offense at these words; consider the argument instead."[21] Listen carefully. First, since Folly is treating such an obscure subject, I soften it with a proverb, saying that Folly has put on a lion skin. I do not simply say "madness and folly" but "a kind of madness and folly," so that you may understand that there is a pious folly and a blessed madness, according to the distinction I proceed to supply. Not satisfied with this, I add the words "kind of" to make it clear that there is an underlying metaphor and that it is not a simple statement. Not content with these distinctions, I beg them to excuse the offense the tone of the words might cause, and I warn them to pay more attention to what is said than to the words in which it is said. And indeed, I said this right in the very statement of my purpose. As a matter of fact, in the whole treatment of the subject, is there anything at all that is not said with piety and circumspection, and even with more reverence than would suit the role of Folly? In that section I preferred momentarily to neglect elegance rather than fail to do justice to the importance of the subject. I preferred offending rhetoric to wounding piety. And finally when the argument was completed, so that I would not offend anyone by having Folly, a humorous character, speak on a very sacred matter, I asked pardon for this fault with these very words: "But indeed I have long since forgotten who I am and have run out of bounds. If anything I said seems too sharp or gossipy, remember that it is Folly and a woman who has spoken."[22]

You see that I continually forestalled any occasion for offense. But the people whose ears are attuned to nothing but propositions, conclusions, and corollaries, do not weigh sufficiently such matters. What about the preface in which I defended my book, where I try to forestall any criticism? I have no doubt that it was sufficient for all sincere men. But what would you do for those individuals who either do not want to be satisfied because of intellectual obstinacy or are too stupid to understand an apology? For just as Simonides said that the Thessalians were too dull to be deceived by him, so you should see that there are certain people who are too stupid to be able to be appeased. Moreover,

---

21. Erasmus, *The Praise of Folly*, trans. Leonard F. Dean (Chicago, 1946), p. 127. See also Olin, *Six Essays*, essay 4.
22. *The Praise of Folly*, trans. Dean, p. 132.

it is not remarkable that they find something to criticize, since all they look for is something to criticize. If anyone should read the writings of St. Jerome in that spirit, he will find a hundred places which can easily be criticized; indeed, there are places in the most orthodox of Christian teachers which could be called heresy. I could say the same of Cyprian, Lactantius, and many others. Besides, who ever heard of bringing a humorous subject before the tribunal of the theologians? But if this is the rule, why don't they take the same pains to investigate everything written or trifled with by the poets of our day? How much offensive matter they will find there, how much that is redolent of ancient paganism! But since these writings are not considered serious, none of the theologians thinks they are any of his business.

Nevertheless, I would not demand that my case be supported by such examples. I would not want anything I wrote in jest to be in any way detrimental to Christian piety. Just give me a reader who understands what I wrote, who is fair and honest, who is eager for knowledge, and not bent on criticism. If a writer would take into account this other class of readers—those first of all, who are endowed with no talent and less judgment, those, secondly, who had no training in literature and were spoiled rather than polished by base and confused learning, and those, finally, who are annoyed at anyone who knows what they are ignorant of and whose only aim is to criticize even what they might easily understand—this man surely would write nothing at all in his desire to avoid criticism. Why does the desire of glory impel these men to criticism? Because nothing is more vainglorious than ignorance joined with the conviction that one knows. Accordingly, since they ardently desire a good name and are not able to attain it by fair means, they prefer to imitate that young man from Ephesus who became famous by setting fire to the most celebrated temple in the world rather than live on in obscurity. And since they cannot produce anything worth reading, they apply themselves wholeheartedly to picking apart the works of famous men.

I speak of other men, not of myself, since I am completely insignificant. And I do not consider my book *Folly* worth a great deal, in case any of you might think that I am disturbed by this affair. What wonder that such men as I have described should choose a few statements and remove them from their context, make some of them out to be scandal-

Erasmus by Holbein, 1515; enlarged detail.

NOVVM TESTAMEN

HIERONVMVS

331

Erasmus by Metsys, 1517: the original (?) at Hampton Court.

Erasmus by Metsys, 1517: the copy (?) at Rome.

Erasmus by Dürer, 1526.

⊕ ‹ERASMI ROTERO
DAMI PARACLESIS. AD LECTO‹
·REM PIVM.

Lactantiu.

ACTANTIVS ille Firmianus,optime lector,cuius linguã unice miratur Hieronymus,Christianæ reli‹ gioni patrocinaturus aduersus ethnicos, cũ primis optat sibi dari eloquentiam,Tullianæ proximã, im probum ratus,opinor, optasse parem.At ego sanè, si quid huiusmodi uotis proficiẽ, tantisper dũ mor‹ tales omneis ad sanctissimũ ac saluberrimũ Christi anæ philosophiæ studiũ adhortor,ac ueluti classicũ canens euoco,uehemẽter optarim eloquentiã mihi

Optat eloquẽ
tiã efficacẽ. dari longe aliã cp fuerit Ciceroni:si minus picturatã quàm fuit illius,certe mul‹ to magis efficacem.Imò si cui uncp talis contigit dicendi uis,qualẽ non omni‹

Mercurius. no sine causa,ueterum poêtarũ fabulæ subnotarũt in Mercurio,qui ceu magica uirga,diuinacp cithara somnũ immittit cũ libet,& idem adimit,quos uult ad in feros impellens,ac rursus ab inferis euocans,Aut qualẽ signarũt in Amphione

Hercules Cel Orpheocp,quorum alter rigida mouisse saxa,alter quercus & ornos traxisse ci
‹ ticus. thara,fingitur.Aut qualẽ Ogmio suo tribuebant Galli, mortaleis omneis cate

Marsyas. nulis,à lingua in aures infixis,quò uellet circũducenti,Aut qualẽ Marsyæ fabu
Socrates. losa tribuit antiquitas,Aut certe,ne nimiũ diu fabulis immoremur, qualẽ So‹
Alcibiades. crati tribũ:it Alcibiades,Pericli uetus comœdia,quæ nó aures tantum mox peri
Pericles. tura uoluptate deliniat,sed quæ tenaces aculeos relinquat in animis auditorũ,
* quæ rapiat, quæ transformet,quæ multo aliũ dimittat auditorem cp acceperit,

Timotheus. Timotheus musicus ille nobilis Dorios occinens modos, Alexandrũ Magnũ ad belli studiũ inflammare solitus legitur.Necp defuerunt olim,qui precamini bus quas Græci uocant ἐπῳδὰς,nihil ducerẽt efficacius.At si quod uscp esset hu‹ iusmodi genus incãtamẽti,si qua uis harmoniæ quæ uerũ habeãt ἐπϑυσίασμ ὸρ, si qua Pithô uere flexanima, eam mihi cupiã in præsentia suppetere, quo rem omniũ saluberrimã omnibus psuadeã.Quancp illud potius optandũ, ut Chri stus ipse cuius negociũ agitur,ita citharæ nostræ chordas tẽperet,ut hæc cantile‹ na penitus afficiat ac moueat animos omniũ.Ad quod quidẽ efficiẽdum, nihil

Veritatis ora opus rhetorũm epicherematis aut epiphonematis.Hoc quod optamus,nó alia
tio quo sim‹ res certius præstet quàm ipsa ueritas,cuius quo simplicior,hoc efficacior est ora
plicior hoc tio.Ac primũ quidẽ nó libet in præsentia refricare querelã illã,nó omnino noua
efficatior. sed heu nimiũ iustã,& haud scio an uncp iustiorẽ cp hisce tẽporibus, cũ tam ar‹
Philosophia dentibus animis in sua quiscp studia,mortales incũbãt,hãc unã Christi philoso
Christi negle‹ phiam à nónullis etiã Christianis rideri,à pleriscp negligi,à paucis tractari,sed
cta

The opening of the *Paraclesis*.

IO. FROBENIVS PIO
LECTORI S. D.

DIVI Hilarij Pictauorū epi
scopi lucubrationes per Erasmū
Roterodamum nó mediocribus
sudoribus emendatas, formulis
nostris, operacǫ nostra, quantum
licuit, ornauimus. Priore æditio,
nem nó damnamus, sed quid in,
tersit, ipse cognosces ex collatio,
ne, lector optime, simulcǫ uale,
bis. Catalogum repeties in proxi
ma pagella.

In officina Frobeniana apud
inclytam Basileam. Anno, M.D.
XXIII. mense Febr.

·CLEOPATRA·

·DIONYSIVS·

Erasmus presents the dedication copy of his edition of Hilary to Carondelet.

Jean de Carondelet by Vermeyen, before 1525.

The opening of St. John's Gospel.

ous, some irreverent, some evil-sounding, and some savoring of impiety and heresy, not because they find these faults there, but because they bring them along themselves! How much more fitting and worthy of Christian simplicity it would be to support the activity of learned men and, if something happens to slip out thoughtlessly, to overlook it or interpret it favorably rather than maliciously to hunt for something to censure, acting like an informer and not a theologian! How much more felicitous it would be to teach or learn in mutual cooperation and, to use the words of Jerome, "to exercise on the playing-fields of learning without fear of incurring injury"! It is an amazing thing to see how there is no middle course for these men. They so read certain authors that they defend them on a trifling pretext, no matter how obvious it is that there is a mistake. They are so hostile to others that nothing can be said so circumspectly that they cannot criticize it on some ground. How much better, instead of doing what they are doing—wounding others and being wounded, wasting their own time and that of others —to learn Greek or Hebrew, or at least Latin, which are so indispensable to the knowledge of Sacred Scripture that I think it extremely impudent for anyone ignoring them to usurp the name of theologian!

Therefore, dear Martin, out of my good will toward you, I will not stop encouraging you, as I have done before, at least to add the knowledge of Greek letters to your studies. You have been exceptionally blessed in your talent; and your compact, bold, fluent, and luxuriant style gives evidence of not only a sound mind but also a prolific one. There is not only a full life ahead of you but one that is vigorous and productive as well. You have already completed the common course of studies with distinction. Believe me, if you add the summit of Greek letters to your very distinguished undertakings, I would dare to predict both to myself and others a great future for you and accomplishments not as yet equaled by any of the modern theologians. But if you hold the view that all human learning should be despised out of love for true piety, and that one arrives at this wisdom much more quickly through a certain transformation in Christ, and if it is your judgment that everything else worth learning can be seen more fully in the light of faith than in the books of men, I would gladly agree with your opinion. But if, as matters now stand, you promise yourself a true understanding of theology without a knowledge of languages and especially of that language in which the majority of the Divine Writings have been handed down, you have strayed far off the path.

And would that I were able to persuade you in this regard as well as I desire, for my desire is as great as my affection for you and my interest in your scholarly pursuits; and my affection is as strong as my interest is boundless. But if I am unable to make it entirely evident to you, I would like you at least to grant this favor to a friend's wishes—that you will make the attempt. I will decline no punishment if you do not finally agree that my advice was friendly and reliable. If my fondness for you means anything, if our common fatherland is at all important, if you put any value on what I would not dare to call my learning but certainly painstaking practice in literary endeavor, if you set any store by age (for I am old enough to be your father), promise me that you will do what I have asked of you, either out of favor or respect if not for logic's sake. So finally, if I convince you of this, I will think myself eloquent, as you always say I am. And if I succeed, both of us will rejoice: I because I gave the advice, you because you followed it. And now you who are the dearest to me of all will be still dearer because I have made you dearer to yourself. But if you do not agree now, I am afraid that when you are older and more experienced, you will approve my suggestion and condemn your own opinion. Then, as often happens, you will see your mistake when it is too late to correct it. I would be able to name for you a great number of men who, already gray-haired oldsters, were rejuvenated in the study of Greek, since they finally realized that without Greek the study of letters was feeble and groping.

But I have already said too much on this point. To return to your letter, you think there is but one way to assuage the ill will of the theologians and regain their former favor, that is, by way of a retraction, to set a *Praise of Wisdom* against the *Praise of Folly*. You earnestly urge and beg me to do this. My dear Dorp, since I disdain no one but myself and since I have a great desire to put all men at peace if possible, I would not hesitate to undertake this labor, if I did not foresee that whatever ill will has arisen among some few small-minded and stupid people would not only remain undiminished but would be even more inflamed. Therefore I think it better, as they say, to leave well enough alone and let sleeping dogs lie. Unless I am mistaken, this serpent will better fade away with time.

Now I come to another part of your letter. You wholeheartedly approve of my work in restoring Jerome, and you urge me on to similar labors. You are encouraging one who is already off to a start. Yet there is not as great a need for people to exhort me on to this work as there is for people to help me with it, so difficult is the task. But I would not want you to believe me in any regard henceforth, if you do not find me reliable on this point. Those whom the *Folly* seriously offends will not approve of this edition of Jerome either. Nor are they much more impartial to Basil, Chrysostom, Nazianzen than they are to me, except that they rage with less restraint against me, although in their wrath they sometimes are not afraid to hurl indignities at even these distinguished men. They fear good scholarship, and they are apprehensive for their absolute power. So that you may know that I am not making a rash prediction, no sooner had the work been started and the news spread abroad than some men of eminent reputation and some distinguished theologians—distinguished, at least, in their own opinion— came running to beg the printer by all that is sacred not to allow any Greek or Hebrew to get involved, saying that these languages were dangerous and possessed no value, being contrived only for curiosity's sake. Even before this time, while I was living in England, I happened to be having a cup of wine with a certain Franciscan, a Scotist of good repute, who seemed in the public eye to know a great deal and to know everything in his own. When I explained to him what I was attempting in Jerome, he was greatly astonished that there was anything in that man's writings that was not understood by the theologians. The man was so ignorant that I would be surprised if he really understood three verses in all Jerome's works. This good fellow added that, if I had any difficulties with the formulas of Jerome, there was a Breton who had written a splendid exposition on the whole subject.

I ask you, my dear Dorp, what can you do with such theologians? What would you pray for, except possibly a good doctor to cure their brains? And yet this is the sort of people who shout the loudest in the assembly of the theologians; and they are the men who decide the fate of Christianity. They fear and dread as though it were dangerous and destructive the very skill which St. Jerome and even aged Origen acquired for themselves at such great pains so that they might truly be theologians. Even Augustine, when he was an elderly bishop, lamented in his *Confessions* that as a young man he had shrunk from the study of those letters which would have been so useful in explaining Sacred Scripture. If there be any danger, I shall not fear the risk which men so wise have invited. If it is a curiosity, I do not want to be holier than Jerome; and let those very men who call what he did a curiosity see the service they do him.

There is extant a very old decree of the papal court on the appointment of instructors to teach certain languages publicly, whereas nowhere was any stipulation made on the teaching of sophistry or of Aristotle's philosophy, probably because the decrees call into question whether it is proper to teach these subjects or not. Besides, the study of these subjects is condemned by many renowned authors. Why do we neglect what the papal authority has ordered and embrace only that about which there is doubt, even disapproval? Yet the same difficulty meets these men in Aristotle as in Sacred Scripture. Everywhere they find that same Nemesis, avenger of the scorned language. They wander aimlessly, dream, strike out blindly, and produce nothing but monstrosities. We owe to these eminent theologians the fact that from the vast multitude of writers whom Jerome catalogued, such a small number survive, since *our masters* could not understand what they wrote. They are also to blame for the fact that St. Jerome's text is so maimed and distorted that those who try to re-edit it have almost as much trouble as Jerome himself had in writing it.

Now indeed, when in the third place you write regarding the New Testament, I wonder what has happened to you or whither your judgment so astute has in the meantime wandered. You do not want me to change anything except where there might be, perhaps, a little clearer meaning in the Greek. You deny that there are faults in the edition we commonly use, and you think that we are forbidden to alter in any way something approved by the agreement of so many ages and so many synods. I ask you, most learned Dorp, if what you write is true, why is it that Jerome, Augustine, and Ambrose had different readings from the ones that we have? Why did Jerome expressly censure and correct many readings which are still contained in this edition? What will you do in the face of such converging testimony, that is, when the Greek codices offer a different reading from ours, when Jerome in making citations uses that reading, when the most ancient Latin texts have the same reading, when its meaning fits better into the context? Are you going to disregard all these facts and still follow your own codex, which might have been corrupted by a copyist? Certainly no one is stating that there are mistakes in the Divine Writings (something you seemed to have suggested); nor is there any question here of that dispute Augustine had with Jerome. The solution to the problem almost stares us in the face, for it would be clear even to a blind man, as they say, that the Greek was often poorly translated because of the ignorance or laziness of a translator, that often the authentic and true text has been corrupted by ignorant copyists (something we see happening every day) or even changed by unskilled or inattentive ones. Who is more indulgent to error: the one who corrects and restores the mistakes, or the one who would sooner see a blunder added than removed, especially since it is the nature of mistakes that one causes another? And what we are changing is of such a nature that the corrections are concerned more with the tone of a passage than with its meaning, although the tone often constitutes a large part of meaning. But it is not seldom that there is a total deviation. And whenever this happens, to what, I ask you, do Augustine, Hilary, and Jerome have recourse but to the Greek sources? Although this practice has been approved even by ecclesiastical decrees, you still hedge and attempt to refute it, or rather evade it with a petty distinction.

You write that in that day the Greek codices had been emended more than the Latin ones, but that now it is just the opposite and that moreover we should not rely on the writings of those who fell away from the Roman Church. I can hardly bring myself to believe that you are really sincere in writing this. What are you saying? Shall we not read the writings of people who fell away from the Christian faith? Why, then, do they give such authority to Aristotle, a pagan who never had anything to do with the faith? The whole Jewish race severed itself from Christ; will the Psalms and the Prophets have no importance in our eyes, since they were written in Hebrew? Enumerate all the points on which the Greeks disagree with orthodox Latins: you will find nothing which has come from the words of the New Testament or which is relevant here. The whole controversy is about the word "hypostatic," about the procession of the Holy Spirit, about the rites of consecration, about the poverty of priests, about the authority of the Roman pontiff. And on none of these points do the Greeks try to prove their claims from falsified texts. And what will you say when you see that Origen, Chrysostom, Basil, and Jerome have explained passages in identical ways? Did someone in their time also falsify the Greek codices? Or who at any time ever discovered the Greek codices altered in even one spot? Finally, why would the Greeks want to interpolate, since they did not defend their doctrines from the text? Add to this the fact that even Cicero admits that the Greek codices were generally more correct than ours in every branch of learning, even though he is rather harsh on the Greeks in other respects. Indeed the separation of the letters, the forms of the letters, and the very strangeness of the script are reasons why the text could not be so easily corrupted or, if some mistake were made, it would be easier to restore the text.

Besides, when you write that we should not put aside our present edition after it has been clearly approved by so many councils, you are acting like the commonplace theologians who are wont to attribute to ecclesiastical authority whatever in any way has crept into public usage. Quote for me even one synod in which this edition was approved. For who could have approved something whose author was unknown? Jerome's preface states that it is not his own. But let us suppose that some synod did approve it. Did it approve it in such a way that we are not allowed to emend it from the Greek sources at all? Did it also approve all the faults which in various ways could have crept into the text? Was the decree of the Fathers formulated in the following words: "We do not know the author of this edition, but nevertheless we approve it. We do not want anything changed, even if the Greek codices are different, no matter how correct they are, even if Chrysostom, Athanasius, or Jerome had a different reading, even if this reading would square better with the evangelical sense, although we have highly approved these very authors in other instances. Further still, we approve by the same authority whatever will have been in the future falsified, corrupted, added, or omitted in any way by undertrained and overconfident copyists or by unskilled, drunken, and negligent ones. We do not want to permit anyone to change a single passage once it has been introduced"? A ridiculous decree, you would say. But it necessarily has to be so, if you would discourage me from my undertaking by the authority of a synod.

Finally, what are we to say when we see that the copies of this edition do not even agree? Did the synod also approve these inconsistencies with the foreknowledge, perhaps, of what changes would be made in each? My dear Dorp, would that the Roman pontiff had enough time to put into effect proper constitutions concerning these matters, in which care might be taken to restore the writings of these authors and to prepare and restore the texts which had been emended. But I would not want these men, by a misnomer called theologians, to sit on this council, these men whose sole aim has been to see that what they have learned should prevail. What did they ever learn that was not most absurd and completely confused? If decision falls to these tyrants, the better authors of antiquity will be rejected and the world will be forced to consider as from oracles their insipid incantations. Their writings possess so little good learning that had I no better training than they, I would rather be an ordinary craftsman than the best man of their class. They are the men who would not want anything restored lest they appear to be ignorant of something. They throw up at us the fictitious authority of councils; they exaggerate the great split in the Christian faith and the dangers to the Church (whose weight they are evidently supporting on their shoulders, whereas they would be better suited to pulling wagons), and they spread other grave warnings among the ignorant and superstitious people. Since they are known among these people as theologians, they thus wish to guard their reputation from damage. They fear that when they cite Sacred Scripture erroneously, as they often do, the authority of Greek or Hebrew truth will be thrown in their faces, and what was thought to be an oracle would soon be clearly seen to be a revery. St. Augustine, a great man and a bishop at the time, was not reluctant to learn even from a year-old boy. Men of their sort would rather turn the world upside down than be forced to admit that they are ignorant of anything that an educated man should know. Yet I see nothing here that particularly involves the purity of the Christian faith, but if such a thing were at stake, this would surely be all the more reason to redouble our efforts.

There is no danger that anyone will immediately desert Christ if he happens to hear that in the sacred books an unskilled or drowsy copyist corrupted something or that some unknown translator made a poor rendition. This danger springs from other causes, which I prudently pass over here. How much more Christian it would be to put aside all conflict and bring forward with good spirit whatever is of advantage for the common good, learning what you do not know without pride and teaching what you do know without jealousy. But if they are too uneducated to be able to teach anything correctly or too proud to learn anything, let them go their way, since there are only a few of them, and let us turn our attention to minds which are either good or promising. I once showed some of my notes which were in a rough draft, still hot from the anvil, as they say, to certain men of utmost impartiality, among whom were renowned theologians and learned bishops. They admitted that from such rough notes a great deal of light had been shed on the understanding of the Divine Writings.

I was quite aware of what you told me concerning Lorenzo Valla, that he had already taken up this task before me.[23] As a matter of fact, I was the first one to publish his notes; and I have also seen the commentaries of Jacques Lefèvre on the Pauline Epistles.[24] Would that these men had so elaborated the subject that there would be no need for my labors. Certainly I consider Valla deserving of the highest praise; he was a rhetorician more than a theologian, who had the diligence in treating of Sacred Scripture to compare the Greek with the Latin, although there are not many theologians who have read the Bible from cover to cover. Yet I disagree with him in a number of places, especially in those which have theological implications. As for Jacques Lefèvre, he was still at work on his commentaries when I set about my undertaking; and it is unfortunate that it did not occur

23. See Selection II, note 8.
24. Jacques Lefèvre d'Étaples (1455–1536) was the great French biblical humanist whose work in many ways parallels that of Erasmus. His edition of and commentary on St. Paul's Epistles appeared in 1512. On Lefèvre, see Augustin Renaudet, *Humanisme et Renaissance* (Geneva, 1958), pp. 201ff., and *The Prefatory Epistles of Jacques Lefèvre d'Étaples and Related Texts*, ed. Eugene F. Rice, Jr. (New York, 1972), *Ep.* 96 (pp. 295–302). See also Selection I, note 13.

to either of us to mention his work to the other even in our intimate conversations. I did not even know what he was about until he brought the work out in published form. I approve his endeavor wholeheartedly. Nevertheless, I disagree with him on some points, regretfully so, because I would gladly be in total agreement with such a good friend, except that more account should be shown truth than friendship, especially in the case of Sacred Scripture.

Still, the reason why you bring these two men to my attention is not sufficiently clear. Are you trying to discourage me from the subject as though it were already pre-empted? But we will see that I have not undertaken this task without reason, even though in the wake of such esteemed men. Or do you mean that theologians do not approve of the work of these two? I do not see what this would add to Lorenzo's old unpopularity. I hear Lefèvre being praised by everyone. And how can you say theirs is the exact task I am undertaking? Lorenzo merely commented on a few passages and that, as it appears, in a very cursory and, as is said, superficial manner. Lefèvre published commentaries only on the Pauline Epistles, translating them after his own fashion, and if there were any difficulties, he merely noted them as they occurred. I have translated the entire New Testament according to the Greek original, with the Greek appended directly to allow for quicker comparison. I added notes separately in which, partly by proofs and partly by the authority of early theologians, I show that what I emended was not changed rashly, lest my corrections should lack credence or my emendations be easily altered. Would that I had been able to accomplish what I tried so hard to do! As far as the Church is concerned, I will have no fears in dedicating my work to any bishop, cardinal, or even Roman pontiff, provided he be like the present one.[25] Finally, I have no doubt that you too will offer your congratulations when the book has been printed, even though you are now trying to discourage me from publishing it, provided you become somewhat acquainted with that language without which it would be impossible to appraise the matter correctly.

See, my dear Dorp, how by one and the same work you have performed a twofold service: one you have performed for the theologians whose views you so carefully represented, and another you have per-

25. Erasmus did dedicate his New Testament to the pope then reigning, Leo X.

formed for me, to whom you have more clearly manifested your affection by your friendly correction. You, in turn, should take in good part my equally unrestrained explanation. And if you are wise, you will assent more to my advice than to the advice of those men, who are eager to draw into their faction your genius, which is so promising, solely for the purpose of strengthening their forces by gaining a leader. Let them pursue better ends if they can; but if they take a poorer course, you must still follow the best one. And if you are not able to better them—which I would want you to strive for—at least be careful that they do not corrupt you. Hence I beg you to plead my case with them just as loyally as you pleaded their cause with me. Endeavor to put these fellows at peace as far as possible and convince them that what I am doing is not intended to insult those who are unfamiliar with this scholarship, but that it is meant to serve the common good. This explanation will suffice for those who are disposed to accept it but will convince no one who prefers to reject it. Then add that I am so minded that should anyone arise who would or could teach a better doctrine, I would be the first to retract my opinions and subscribe to his point of view.

Extend my cordial regards to John Paludanus, and see to it that you bring him in on this controversy over *Folly* by reason of the commentaries dedicated to him by our friend Lister.[26] Please commend me earnestly to the learned Nevius, and to the cultured Nicholas of Beveren, provost of St. Peter's.[27] I admire and revere for your sake Abbot Menardus, whom you praise so highly;[28] I have no doubt the praise is deserved, since you are trustworthy; and I do not forget to mention him very honorably in my letters whenever there is a fitting occasion. Health and farewell, Dorp, dearest of men.

Antwerp, 1515

26. John Paludanus was a professor of oratory at Louvain and a close friend of Erasmus. Gerard Lister, a former student of Paludanus, annotated *The Praise of Folly* for the edition published by Froben in early 1515.

27. Nevius was the principal of the Collège du Lis at Louvain. Nicholas of Beveren, provost of St. Peter's church at Utrecht, was a member of the noble house of Veere and Beveren. He was living in Louvain at this time.

28. Menardus, abbott of the Benedictine abbey at Egmond, was a close friend and patron of Dorp.

IV

The *Paraclesis*

The *Paraclesis* is the preface to Erasmus' Greek and Latin edition of the New Testament, which Froben first published in February 1516.[1] The word itself is Greek and means a summons or exhortation. In this context it is a summons or exhortation to the Christian to study Holy Scripture, where alone he will find the teachings of Christ in all their fullness and life. These incomparable writings, Erasmus declares in his concluding words, "bring you the living image of His holy mind and the speaking, healing, dying, rising Christ Himself, and thus they render Him so fully present that you would see less if you gazed upon Him with your very eyes."

The *Paraclesis* is one of the great classic statements of Erasmus' biblical humanism.[2] Its argument is simple and somewhat repetitive, and the essay, as important as it is, would seem to have been written in haste. Yet it is a moving and even powerful document, and it expresses as well as any other single work the religious ideals of Erasmus. There is frequent use and a definition in it of the famous Erasmian term "the philosophy of Christ." It also contains the oft-quoted passage of Erasmus wherein he hopes that Holy Scripture will be translated into the vernacular and be read by all and that the farmer and the weaver will sing verses from it at their work.

The illustrious Lactantius Firmianus, good reader, whose eloquence Jerome especially admires, as he begins to defend the Christian religion against the pagans desires especially an eloquence second only to Cicero's be given him, thinking it wrong, I believe, to want an

---

1. The Latin text is in *Desiderius Erasmus Roterodamus: Ausgewählte Werke*, ed. Hajo Holborn (Munich, 1933), pp. 139–49. The present translation was made by the editor from the Holborn edition. The only other English translation, insofar as the editor knows, is a rather quaint early one attributed to William Roy and published at Marburg in Hesse in 1529. See Plate 5.

2. For appraisals of the *Paraclesis*, see Phillips, *Erasmus and the Northern Renaissance*, pp. 77–85, and Jacques Etienne, *Spiritualisme érasmien et théologiens louvanistes* (Louvain, 1956), pp. 18–22.

equal eloquence.[3] But I indeed might heartily wish, if anything is to be gained by wishes of this kind, so long as I exhort all men to the most holy and wholesome study of Christian philosophy and summon them as if with the blast of a trumpet, that an eloquence far different from Cicero's be given me: an eloquence certainly much more efficacious, if less ornate than his. Or rather [I might wish for that kind of eloquence], if such power of speech was ever granted anyone, as the tales of the ancient poets not entirely without cause attributed to Mercury, who as if with a magic wand and a divine lyre induces sleep when he wishes and likewise snatches sleep away, plunging whom he wished into hell and again calling them forth from hell; or as the ancient tales assigned to Amphion and Orpheus, one of whom is supposed to have moved hard rocks, the other to have attracted oaks and ashes with a lyre; or as the Gauls ascribed to their Ogmius, leading about whither he wished all men by little chains fastened to their ears from his tongue; or as fabled antiquity attributed to Marsyas; or really, lest we linger too long on fables, as Alcibiades imputed to Socrates and old comedy to Pericles, an eloquence which not only captivates the ear with its fleeting delight but which leaves a lasting sting in the minds of its hearers, which grips, which transforms, which sends away a far different listener than it had received. One reads that the noble musician Timotheus, singing Doric melodies, was wont to rouse Alexander the Great to a desire for war. Nor were they lacking in former times who considered nothing more effective than the entreaties which the Greeks call *epodes*. But if there were any such kind of incantation anywhere, if there were any power of song which truly could inspire, if any Pytho truly swayed the heart, I would desire that it be at hand for me so that I might convince all of the most wholesome truth of all. However, it is more desirable that Christ Himself, whose business we are about, so guide the strings of our lyre that this song might deeply affect and move the minds of all, and, in fact, to accomplish this there is no need for the syllogisms and exclamations of the orators. What we desire is that nothing may stand forth with greater certainty than

3. Lactantius Firmianus was an early fourth-century Christian writer, and the author of a defense of the Christian faith entitled *Institutiones divinae*. He had a reputation for great eloquence.

the truth itself, whose expression is the more powerful, the simpler it is.

And in the first place it is not pleasing to renew at the present time this complaint, not entirely new but, alas, only too just—and perhaps never more just than in these days—that when men are devoting themselves with such ardent spirit to all their studies, this philosophy of Christ alone is derided by some, even Christians, is neglected by many, and is discussed by a few, but in a cold manner (I shall not say insincerely). Moreover, in all other branches of learning which human industry has brought forth, nothing is so hidden and obscure which the keenness of genius has not explored, nothing is so difficult which tremendous exertion has not overcome. Yet how is it that even those of us who profess to be Christian fail to embrace with the proper spirit this philosophy alone? Platonists, Pythagoreans, Academics, Stoics, Cynics, Peripatetics, Epicureans not only have a deep understanding of the doctrines of their respective sects, but they commit them to memory, and they fight fiercely in their behalf, willing even to die rather than abandon the defense of their author. Then why do not we evince far greater spirit for Christ, our Author and Prince? Who does not judge it very shameful for one professing Aristotle's philosophy not to know that man's opinion about the causes of lightning, about prime matter, about the infinite? And neither does this knowledge render a man happy, nor does the lack of it render him unhappy. And do not we, initiated in so many ways, drawn by so many sacraments to Christ, think it shameful and base to know nothing of His doctrines, which offer the most certain happiness to all? But what purpose is served to exaggerate the matter by controversy, since it is what I might call a kind of wicked madness to wish to compare Christ with Zeno or Aristotle and His teaching with, to put it mildly, the paltry precepts of those men? Let them magnify the leaders of their sect as much as they can or wish. Certainly He alone was a teacher who came forth from heaven, He alone could teach certain doctrine, since it is eternal wisdom, He alone, the sole author of human salvation, taught what pertains to salvation, He alone fully vouches for whatsoever He taught, He alone is able to grant whatsoever He has promised. If anything is brought to us from the Chaldeans or Egyptians, we desire more eagerly to examine it because of the fact that it comes from a strange world, and part of its value is to have come from far off; and oftentimes we are anxiously tormented by the fancies of an insignificant man, not to say an impostor, not only to no avail but with great loss of time (I am not adding a more serious note, for the matter as it stands is most serious). But why does not such a desire also excite Christian minds who are convinced—and it is a fact—that this teaching has come not from Egypt or Syria but from heaven itself? Why do not all of us ponder within ourselves that this must be a new and wonderful kind of philosophy since, in order to transmit it to mortals, He who was God became man, He who was immortal became mortal, He who was in the heart of the Father descended to earth? It must be a great matter, and in no sense a commonplace one, whatever it is, because that wondrous Author came to teach after so many families of distinguished philosophers, after so many remarkable prophets. Why, then, out of pious curiosity do we not investigate, examine, explore each tenet? Especially since this kind of wisdom, so extraordinary that once for all it renders foolish the entire wisdom of this world, may be drawn from its few books as from the most limpid springs with far less labor than Aristotle's doctrine is extracted from so many obscure volumes, from those huge commentaries of the interpreters at odds with one another—and I shall not add with how much greater reward. Indeed, here there is no requirement that you approach equipped with so many troublesome sciences. The journey is simple, and it is ready for anyone. Only bring a pious and open mind, possessed above all with a pure and simple faith. Only be docile, and you have advanced far in this philosophy. It itself supplies inspiration as a teacher which communicates itself to no one more gladly than to minds that are without guile. The teachings of the others, besides that fact that they give hope of a false happiness, drive off the natural talents of many by the very difficulty, it is clear, of their precepts. This doctrine in an equal degree accommodates itself to all, lowers itself to the little ones, adjusts itself to their measure, nourishing them with milk, bearing, fostering, sustaining them, doing everything until we grow in Christ. Again, not only does it serve the lowliest, but it is also an object of wonder to those at the top. And the more you shall have progressed in its riches, the more you shall have withdrawn it from the shadow of the power of any other. It is a small affair to the little ones and more than the highest affair to the great. It casts aside no age, no sex, no fortune or position in life. The sun itself is not as common and accessible to all as is Christ's teaching. It keeps no one at a distance, unless a person, begrudging himself, keeps himself away.

Indeed, I disagree very much with those who are unwilling that Holy Scripture, translated into the vulgar tongue, be read by the uneducated, as if Christ taught such intricate doctrines that they could scarcely be understood by very few theologians, or as if the strength of the Christian religion consisted in men's ignorance of it. The mysteries of kings, perhaps, are better concealed, but Christ wishes His mysteries published as openly as possible. I would that even the lowliest women read the Gospels and the Pauline Epistles. And I would that they were translated into all languages so that they could be read and understood not only by Scots and Irish but also by Turks and Saracens. Surely the first step is to understand in one way or another. It may be that many will ridicule, but some may be taken captive. Would that, as a result, the farmer sing some portion of them at the plow, the weaver hum some parts of them to the movement of his shuttle, the traveler lighten the weariness of the journey with stories of this kind! Let all the conversations of every Christian be drawn from this source. For in general our daily conversations reveal what we are. Let each one comprehend what he can, let him express what he can. Whoever lags behind, let him not envy him who is ahead; whoever is in the front rank, let him encourage him who follows, not despair of him. Why do we restrict a profession common to all to a few? For it is not fitting, since baptism is common in an equal degree to all Christians, wherein there is the first profession of Christian philosophy, and since the other sacraments and at length the reward of immortality belong equally to all, that doctrines alone should be reserved for those very few whom today the crowd call theologians or monks, the very persons whom, although they comprise one of the smallest parts of the Christian populace, yet I might wish to be in greater measure what they are styled. For I fear that one may find among the theologians men who are far removed from the title they bear, that is, men who discuss earthly matters, not divine, and that among the monks who profess the poverty of Christ and the contempt of the world you may find something more than worldliness. To me he is truly a theologian who teaches not by skill with intricate syllogisms but by a disposition of mind, by the very expression and the eyes, by his very life that riches should be disdained, that the Christian should not put his trust in the supports of this world but must rely entirely on heaven, that a wrong should not be avenged, that a good should be wished for those wishing ill, that we should deserve well of those deserving ill, that all good men should be loved and cherished equally as members of the same body, that the evil should be tolerated if they cannot be corrected, that those who are stripped of their goods, those who are turned away from possessions, those who mourn are blessed and should not be deplored, and that death should even be desired by the devout, since it is nothing other than a passage to immortality. And if anyone under the inspiration of the spirit of Christ preaches this kind of doctrine, inculcates it, exhorts, incites, and encourages men to it, he indeed is truly a theologian, even if he should be a common laborer or weaver. And if anyone exemplifies this doctrine in his life itself, he is in fact a great doctor. Another, perhaps, even a non-Christian, may discuss more subtly how the angels understand, but to persuade us to lead here an angelic life, free from every stain, this indeed is the duty of the Christian theologian.

But if anyone objects that these notions are somewhat stupid and vulgar, I should respond to him only that Christ particularly taught these rude doctrines, that the Apostles inculcated them, that however vulgar they are, they have brought forth for us so many sincerely Christian and so great a throng of illustrious martyrs. This philosophy, unlettered as it appears to these very objectors, has drawn the highest princes of the world and so many kingdoms and peoples to its laws, an achievement which the power of tyrants and the erudition of philosophers cannot claim. Indeed I do not object to having that latter wisdom, if it seems worthwhile, discussed among the educated. But let the lowly mass of Christians console themselves certainly with this title because, whether the Apostles knew or other Fathers understood these subtleties or not, they surely didn't teach them. If princes in the execution of their duties would manifest what I have referred to as a vulgar doctrine, if priests would inculcate it in sermons, if schoolmasters would instill it in students rather than that erudition which they draw from the fonts of Aristotle and Averroës, Christendom would not be so disturbed on all sides by almost continuous war, everything would not be boiling over with such a mad desire to heap up riches by fair means or foul, every subject, sacred as well as profane, would not be made to resound everywhere with so much noisy disputation, and, finally, we would not differ from those who do not profess the philosophy of Christ merely in name and ceremonial. For upon these three ranks of men principally the task of either renewing or advancing the Christian religion has been placed: on the princes and the magistrates who serve in their place, on the bishops and their delegated priests, and on those who instruct the young eager for all knowledge. If it happen that they, having laid aside their own affairs, should sincerely cooperate in Christ, we would certainly see in not so many years a true and, as Paul says, a genuine race of Christians everywhere emerge, a people who would restore the philosophy of Christ not in ceremonies alone and in syllogistic propositions but in the heart itself and in the whole life. The enemies of the Christian name will far more quickly be drawn to the faith of Christ by these weapons than by threats or arms. In the conquest of every citadel nothing is more powerful than the truth itself. He is not a Platonist who has not read the works of Plato; and is he a theologian, let alone a Christian, who has not read the literature of Christ? Who loves me, Christ says, keeps my word, a distinguishing mark which He himself prescribed. Therefore, if we are truly and sincerely Christian, if we truly believe in Him who has been sent from Heaven to teach us that which the wisdom of the philosophers could not do, if we truly expect from Him what no prince, however powerful, can give, why is anything more important to us than His literature? Why indeed does anything seem learned that is not in harmony with His decrees? Why in the case of this literature that should be revered do we also allow ourselves, and I shall say almost to a greater extent than do the secular interpreters in the case of the imperial laws or the books of the physicians, to speak whatever comes to mind, to distort, to obscure? We drag heavenly doctrines down to the level of our own life as if it were a Lydian rule, and while we seek to avoid by every means appearing to be ignorant and for this reason gather in whatever is of account in secular literature, that which is of special value in Christian philosophy I shall not say we corrupt, but—and no one can deny it—we restrict to a few, although Christ wished nothing to be more public. In this kind of philosophy, located as it is more truly in the disposition of the mind than in syllogisms, life means more than debate, inspiration is preferable to erudition, transformation is a more important matter than intellectual comprehension. Only a very few can be learned, but all can be Christian, all can be devout, and—I shall boldly add—all can be theologians.

Indeed, this philosophy easily penetrates into the minds of all, an action in especial accord with human nature. Moreover, what else is the philosophy of Christ, which He Himself calls a rebirth, than the restoration of human nature originally well formed? By the same token, although no one has taught this more perfectly and more effectively than Christ, nevertheless one may find in the books of the pagans very much which does agree with His teaching. There was never so coarse a school of philosophy that taught that money rendered a man happy. Nor has there ever been one so shameless that fixed the chief good in those vulgar honors and pleasures. The Stoics understood that no one was wise unless he was good; they understood that nothing was truly good or noble save real virtue and nothing fearful or evil save baseness alone. According to Plato, Socrates teaches in many different ways that a wrong must not be repaid with a wrong, and also that since the soul is immortal, those should not be lamented who depart this life for a happier one with the assurance of having led an upright life. In addition, he teaches that the soul must be drawn away from the inclinations of the body and led to those which are its real objectives although they are not seen. Aristotle has written in the *Politics* that nothing can be a delight to us, even though it is not in any way despised, except virtue alone. Epicurus also acknowledges that nothing in man's life can bring delight unless the mind is conscious of no evil, from which awareness true pleasure gushes forth as from a spring. What shall we say of this, that many—notably Socrates, Diogenes, and Epictetus—have presented a good portion of His teaching? But since Christ both taught and presented the same doctrine so much more fully, is it not a monstrous thing that Christians either disregard or neglect or even ridicule it? If there are things that belong particularly to Christianity in these ancient writers, let us follow them. But if these alone can truly make a Christian, why do we consider them as almost more obsolete and replaced than the Mosaic books? The first step, however, is to know what He taught; the next is to carry it into effect. Therefore, I believe, anyone should not think himself to be Christian if he disputes about instances, relations, quiddities, and formalities with an obscure and irksome confusion of words, but rather if he holds and exhibits what Christ taught and showed forth. Not that I condemn the industry of those who not without merit employ their native intellectual powers in such subtle discourse, for I do not wish anyone to be offended, but that I think, and rightly so, unless I am mistaken, that that pure and genuine philosophy of Christ is not to be drawn from any source more abundantly than from the evangelical books and from the Apostolic Letters, about which, if anyone should devoutly philosophize, praying more than arguing and seeking to be transformed rather than armed for battle, he would without a doubt find that there is nothing pertaining to the happiness of man and the living of his life which is not taught, examined, and unraveled in these works. If we desire to learn, why is another author more pleasing than Christ Himself? If we seek a model for life, why does another example take precedence for us over that of Christ Himself? If we wish some medicine against the troublesome desires of the soul, why do we think the remedy to be more at hand somewhere else? If we want to arouse a soul that is idle and growing listless by reading, where, I ask, will you find sparks equally alive and efficacious? If the soul seems distracted by the vexations of this life, why are other delights more pleasing? Why have we steadfastly preferred to learn the wisdom of Christ from the writings of men than from Christ Himself? And He, since He promised to be with us all days, even unto the consummation of the world, stands forth especially in this literature, in which He lives for us even at this time, breathes and speaks. I should say almost more effectively than when He dwelt among men. The Jews saw and heard less than you see and hear in the books of the Gospels, to the extent that you make use of your eyes and ears, whereby this can be perceived and heard.

And what kind of a situation is this, I ask? We preserve the letters written by a dear friend, we kiss them fondly, we carry them about, we read them again and again, yet there are many thousands of Christians who, although they are learned in other respects, never read, however, the evangelical and apostolic books in an entire lifetime. The Mohammedans hold fast to their doctrines, the Jews also today from the very cradle study the books of Moses. Why do not we in the same way distinguish ourselves in Christ? Those who profess the way of life of Benedict hold, study, absorb a rule written by man, and by one nearly uneducated for the uneducated. Those who are in the Augustinian order are well versed in the rule of their founder. The Franciscans reverence and love the little traditions of their Francis, and to whatever corner of the earth they go, they carry them with them; they do not feel safe unless the little book is on their person. Why do these men attribute more to a rule written by man than does the Christian world to its rule, which Christ delivered to all and which all have equally professed in baptism? Finally, although you may even cite a thousand rules, can anything be holier than this? And I wish that this may come to pass: just as Paul wrote that the law of Moses was not full of glory compared with the glory of the Gospel succeeding it, so may all Christians hold the Gospels and Letters of the Apostles as so holy that in comparison with them these other writings do not seem holy. What others may wish to concede to Albert the Great, to Alexander, to Thomas, to Egidio, to Richard, to Occam, they will certainly be free, as far as I am concerned, to do, for I do not want to diminish the fame of anyone or contend with the studies of men that are now of long standing.[4] However learned these may be, however subtle, however seraphic, if they like, yet they must admit that the former are the most tried and true. Paul wishes that the spirits of those prophesying be judged whether they are of God. Augustine, reading every kind of book with discretion, asks nothing more than a just hearing also for his own works. But in this literature alone [i.e., Holy Scripture] what I do not comprehend, I nevertheless revere. It is no school of theologians that has attested this Author for us but the Heavenly Father Himself through the testimony of the divine voice, and He has done this on two occasions: first at the Jordan at the time of the Baptism, then on Mount Tabor at the Transfiguration. "This is my beloved Son," He says, "in whom I am well pleased; hear Him."[5] O solid and truly irref-

---

4. The names are those of medieval theologians: Albert the Great, Alexander of Hales, Thomas Aquinas, Egidio of Rome, Richard of St. Victor, and William of Occam.
5. Matthew 3:17; 17:5.

ragable authority, as the theologians say! What is this phrase, "Hear Him"? Certainly He is the one and only teacher, let us be the disciples of Him alone. Let each one extol in his studies his own author as much as he will wish, this utterance has been said without exception of Christ alone. A dove first descended on Him, the confirmation of the Father's testimony. Peter next bears His spirit, to whom the highest Pastor three times entrusted the feeding of His sheep, feeding them without a doubt, however, on the food of Christian doctrine.[6] This spirit was born again, as it were, in Paul, whom He himself called a "chosen vessel" and an extraordinary herald of His name.[7] What John had drawn from that sacred font of His heart, he expressed in his own writings. What, I pray, is like this in Scotus (I do not wish that this remark be taken as a pretext for abuse), what is like this in Thomas? Nevertheless, I admire the talents of the one, and I also revere the sanctity of the other. But why do not all of us apply ourselves to philosophy in these authors of such great value? Why do we not carry them about on our persons, have them ever in our hands? Why do we not hunt through these authors, thoroughly examine them, assiduously investigate them? Why devote the greater part of life to Averroës rather than to the Gospels? Why spend nearly all of life on the ordinances of men and on opinions in contradiction with themselves? The latter, in fact, may now be the views of the more eminent theologians, if you please; but certainly the first steps of the great theologian in the days to come will be in these authors [of Holy Scripture].

Let all those of us who have pledged in baptism in the words prescribed by Christ, if we have pledged sincerely, be directly imbued with the teachings of Christ in the midst of the very embraces of parents and the caresses of nurses. For that which the new earthen pot of the soul first imbibes settles most deeply and clings most tenaciously. Let the first lispings utter Christ, let earliest childhood be formed by the Gospels of Him whom I would wish particularly presented in such a way that children also might love Him. For as the severity of some teachers causes children to hate literature before they come to know it, so there are those who make the philosophy of Christ sad and morose, although nothing is more sweet than it. In these studies, then, let them

6. John 21:15ff.
7. Acts 9:15.

engage themselves until at length in silent growth they mature into strong manhood in Christ. The literature of others is such that many have greatly repented the effort expended upon it, and it happens again and again that those who have fought through all their life up to death to defend the principles of that literature, free themselves from the faction of their author at the very hour of death. But happy is that man whom death takes as he meditates upon this literature [of Christ]. Let us all, therefore, with our whole heart covet this literature, let us embrace it, let us continually occupy ourselves with it, let us fondly kiss it, at length let us die in its embrace, let us be transformed in it, since indeed studies are transmuted into morals. As for him who cannot pursue this course (but who cannot do it, if only he wishes?), let him at least reverence this literature enveloping, as it were, His divine heart. If anyone shows us the footprints of Christ, in what manner, as Christians, do we prostrate ourselves, how we adore them! But why do we not venerate instead the living and breathing likeness of Him in these books? If anyone displays the tunic of Christ, to what corner of the earth shall we not hasten so that we may kiss it? Yet were you to bring forth His entire wardrobe, it would not manifest Christ more clearly and truly than the Gospel writings. We embellish a wooden or stone statue with gems and gold for the love of Christ. Why not, rather, mark with gold and gems and with ornaments of greater value than these, if such there be, these writings which bring Christ to us so much more effectively than any paltry image? The latter represents only the form of the body—if indeed it represents anything of Him—but these writings bring you the living image of His holy mind and the speaking, healing, dying, rising Christ Himself, and thus they render Him so fully present that you would see less if you gazed upon Him with your very eyes.

V

Letter to Paul Volz

14 August 1518

This letter was written as the preface to the new edition of the *Enchiridion militis Christiani* which Froben published in the summer of 1518.[1] It is addressed to Paul Volz, abbot of the Benedictine monastery of Hugshofen, near Schlettstadt (Sélestat) in Alsace, a man whose life Erasmus considered an example of the precepts which he himself set down in the *Enchiridion*. Volz (1480–1544) had become a Benedictine in 1503 and had been elected abbot of Hugshofen in 1512, at which time he undertook the reform of his monastic community. He was also associated with the literary circle of Schlettstadt, which included such humanists as Beatus Rhenanus and Jacob Wimpfeling. By 1526 he had gone over to Protestantism, though as "an Erasmian who had strayed into Lutheranism" he had some difficulties in the Lutheran fold.[2] He remained always on good terms with Erasmus, and Erasmus left him a small sum in his will.

The letter is an important statement of Erasmus' basic themes and has been called "a veritable Erasmian manifesto of the religion of pure spirit."[3] Both the scholastic theologians and the monks come in for some harsh criticism because of their departure from the pure and simple "philosophy of Christ." It contains many interesting features: an emphasis on the conversion of the Turks rather than war against them, for which purpose a commission of pious and learned men would draw up a concise statement of Christian doctrine; a fairly obvious reference to Luther's Ninety-five Theses; and, in the version here presented, a significant addition, which Erasmus inserted in 1529, explaining the laudable purpose and character of early monasticism.

The letter was translated into German in 1520 by Luther's close friend Spalatin and was published the following year. An English translation,

1. The Latin text is in Allen, III 361–77. A previous English version attributed to William Tyndale was published in London in 1533 along with the *Enchiridion*. Erasmus, *Enchiridion militis Christiani: An English Version*, ed. Anne M. O'Donnell, S.N.D., was published at Oxford in 1981. The present translation was made by the editor from Allen with reference to the Tyndale text.
2. *Douze Lettres d'Erasme*, edd. Roland Crahay and Marie Delcourt (Paris, 1938), p. 76. See also Allen, II 159.
3. A. Renaudet, *Etudes érasmiennes* (Paris, 1939), p. 175.

prefacing the *Enchiridion* in Latin, appeared in 1533 and is attributed to William Tyndale. The *Enchiridion* itself was originally written in 1501 and was published for the first time at Antwerp in 1503.

To the Reverend Father in Christ, Paul Volz,
most devout Abbot of the monastery of Hugshofen,
greetings from Desiderius Erasmus of Rotterdam:

Although that little book entitled *Enchiridion militis Christiani*, which I had once written for myself alone and for an untutored friend, began to be less displeasing, most virtuous father, after I learned that it was approved by you and by others like you—who, endowed as you yourselves are with pious learning and with learned piety, would certainly not approve anything that is not pious as well as learned—it nevertheless begins now almost to please when I see that even though it has often been printed, it is ever in demand as if it were a new work, unless the printers are completely deceiving me. Yet that remark repeatedly troubles my mind which a certain learned friend once expressed very wittily (he was joking, but I wish that there were neither truth nor wit in it!): "I see more sanctity in the book than in its author." And this is all the more distressing to me, because the same jest applies to him whose conversion was the chief aim of the work, since indeed this man has not so much torn himself away from the court as immersed himself more deeply in it day by day, with what increase of piety I know not, but I do know to what great disaster, as he himself admits. Nevertheless, I do not entirely grieve for my friend, for, though he has not wished to follow my warnings, some day with misfortune as the teacher he may return to his senses. As for me, though up to now I continue to struggle forward, my guardian spirit assails me with so many mishaps and trials that Homer's Ulysses seems like another Polycrates alongside me.

I do not altogether regret this work, however, if it arouses in so many the desire for true piety. Nor do I think that every kind of reproach should be leveled against me if I fall short of my own counsels. First of all, it is a part of piety to wish truly to become pious; and I do not believe that a heart filled with such intentions should be disdained, even if at times the effort is not crowned with success. One must ever make the effort throughout life, and success on occasion comes to him who has tried again and again. But he has traveled a good part of a difficult journey who has become well acquainted with the way. Therefore I am not moved by the jests of those who scorn this little book as not being learned enough or as one which could be written by any schoolboy, because it does not discuss the questions of the Scotists. As if nothing is learned without these! Let this little book not be sharp-witted provided it be pious. Let it not prepare a person for the mental gymnastics of the Sorbonne but for Christian peace of soul. Let it not contribute to theological argument but to a theological life. What is to be gained by discussing that which everyone discusses? Who today is not occupied with theological questions? With what else are the swarms of schoolmen concerned? There are almost as many commentaries on the *Sentences* as there are theologians.[4] What other kind or category of manual writer is there except those who blend over and again one manual with another and, in the fashion of a pharmacist, repeatedly concoct the old out of the new, the new out of the old, one out of many, and many out of one? How could the great mass of these volumes teach us to live properly when not even a lifetime is enough to read them? It is as if a doctor would prescribe to a patient seriously ill that he read the books of Jacobus a Partibus and all others of a similar character, wherein he will find the remedy to restore his health. But in the meantime the patient dies, nor will there be anyone who can be helped.

In such a fleeting life it is necessary to have a ready remedy at hand. In how many volumes do these writers give instruction about restitution, confession, vows, scandal, and innumerable other matters? And though they examine minutely each single topic and so define each as if they mistrusted the abilities of all the other writers, indeed even as if they mistrusted the goodness of Christ, while they set forth precisely how He ought to reward or punish each deed, yet they fail to agree among themselves, nor do they often explain anything clearly if they are more closely consulted. There is so great a variety either of abilities or of circumstances. Moreover, even though they define everything truly and correctly, and aside from the fact that these questions are treated in a cold and meager way, how many have the time to read

4. See Selection II, note 13.

such volumes? Who can carry around with him Aquinas' *Secundae secunda*? And yet it is important for all to live a good life, the path to which Christ intended to be accessible to all, not by way of a difficult labyrinth of argument but by a sincere faith and by an unfeigned charity which a confident hope accompanies. Finally, let the great masters, who of necessity are few in numbers, study these huge volumes; nonetheless, the untrained multitude for whom Christ died must be considered. However, he has taught the chief part of Christian piety who has enkindled the love for it. That wise king instructing his son in true wisdom devotes even more effort to encouraging him than to teaching him, as if to love wisdom is almost to obtain it. What is disgraceful in the case of lawyers and doctors who industriously complicate their art so that at the same time their income may be larger and their prestige among the unskilled may be greater, that would be far more disgraceful to do in the case of the philosophy of Christ. Rather we must strive to render this art as simple as possible and accessible to all. Let our aim be not to appear learned but to lead as many as possible to a Christian life.

War is now being prepared against the Turks, and regardless of the plan behind it we must pray that it be turned not to the advantage of a certain few but to the common good of all. But what do we think would happen if we set before the vanquished (for I don't believe that we shall put them all to the sword), in order to win them to Christ, the works of Occam or Durandus or Scotus or Gabriel or Alvarus? What will they think, what impression will they get (for they are certainly men, if nothing else) when they hear those thorny and intricate arguments about instances, formalities, quiddities, and relationships? Especially when they see those great professors of religion disagreeing about these matters among themselves to the point that they frequently grow pale and insult and spit at one another and sometimes even exchange blows, or when they see the Dominicans contending at close hand and afar in behalf of their Thomas, and the Franciscans guarding with joined shields their most subtle and seraphic doctors, some speaking as nominalists, others as realists. What, indeed, will they think if they see that the question is so difficult that it has never adequately been settled what words should be used in speaking of Christ? As though one is dealing with some wayward spirit who is evoked to your own destruction if prescribed words are not carefully followed and not, instead, with the most merciful Saviour, who demands only that we live a pure and simple life. I implore you by the everlasting God, what will happen in this state of affairs, especially if our morals and our life correspond to this arrogant teaching? If the Turks should observe our ambition because of our loud, tyrannical clamoring, our avarice because of our plundering, our lust because of our debauchery, our cruelty because of our oppressive rule, how shall we press upon them the doctrine of Christ, so contrary to all these things? The most efficacious way of overcoming the Turks would be if they beheld that which Christ taught and exemplified shining forth in our own lives, if they perceived that we do not covet their empires nor thirst after their gold nor seek their possessions, but strive for nothing except their salvation and Christ's glory. This is that true, authentic, and efficacious theology which in times gone by subdued for Christ both the pride of the philosophers and the unconquered scepters of the princes. And if we act thus, Christ Himself will be with us.

And indeed it is not fitting that we proclaim ourselves good Christians with this argument if we kill as many as possible, but rather if we save as many as possible; not if we sacrifice many thousands of infidels to Hell, but if we render faithful as many of the infidels as possible; not if we curse them with dire execrations, but if we desire and devoutly pray that Heaven grant them deliverance and a better attitude of mind. And if this be not our disposition, it will sooner come to pass that we shall degenerate into Turks rather than win the Turks to our side. And although the dice of war, ever uncertain, fall favorably, it will happen that the pope or his cardinals perhaps may rule more widely, but not Christ, whose kingdom flourishes at last only if piety, charity, peace, and chastity thrive. This rule we trust shall be under the leadership and guidance of the excellent Leo X, unless he is diverted from his endeavors for what is best into another direction by the surge of human affairs. Christ Himself declares that He is the protector and prince of the heavenly kingdom, which has a splendor only if what is heavenly is triumphant.

For Christ certainly did not die so that the might, the wealth, the arms, and the rest of the pomp of a worldly kingdom, which once were in the hands of the pagans, or at least of secular princes not so very different from the pagans, be now turned over to some priests. In my opinion we should seriously consider influencing their minds with letters and tracts long before we resort to arms. But with what kind of letters? Not with threatening letters, not with tyrannical letters, but with letters which truly breathe a paternal charity, which echo the heart of Peter and Paul, and which not only bear an apostolic inscription but have the flavor of apostolic power. I say this not because I do not know that the whole font and course of Christian philosophy is concealed in the Gospels and Epistles, but because the strange and frequently involved language as well as the figures of speech and oblique metaphors give such difficulty that even we ourselves must often make a great effort before we understand them. Thus, in my opinion, it would be most convenient if the task were assigned to some men as pious as they are learned to draw together in a short statement the whole philosophy of Christ from the most pure sources of the Gospels and the Epistles and from the most approved interpreters, and to do this with simplicity insofar as it is still learned and with brevity insofar as it is still clear. Let those things which pertain to faith be related in as few propositions as possible. Let those things which pertain to the way of life be communicated also in a few statements, and let them be transmitted in such a way that they [the recipients] may understand that the yoke of Christ is sweet and agreeable, not harsh, that they have found fathers, not tyrants, shepherds, not robbers, and that they are called to salvation, not dragged away into slavery. They also are men, nor are their hearts of iron or steel. They can be softened, they can be won over by friendly acts, whereby even wild beasts are tamed. And especially efficacious is Christian truth. But the Roman pontiff shall order at the same time those to whom he wishes to assign this work not to depart in any way from the model of Christ nor anywhere to show regard for the desires and passions of men.

It was such a book that I had in mind to produce at the time when I pounded out the *Enchiridion*. I saw that the mass of Christians had been corrupted not only in their feelings but also in their opinions. I carefully considered that very many of those who profess to be shepherds and teachers abused the titles of Christ for their own advantage, to say nothing whatsoever in the meanwhile about those at whose command and prohibition human affairs are sent scurrying in all directions, and at whose vices, although they are public, one is scarcely permitted to groan. And in such great darkness, amid such worldly confusion, in the face of so great a variety of human opinions, where should we have recourse rather than to the truly sacred anchor of the Gospel teaching? Who, truly pious, does not see and lament over this age, the most corrupt by far? When did tyranny, when did avarice ever hold sway more widely or with more impunity? When was more attention ever paid to ceremonies? When has injustice abounded more freely? When has charity grown so cold? What is asserted, what is read, what is heard, what is proposed except that which savors of ambition and greed? Oh, how unhappy we would be if Christ had not left us some sparks of His teaching and living and the everlasting veins, as it were, of His own mind. Therefore we must strive in this direction so that, after we have set aside the coals of men, we may stir up these sparks—I willingly use the Pauline word—and we may explore these veins until we find the living water flowing to eternal life. We delve deep down into our earth in order to mine that which nourishes our vices. Are we not, then, to turn over the richest earth of Christ in order to obtain the salvation of souls? No cold blast of vice ever so extinguished the flame of charity that it could not be restored from this flintstone. The stone is Christ, but this stone is a seedbed of heavenly fire and has veins of living water. Abraham in times past dug wells in all the land, seeking everywhere veins of living water. But these same wells, having been filled up with earth by the Philistines, were reopened by Isaac and his servants; and not content with restoring the former wells, he also dug new ones. Once again the Philistines incite quarrels and strife, yet he does not stop his digging.[5]

And in these times Philistines are not entirely lacking to whom the earth is more pleasing than the lively bubbling of springs; indeed, those who have a taste for earthly things and turn aside to earthly desires, force the teaching of the Gospel, which they make a servant to human ambition, into compliance with base profit and their own tyranny. And if any Isaac or anyone from his family should dig and discover some pure vein, immediately they raise a clamor and cry out against him, well aware that this vein would check their profit and hinder their ambition, although it served the glory of Christ. Then

5. Genesis 26:14–22.

they throw earth in and stop up the vein with a corrupt interpretation and drive away the digger, or at least they so defile the water with mud and filth that he who drinks it henceforth imbibes more slime and dirt than pure liquid. They do not wish that they who thirst after justice should drink of pure liquid, but they lead them to their own worn-out cisterns which contain rubble but not water. Nevertheless, the real children of Isaac, the true worshipers of Christ, must not be wearied by this labor. For those men who cast earth onto the wellsprings of the Gospel also wish to be considered among the worshipers of Christ, so that among Christians now it is not at all safe to teach Christ purely. So great has the strength of the Philistines become, waging war in behalf of the earth, preaching earthly things in place of what is heavenly, human precepts in place of the divine, that is to say, preaching not what serves Christ's glory but what is to the profit of those who trade in indulgences, agreements, dispensations, and similar bargains. And they do this with greater danger because they cloak their cupidity with the titles of great princes, of the supreme pontiff, and even of Christ Himself. But yet no one more truly carries out the task of the pope than he who teaches purely the heavenly philosophy of Christ, of which the pope is the first teacher. No one deserves better of princes than he who labors that the commonweal may flourish as greatly as possible and may be burdened with the least possible oppression.

But here someone from the army of the schools will shout: "It is easy for anyone to prescribe in general what is to be followed and what is to be avoided; but in the meantime what will the response be to those who seek advice on so many specific matters and particular cases?" First, there are too many kinds of human affairs to permit a sure response to each one of them. Secondly, so great is the variety of circumstances that unless they are known, one cannot even give a certain reply. Finally, I do not know if these men have a sure answer to give, especially since they disagree about most things among themselves. And those who are the more sensible in this contingent are not accustomed to reply thus: "You shall do this, you shall avoid that"; but rather: "In my opinion this is the safer course, this I think is tolerable." But if we have that simple and clear eye of the Gospel, if the house of our soul has the lamp of pure faith set on the lampstand, those petty matters will easily be dispersed as if they were shadows. If the rule of

Christian charity is at hand, everything else will easily conform to it. But what must you do when this rule will clash with those practices which have been accepted in the public usage of the ages and which have been sanctioned by the laws of princes? For this frequently occurs. You may not condemn what princes do in the fulfillment of their duty. But on the other hand, do not corrupt the heavenly philosophy of Christ with human decrees. Let Christ remain that which He is, the center with a number of circles surrounding Him. Do not move the target from its own central position.[6] Those who are nearest to Christ, priests, bishops, cardinals, popes, and all whose duty it is to follow the Lamb wheresoever He shall go, let them embrace what is most pure, and as far as they can, let them transfer this to those nearest to them. The second circle comprises secular princes, whose arms and whose laws serve Christ in their own fashion, either while in just war they overcome the enemy and defend the public peace, or while with lawful punishment they restrain evildoers. And yet because they are of necessity engaged in those affairs which are connected with the lowest dregs of the earth and with the business of the world, there is the danger that they might slip farther from the center, that they might wage war not for the commonweal but for their own pleasure, that under the pretext of justice they might vent their fury even on those whom clemency could restore, that under the title of lord they might plunder the people whose property they had the duty to protect.

Moreover, as Christ like a fountain of everlasting fire draws next to Him the order of priests and makes them fiery and purifies them from all earthly stain, so it is the duty of priests, and especially of the highest priests, to call princes to their side, as far as they may. If war should break out anywhere, let the popes strive for a settlement of the issues without bloodshed, or, if that is impossible, since there are tempests in human affairs, at least let them do their best that war be waged with less bloodshed and not be drawn out for a long time. In former times the bishops' authority intervened even in cases of just penalties and repeatedly wrested the guilty one from the hands of the judges, as Augustine openly bears witness in his letters. For certain things are so necessary to the order of the commonwealth that Christ

---

6. The notion of Christ as target (*scopus*) is also in the *Enchiridion*; see "The Fourth Rule" in *The* ENCHIRIDION *of Erasmus*, trans. Himelick.

nevertheless has ignored them in part, in part has rejected them, and in part has neither disapproved nor approved, as if He closed His eyes at them. He does not recognize the coin of Caesar nor the inscription on it. Thus it is that He orders tribute to be paid if it is due, as if it is of little concern to Him, provided that that which is due to God is given Him. He neither condemns nor openly absolves the adulterous woman, but He bids her not to repeat her crime. Concerning those condemned by Pilate, whose blood he had mixed with their sacrifices, He does not pronounce whether they suffered this rightly or wrongly, but He threatens a like destruction for all unless they return to their senses. Moreover, when He was asked to settle the division of an inheritance, He openly refused the task, as if to judge such crass issues was unworthy of Him who taught heavenly things. On the other hand, there are things which He openly abominates. He thunders "Woe!" against the greedy Pharisees, the hypocrites, the exalted rich. He never rebukes the Apostles more sharply than when they are moved by the desire for revenge or the stirrings of ambition. To those asking if they should bid fire come down from heaven to consume the city which had shut them out, He says, "You know not of what spirit you are." When Peter attempts to call Him away from the cross and back to the world, He calls him Satan. In how many ways and how often does He recall those disputing over first rank to a different frame of mind! Also there is that which He explicitly teaches and prescribes: not to resist evil, to deserve well of enemies, to be gentle of soul, and other precepts of the same character.

These injunctions must be sorted out and each must be arranged in its proper place. Let us not therefore immediately make Christ the author of that which is done by princes or secular officials, nor claim that it is done by divine right, as they now say. Certain gross matters are dealt with by these men, not entirely possessing a Christian purity but which nevertheless must not be reproached, inasmuch as they are necessary for the maintenance of order. For by the service of these men we are not made good, but less evil, and those who are evil do less harm to the commonwealth. Therefore their honor is due to them, since they do in some manner serve divine justice and the public peace, without which the work of piety is sometimes thrown into confusion. They should be honored when they perform their duty, they should perhaps be endured when they exercise their power in their own interests, lest a greater evil arise. For the image, or rather the shadow, of divine justice gleams in them also, which however ought to shine forth with far greater sharpness, clarity, and purity in the morals and laws of priests. An image is reflected in one way in iron, in another way in a mirror of glass.

In the third circle let us place the common people, as the grossest part of this world, but gross as it is still belonging to the body of Christ. For not only are the eyes members of the body but also the legs, feet, and the less honorable parts. Thus forbearance must be shown them so that they may always be called, as far as it can be done, to that which is more approved by Christ. For in the body of Christ he who was at one time the foot can become the eye. And as princes, if they are reprobate, should not be embittered by loud reproaches lest, according to the opinion of Augustine, provoked, they stir up more serious tragedies, so the weak people, after the example of Christ who endured and supported His disciples with such gentleness, should be endured and supported with fatherly indulgence until little by little they grow strong in Christ. For piety also has its infancy, its adolescence, its time of full and vigorous strength. Yet all must strive toward Christ, each according to his own strength. Each of the elements has its own place. Fire, however, which occupies the highest place, little by little draws all the others to it and, as far as it can, transforms them into its own nature. It turns clear water into air, the thin air it transforms into itself. Paul made many allowances for the Corinthians, distinguishing meanwhile between what he set forth in the name of the Lord to those who were perfect and what he permitted in his own name to those who were weak; yet he had this hope, that they may make progress. Again, he was anxious over the Galatians until Christ be formed in them.

Now there will be no great contention with the man who will think that this circle ought to be assigned rather to the princes. And indeed, if we are appraising morals, you will scarcely see other Christians more gross; I am speaking of the majority, not of all. But whatever is beyond the third circle, that should be always and everywhere abhorred. This category includes ambition, greed, lust, anger, vengeance, envy, slander, and the other vices, which then indeed become irremediable when, made attractive in the guise of piety and duty, they creep into the higher circles; that is, when under the pretext of justice and the law we behave as a tyrant, when through an opportunity afforded by religion we look to our gain, when under the pretense of defending the Church we strive for worldly power, when that is commanded as if serving the cause of Christ which is farthest from the teaching of Christ. Accordingly everyone must be given a target toward which he must strive. But there is only one target, namely, Christ and His most pure teaching. Therefore if you set forth a worldly target in place of the heavenly one, that man who strives to advance will not have the goal for which he may rightly make the effort. That which is highest must be fixed upon by all of us so that we may at least attain that which is mediocre.

Nor should we banish any kind of life from this target. The perfection of Christ is in the dispositions, not in the mode of life; in the soul, not in what a person wears or eats. There are among the monks those who are hardly admitted into the outermost circle; and yet I speak of those who are good but weak. There are among the twice married those whom Christ considers worthy of the first circle.[7] Nor, in fact, is injury done in the meantime to any profession of life if what is best and most perfect is set forth before all. Unless by chance it is thought that Plato had insulted all cities because in his *Republic* he set forth the model of such a commonwealth as could not hitherto be seen, or that Quintilian offended the whole class of orators because he invented such a model orator as thus far did not exist. Are you far distant from the archetype? You should not give up but should encourage yourself to go forward. You are not far off? You should urge yourself to come nearer. For no one has advanced so far that he does not have farther to go.

Every kind of life, however, has certain perils connected with it which cause a degeneration. He who clearly points out these dangers does not detract from an order but acts in its interest. The happiness of princes, for instance, is exposed to tyranny and a prey to folly, flattery, and pleasure. The man who shows what must be avoided deserves well of the order of princes. Nor does he diminish the majesty of these princes, in which they glory, who explains on what the true majesty of princes depends, who reminds them of what they swore when they undertook their princely office and of what their obligations are to

7. An obvious reference to Thomas More.

their people and to their magistrates. Ecclesiastical princes have a near affinity with two vices above all, avarice and ambition. As if perceiving this beforehand, that first shepherd after Christ warns the bishops to feed their flocks, not to rob or flay them; and not to feed them for the sake of base gain but out of a free and ready will, nor to lord it over them, but to rouse them to piety by the examples of their lives rather than by threats or commands. Will he then be seen to detract from the priestly order who reminds them by what means bishops are truly great, powerful, and rich? Moreover, the class of monks is practically the companion, besides other vices, of superstition, pride, hypocrisy, and disparagement. He then does not forthwith condemn their way of life who warns wherein true religion is located, and how far distant truly Christian piety is from pride and genuine charity from deceit, and how venomous language is at odds with pure religion, especially if he shows what should be avoided in such a gentle way that no man is marked out nor any class attacked. What, however, in the course of human affairs is so fortunate that it has no vices accompanying it? Therefore, just as he aids, not injures, the health of the body whosoever makes known what is harmful or beneficial to true health, so he does not draw men away from religion but rather exhorts them to it, who shows how true religion can be corrupted and restored.

For I hear that certain men so interpret the precepts of this little book as if they estrange men's minds from the monastic life, because less is attributed to ceremonies than certain men who attribute far too much wish, nor also is much conceded to human ordinances. And what is more, nothing can be said so cautiously that the wicked do not turn it into some false accusation or into an occasion for sin, with the result that now it is hardly safe to give any suitable advice. If anyone should deter men from the wars which, more than the pagans ever did, we have been waging now for some time and for objectives of no importance, he is marked out by the tricksters as if he holds with those who deny that Christians should wage any war. For we have made heretics out of the authors of this opinion because some pope seems to approve of war. He is not censured, however, who, contrary to the teaching of Christ and the Apostles, blows the trumpet to summon men to war for any and every cause. If anyone recalls that it is truly apostolic to draw the Turks to religion with the help of Christ rather than by arms, he is immediately suspected of teaching, as it were, that the Turks should in no way be checked if they attack Christians. If anyone praises the simplicity of the Apostles and comments on the extravagance of these times, there are those who reprimand him as favoring the Ebionites. If anyone more emphatically urges that those who are married should be joined together more by piety and the agreement of their minds than by the embrace of their bodies and that they should live their married life so purely that it resembles virginity as closely as possible, he comes under suspicion of holding with the Marcionites the idea that all sexual intercourse is impure. If anyone warns that disputations, particularly theological ones, should be free from a vain pertinacity in having one's own way and in maintaining one's own opinions and free also from that theatrical ambition to display one's strength, he is improperly arraigned as if he condemned all the schools. For St. Augustine, when he warns the dialecticians to be on their guard against a love of quarreling, does not condemn dialectics but exposes a vice connected with it, so that it might be avoided.[8]

Likewise, if anyone reproaches the perverse judgment of the crowd, which assigns first place among the virtues to those in the lowest class and, on the other side, detests most furiously those vices which are the least wicked when there are far more terrible ones, and vice versa, immediately he is hailed into court as if he is in favor of those vices before which he places a more serious vice or as if he damns those good deeds to which he prefers others as more holy. For instance, if anyone warns that it is safer to trust in good deeds than in papal pardons, he certainly does not condemn these pardons but gives preference to that which is of greater certainty according to Christ's teaching. Likewise, if anyone admonishes that those do better who work hard at home to support their wife and children than if they go off to see Rome, Jerusalem, or Compostella and that the money spent on a long and perilous journey is more devoutly given to the good and deserving poor, he does not condemn the pious disposition of such pilgrims but prefers that which is closer to true piety.[9]

8. *De doctrina Christiana* 2.31.48.
9. The above two sentences seem to refer to Luther's warnings about papal pardons in his Ninety-five Theses, specificially to Theses 41 to 46. These were now in wide circulation and the great controversy inaugurated by them had begun. See Luther's comment regarding this preface in his first letter to Erasmus (CWE 6: *Ep.* 933).

Now indeed it is not only in our times that certain vices are detested just as if they were the only vices, while we treat others lightly as if they were not vices, although they may be more terrible than the ones we so execrate. Augustine complains in his letters that among the Africans the one charge of lust is imputed as a vice to priests, whereas avarice and drunkenness are construed almost as praise. We magnify this one vice in tragic style, viewing it again and again as a dreadful crime for the same hands to touch the body of Christ which have touched the body of a prostitute. Nor are they lacking who, too much in the manner of a tragedy, have dared to assert publicly that it is a lesser fault for a woman to have intercourse with a brute beast than with a priest. The man who rebukes these shameless statements does not necessarily approve of incontinent priests, but he warns that those vices are disregarded which should have been given greater attention. The priest is a gambler, an old war horse or public brawler, an ignoramus, one completely immersed in worldly affairs, one devoted to the evil service of evil princes, yet they do not cry out in like manner against him who totally worldly performs the sacred mysteries. The priest is a deceiver who with his poison tongue and his fabricated lies ruins the reputation of an innocent man who has even deserved well, why then at this point do we not cry out, "Oh, shocking crime! With your tongue stained with the poison of hell, with your mouth whereby you slay an innocent man, you take unto yourself and consume the body of Him who has died even for the reprobate"? But we so disregard this evil that those who profess the most strict religious observances almost take praise from it. They deserve to be reprehended who openly maintain concubines at home and give thereby a dangerous example to the people. Who denies it? But this other vice is much more hateful to Christ. He who prefers honey does not therefore disapprove of butter; nor does he recommend fever who warns that madness is more to be avoided. And it is not easy to say how great a corruption of morals springs from perverse judgments of this kind.

Certain things have now been received into the rank of the virtues in such a way that they have the mask rather than the essence of piety, to the extent that, unless you take care, they utterly extinguish true piety. If there were concealed the blight of an indifferent religion in ceremonies, Paul in all his Epistles would not have become so violently angry at these. Nevertheless, in any case we do not condemn ceremonies moderately observed, but we do not allow that in these we have the beginning and end of sanctity, as they say. St. Augustine even forbade the clergy whom he maintained at home to wear striking attire; and [his attitude was that] if they wished to find favor with the people, let them find favor by their morals, not their dress. Nowadays how much new and wonderful raiment there is! However, I do not inveigh against that; this I wonder at, that too much is attributed to those things which perhaps by right could be reprehended, and on the other hand so little to those things which alone should receive attention. I do not reproach the Franciscans or Benedictines because they prize their own rule but because certain of these men ascribe more to their own rules than to the Gospel. Would that this charge did not apply to most of them! I do not belabor the point that some live on fish, others on beans and herbs, others on eggs, but I warn emphatically that they err who in a Judaic spirit put on the conviction of justice because of this and who, because of this kind of nonsense invented by little men, place themselves before others, while they do not consider it a vice to assail another's reputation with their lies. Christ nowhere prescribes anything about the choice of food, nor do the Apostles, but Paul often advises to the contrary. Christ abhors poisonous defamation, the Apostolic Epistles abominate it. And yet in the former case we wish to appear scrupulous, and in the latter we are brave and intrepid. Does he, I beg, seem to harm religion who gives these admonitions not only in a general way but also with love? However, who is so foolish that he wishes to be considered eloquent for bringing to light the vices of monks? But these men are afraid that they will have fewer listeners and then that fewer people will present themselves for admission into their flock. Yet no one is more obedient and subject to authority, to use the Pauline expression, than he who, after he has drunk in the spirit of Christ, begins to be free. True charity takes account of everything good, endures everything, refuses nothing, is obedient to those in authority, not only to those who are benign and agreeable but even to those who are harsh and surly.

But yet those in power must in the meantime be on guard lest they turn another's obedience into their own tyranny and lest, on that account, they prefer men who are superstitious rather than pious because they may be more obedient to every nod. They delight in being called fathers. But what father in the flesh desires his children always to be infants so that he may have more control over them for his own pleasure? On the other hand, those who make progress toward the liberty of Christ should take care in the beginning lest they make liberty a pretext for sensuality, as Paul warns, or lest they make liberty a cloak for malice, according to Peter's teaching. But if one or another has abused this liberty, it is not necessarily right that everyone be kept in a perpetual Judaism because of this. Whoever is observant will discover that no one among such persons draws more tightly the snares of ceremonies than those who hold sway under this pretense and live by their belly, not by Christ.

Yet in fact, it is not that they fear that the race of Essenes might not be propagated among so great a variety of temperaments and spirits, inasmuch as it happens that there is indeed nothing anywhere so absurd that many do not seek after it. Nevertheless, these men ought to be more desirous of having sincere and true professors of religion than of having many. And would that the law provided that no one might be entangled in snares of this kind before his thirtieth year, before he himself came to know himself or the power of true religion was known! On the other hand, those who conduct their business like the Pharisees, traveling over land and sea to make one convert, nowhere fail to find inexperienced youths whom they inveigle into their net and take prisoner. There is a vast number of fools and simple people everyplace. I should certainly desire, nor do I doubt that everyone truly pious desires the same, that the religion of the Gospel so penetrate the hearts of all that no one, satisfied with it, may seek a Benedictine or Franciscan religion; nor do I doubt that Benedict himself or Francis desires the same. Moses applauds when obscured by the glory of Christ; they also should applaud if, for love of the law of the Gospel, human constitutions are of small account to us. I should wish that all Christians live in such a way that those who alone are now called religious appear not religious enough. And today this is true in many cases; why conceal obvious facts? And yet in former times the first origin of the monastic life was a withdrawal from the barbarism of the idolaters. The rules of the monks following soon after this were nothing else than a calling back to Christ. The courts of princes were at one time more Christian in title than in life. Then the disease of ambition and avarice laid hold of the bishops. The people likewise lost the warmth of that primitive charity. Hence Benedict earnestly sought a retreat, and after him Bernard, and then one and another. These chosen few agreed in nothing else than in a pure and simple Christianity.

But if anyone examines more attentively the life and rules of Benedict, Francis, or Augustine, he will observe that what they wished was only to live with willing friends in liberty of spirit close to the Gospel teaching; and that they had been forced to prescribe to some extent about clothing and food and other outward matters, undoubtedly fearful lest more be attributed, as is often the case, to the human ordinances of men than to the Gospel. They dreaded wealth, they fled honors, even ecclesiastical ones. They labored with their hands not only that they themselves might not be a burden to anyone but that there might be an abundance from which to help others in need. They occupied mountain peaks, they nested in marshy places, they dwelt in sandy and abandoned regions. At length they tamed a great multitude of men without reproaches, scourgings, and prisons but by teaching alone, by counsel, by service, and by the example of their lives. Such were the monks whom Basil loves and praises, whom Chrysostom defends; there was complete agreement among these men, as Saint Jerome writes to Marcella, that the troop of monks and virgins is the flower and the most precious jewel among the ornaments of the Church. It is wonderful to relate how today monks of every kind flatter themselves with this statement. But we shall allow them to embrace the praise if at the same time they embrace the example. Moreover, the most prudent man suggests this image of the monks whom he has judged worthy of that title: "A dissonant voice indeed," he says, "but one religion. Almost as many choruses of psalm singers as different kinds of people. Meanwhile, and this is certainly the very first virtue among Christians, they arrogate nothing to themselves because of the control of their pride. All strive for humility. Whoever shall have been last, this man is considered first. In their dress there is no distinction, no admiration. It is the cause neither of blame nor of praise however one has been pleased to conduct himself. Fasts also exalt no one, nor is deference paid to total abstinence, nor is a moderate satiety condemned. Each one stands or falls in the sight of his Lord. No one judges another, lest he be judged by the Lord; and what is customary in very many regions, to censure oneself severely, does not entirely prevail here." Thus far this man has painted the picture of the best monks; whoever wishes may compare it with the morals of these times.[10]

Such were the origins of monasticism, such were the patriarchs. Then gradually in the course of time ceremonies increased with riches, genuine piety and simplicity grew cold. And although we see that monasteries everywhere have degenerated to morals that are more than profane, yet the world is burdened with new institutions, as if they also were not going to decline in the same way a short time after. In former times, as I have said, the life of the monks was a withdrawal to solitude. Now they are called monks who are completely occupied in the midst of worldly business, clearly exercising a certain despotic control over human affairs. And yet on account of their attire, on account of some title, they arrogate so much virtue to themselves that in comparison they do not regard others as Christians. Why do we so limit the profession of Christ, which he wished to extend most widely? If we are moved by splendid appellations, I beseech you, what else is a city but a great monastery? Monks are obedient to their abbot or to those placed in charge; citizens submit to the bishop and their pastors, whom Christ Himself, not the authority of men, has set over them. The former live in idleness and are nourished by the generosity of others, possessing in common what has come to them without hard work (I say nothing, meanwhile, about those who are corrupt); the latter, each in proportion to his own wealth, share what they have acquired by their own industry with those in need. Moreover, concerning the vow of chastity, I would not dare to set forth how trifling the difference is between ordinary celibacy and chaste marriage. Finally, we shall not at all miss those three vows devised by men in that person who sincerely and purely has kept first that one and only vow which in baptism we made not to man but to Christ. Now if you compare the bad with the bad from each group, the latter without question are better. But if you compare the good with the good, the difference is

---

10. Erasmus added this entire paragraph on early monasticism to the letter when it was published in the Basel *Opus epistolarum* of 1529. It is not found in Tyndale's translation, since he obviously used the earlier edition of the *Enchiridion*.

very small; if, however, there is any difference, it is only that they seem to be more religious who practice their religion with less coercion. Therefore it remains that one should neither be foolishly pleased with himself on account of a kind of life different from others nor should he despise or condemn another way of life. But in every kind of life let this be the common endeavor of all, that we strive, each according to his own ability, toward that target, which is Christ, set up before us all; and let us exhort and also aid one another toward this goal, neither envying those who hasten on before us in this race nor disdaining the weak who are not yet able to overtake us. At last, when each has done what he could, let him not be like that Pharisee in the Gospel who boasts of his good works before God, "I fast twice a week," etc., but in accordance with Christ's counsel let him say, and let him say from the heart, "I am a useless servant, I have done only what I had to do," and let him say this to himself, not merely to others. No one is more truly trusting than he who is distrustful to this extent. No one is farther from true religion than he who very much seems to himself to be religious. Nor is the situation ever worse with respect to Christian piety than when what is of the world is twisted toward Christ and when the authority of men is preferred to divine authority. We must unite under that one head if we wish to be truly Christian. Moreover, he obeys Christ, not man, who obeys a man calling him to Christ. And he who endures false, cruel, and tyrannical men who teach that which serves not religion but their own domination, he practices Christian patience, provided that what these teachers bid is only injurious and not also unholy. Otherwise it will be fitting to have that Apostolic response at hand: "We must obey God rather than men."

But we have long since exceeded an epistle's length, to such an extent does the time escape our notice when we converse most pleasantly with a most agreeable friend. The book under Froben's imprint, reborn, as it were, and much more polished and free from faults than before, flies to your breast. Certain fragments of our earlier studies have been added. Moreover, it seemed proper that this edition, such as it is, should be linked with you above all, so that he who has taken the precepts of upright living from Erasmus may have an example from Volz immediately at hand. Farewell, good father and outstanding light of the true religion.

Admonish Sapidus[11] with my words that he truly resemble his name, that is, that he continue to be like himself; and Wimpfeling[12] that he make ready his armor, soon to engage the Turks, seeing that he has now waged war long enough with priests who keep concubines. I hope that we shall sometime see him a bishop, conspicuous with his two-horned miter and staff, borne aloft on a mule. But, joking aside, in my name extend many greetings both to them and Ruserus[13] and to other friends. Now and then in pure and devout prayers commend the welfare of your Erasmus to the All-good and All-powerful Christ.

Basel,
The Vigil of the Assumption of the Virgin Mother, 1518

11. Sapidus is Johann Witz, a scholar and teacher at Schlettstadt and a prominent member of the literary circle there.

12. Jacob Wimpfeling, former rector of the University of Heidelberg, was one of the most distinguished of the German humanists. His last years (1515–1528) were spent at Schlettstadt.

13. Johann Ruserus was a priest at Schlettstadt and a former editor for the Schürer press in Strasburg.

VI

Letter to Albert of Brandenburg
19 October 1519

Albert of Brandenburg (1490–1545) was the young archbishop of Mainz, whose elevation to that important see in 1514 involved large payments to Rome, which in turn occasioned the granting and preaching of the special indulgence that Luther attacked in his Ninety-five Theses. There is therefore a certain irony in Erasmus' addressing this letter, so favorable to Luther, to the man who bore at least some responsibility for the original indulgence controversy. That, of course, was not the point that Erasmus had in mind when he wrote the archbishop. He wished to explain clearly his position with regard to Luther in view of the accusations that now linked him with the Wittenberg reformer, and he desired to alert his distinguished correspondent to the base motives and questionable tactics of those who attacked Luther and himself. The letter is remarkably frank and incisive, considering to whom it was sent, and it is one of the fullest expressions of Erasmus' mind on the Lutheran controversy as it developed through 1519.[1]

Albert himself was an educated man and favorable to the new learning. He had written Erasmus in September 1517 to congratulate him on his edition of the New Testament, and Erasmus had subsequently dedicated his *Ratio verae theologiae*, or *Methodus*, to him. They continued to correspond in 1519. Thus the letter here presented did not arrive entirely out of the blue, and it is particularly interesting to see how Erasmus deftly leads into his subject from his opening words of appreciation for the gold cup Albert had sent him through their mutual friend Ulrich von Hutten. Erasmus was at the University of Louvain at this time, where once again he had become an object of suspicion and attack because of the growing alarm over Luther.

The letter, though a private one for the archbishop, was soon in wide circulation. Unauthorized versions were published in 1520 in Cologne, Wittenberg, and Nuremberg, and as a result Erasmus included it in a collection of his letters published by Froben in 1521.

1. The Latin text is in Allen, IV 96–107; the present translation was made by the editor from Allen.

To the most reverend Father in Christ,
Albert, Cardinal Archbishop,
greetings from Erasmus of Rotterdam, theologian:

Many greetings, most reverend Prelate and most illustrious Prince. I received Your Highness' gift, as beautiful and as striking in its material as in its workmanship, and worthy indeed of being sent by such a Prince; but I do not know if its recipient Erasmus, for whom it is more fitting to drink from glass or earthenware than from goblets of gold, is worthy of it. Even if it had been a glass goblet, I would have placed it among my most prized possessions, especially because so distinguished a man had sent it. Moreover, your gift, most welcome in itself, was graciously presented to me by our friend Hutten, who informed me that it is called a cup of love, as if sacred to the Graces, the reason being, I suppose, that when two are joined together by it, as in a kiss, they become one. He added that your cup had the power of binding together in the closest friendship those who drank from it. Wishing to test this, I drank from your cup the health of the most reverend Cardinal Guillaume de Croy when he visited my study recently, and he in turn drank mine. This youth is a most fortunate young man, and his talents seem worthy of his great good fortune.

But I am sorry that your gift did not arrive sooner. For recently the theologians of Louvain and I made peace, with the understanding that they would restrain the disparaging tongues which they provoke and I, as far as I could, would continue to curb the pens of my friends. At the banquet concluding this arrangement (for nothing is consecrated here without a drinking party) I would have produced your cup, if I had had it, and if each one had drunk from it, perhaps our peace would have been launched under more favorable auspices. For our friendship, never completely restored, has now been disrupted because of a letter of mine which has been misunderstood and badly interpreted, and thus, after a brief calm, the rising storm seems more violent than before.[2] I do not doubt that this is the work of Satan, who

2. The letter Erasmus refers to is a courteous and friendly one he wrote Luther on 30 May 1519 (CWE 6: *Ep.* 980). It had evidently just become known at Louvain, probably through Jacob Hochstrat, the Dominican inquisitor at Cologne, who had recently arrived at Louvain to encourage the condemnation of Luther's opinions there. See Etienne, *Spiritualisme érasmien*, pp. 98–99.

hates nothing worse than concord among Christians and on that account tries in every way to disturb somehow or other the tranquillity of life and of learning, and he does this under the pretext of piety in order to do even greater harm.

And so it is that there are a few facts on this subject which it is in my interest that you know, if the pressure of Your Eminence's affairs permits it; and perhaps it is of importance to you as well, as it certainly is to the cause of learning, which, in justice, the best men must support against the worst. In the first place, I must declare that I never had anything to do either with the affair of Reuchlin[3] or with the case of Luther. Cabala and Talmud, whatever they are, never had any appeal to me. Those bitter clashes between Reuchlin and the supporters of Jacob Hochstrat have greatly displeased me. Luther couldn't be more unknown to me, and I have not yet had the time to read his books beyond merely sampling a few pages. If he has written well, no praise is due me; if not, I should not be held accountable. I observe this, however, that the best men are the least offended by his writings, not that they approve everything, I suppose, but that they read them in the spirit in which we read Cyprian and Jerome, or rather Peter Lombard, certainly with considerable allowance.

I was sorry that Luther's books were published; and when some or other of his writings first came into view, I made every effort to prevent their publication, chiefly because I feared a disturbance might result from them. Luther had written, in my opinion, a very Christian letter to me, and I replied, advising him in passing not to write anything seditious, nor against the Roman pontiff, nor too arrogantly and passionately, but rather to preach the Gospel teaching in a sincere spirit and with all gentleness. I did this politely, so to accomplish more. I added that there were some here who favored him, with the hope that he might adapt himself more readily to their judgment. Certain simpletons have interpreted this to mean that I favor Luther. Since none of these men have admonished Luther up to now, I alone have admonished him. I am neither Luther's accuser nor his defender, nor am I answerable for him. I would not dare to judge the spirit of

---

3. The "affair of Reuchlin" refers to the long and bitter quarrel between Johann Reuchlin, the German scholar and Hebraist, and those who sought his condemnation for heresy because of his defense of the study of Hebrew literature. Hochstrat led the opposition to Reuchlin.

the man, for that is a most difficult task, especially when it is a question of his condemnation. Yet, if I were favorably inclined to him as a good man, which even his enemies admit him to be, or as an accused person, which the laws permit even to sworn judges, or as one oppressed, following the dictates of humanity—indeed, as one oppressed by those who under the false pretext of being devout fight against learning—if I were inclined thus to take his part, what reproach would there be, provided I did not become involved myself in his cause? In short, I think it is only Christian to support Luther this far, for if he is innocent, I do not want him crushed by a faction of rogues, and if he is in error, I wish him to be corrected, not destroyed. This approach agrees better with the example of Christ, who, according to the prophet, did not extinguish the smoking flax, nor break the bruised reed.

I should wish that that heart, which seems to hold certain bright sparks of evangelical doctrine, be not crushed but rather be corrected and called to preach the glory of Christ. At the present moment, however, certain theologians with whom I am acquainted neither admonish nor instruct Luther; they only defame the man before the people with their insane cries and lacerate him with their savage and virulent abuse, speaking of nothing else but heresies and heretics. It cannot be denied that a most unpleasant outcry has been raised here among the people by persons who have not yet seen Luther's books. It is certain that some have expressly condemned what they have not understood. For example, Luther had written that we are not bound to confess mortal sins unless they are "manifest," meaning by that term "known to us when we confess." A certain Carmelite theologian,[4] explaining "manifest" in this context as sins "openly committed," shouted about this in an extraordinary fashion simply because he did not understand the question. It is certain that they have condemned as heretical in Luther's books statements which are regarded as orthodox and even edifying in the works of Bernard and Augustine.

I warned these men in the beginning to refrain from such outbursts and instead to present their case in writings and arguments. First, I advised them not to condemn publicly what they have not read, or

4. This would appear to be Egmondanus, prior of the Carmelites at Louvain and one of Erasmus' most persistent critics.

rather what they have not seriously considered (I will not say what they have not understood). Secondly, I told them that it is unbecoming for theologians, whose judgment should carry great weight, to do anything by raising a commotion, and that they should not rage against a man whose life was approved by all. Finally, I said that perhaps it is not safe to touch on such topics before a mixed crowd, in which there are many to whom the confession of secret sins is intensely displeasing. If such persons hear that there are theologians who deny that we have to confess all sins, they will quickly seize upon and hold this perverse notion.

Although any judicious man would consider, as I did, that this was sensible advice, nevertheless, as a result of these friendly admonitions they conceived the idea that Luther's books were for the most part mine and that they were written at Louvain; yet there is not a letter in them that is mine, nor were they published with my knowledge or consent. Relying on this completely false suspicion, however, and without bringing their complaints to me, they provoked many tragic scenes here, worse than any I have seen thus far in my life. Besides, while the proper task of theologians is to instruct, I now observe that many do nothing but constrain or destroy and extinguish, though Augustine, even in the case of the Donatists, who were not only heretics but also savage brigands, does not approve of those who only use force and do not instruct. Men, whom gentleness especially becomes, seem to thirst for nothing except human blood, and they eagerly desire only that Luther be seized and destroyed. But this is to play the part of the executioner, not the theologian. If they wish to show themselves as great theologians, let them convert the Jews, let them convert to Christ those who are strangers to Christ, let them correct the public morals of Christians, than which there is nothing more corrupt, not even among the Turks. How is it right that he should be carried off to punishment who in the first place proposed for debate those propositions which the theological schools have always debated and have even questioned? Why should he be struck down, who desires to be taught, who submits to the judgment of the Apostolic See, who entrusts himself to the judgment of the universities? And if he does not deliver himself into the hands of those who would rather destroy him than correct him, there should be no cause for surprise.

At the outset the sources of this evil must be examined. The world is weighed down with human ordinances, burdened with scholastic opinions and dogmas, oppressed by the tyranny of the mendicant friars, who, though they are attendants upon the Roman see, nevertheless have achieved such power and numbers that they are formidable to the Roman pontiff himself and even to kings. When the pope acts in their behalf, he is more than God; but when things work against their advantage, he is no more than a dream. I do not condemn all of them, but very many are of the kind who do their best to ensnare the consciences of men for their own profit and power. And, having set aside modesty, they had undertaken to preach, to the exclusion of Christ, nothing save their own new and increasingly more shameless dogmas. They preached indulgences in such a way that even the ignorant could not bear it. Due to this and many other similar causes, the vigor of the Gospel teaching was gradually disappearing. And it looked as if, with things ever heading for the worse, the spark of Christian piety, whence an extinct charity could be rekindled, would at last be totally put out. The sum of religion was tending toward a more than Jewish ceremonial. Good men bemoan and deplore all this. Even the theologians themselves, who are not monks, and even some monks, admit this in their private conversations.

It was this, in my opinion, which at first drove Luther to dare oppose the intolerable shamelessness of certain monks. How may I form any other opinion about him who seeks neither honors nor wealth? I am not questioning at present the propositions they object to in Luther, I am only discussing the kind they are and the occasion for them. Luther dared to challenge indulgences, but others previously had made rather extravagant assertions about them. He presumed to speak rather reservedly about the power of the Roman pontiff, but others had first written with far too little reserve about it, particularly three Dominicans: Alvarus, Sylvester, and the cardinal of San Sisto.[5] He dared to make little of the principles of Thomas, but the Dominicans almost

---

5. Alvarus Pelagius was a fourteenth-century Spanish theologian (and a Franciscan!). Sylvester Prierias was at this time the Master of the Papal Palace. He wrote a critical report for the Curia on the Ninety-five Theses in early 1518. The cardinal of San Sisto is the distinguished Cardinal Cajetan, who was at this time general of the Dominicans. As papal legate in Germany, he had interviewed Luther at the Diet of Augsburg in October 1518 and had subsequently pressed for Luther's apprehension.

prefer these to the Gospels. He ventured to disperse several scruples about the nature of confession, but here the monks endlessly ensnare men's consciences. He was bold enough to disregard to some extent scholastic principles, but the schoolmen themselves attribute too much to them, though they differ considerably among themselves about them and at the end repeatedly change their views, introducing new ideas in place of the old.

Pious minds were troubled when they heard in the universities scarcely any discussion of evangelical doctrine and observed that the sacred writers approved of old by the Church were now regarded as obsolete; and even in sermons they heard very little about Christ but much about the power of the pope and the opinions of modern authors. All this eloquence now openly displayed self-advantage, servility, ambition, and deceit. This must be blamed, in my opinion, even if Luther has written somewhat intemperately. Whoever favors evangelical doctrine, favors also the Roman pontiff, who is the chief herald of the Gospel, as the other bishops are the heralds of the same. All bishops serve in the place of Christ, but the Roman pontiff is pre-eminent among them. He must be considered as favoring nothing more than the glory of Christ, whose minister it is his glory to be. They deserve very ill of him who in their flattery attribute powers to him which he himself does not acknowledge and which are not to the advantage of the Christian flock. And further, some who are behind these tragic scenes are not motivated by zeal for the pope, but they misuse his power for their own profit and supremacy. We have, so I think, a good pope. But in such a rush of events there is much of which he is ignorant; and there are certain things he cannot achieve, even if he wishes, for, as Virgil says, "the charioteer is borne by the horses, nor does the chariot respond to the reins." Therefore, he contributes to the virtue of his pontificate who encourages that which especially is worthy of Christ. It is plain, however, that there are those who incite His Holiness against Luther, and indeed against all who dare murmur against their dogmas. But the greatest princes should seek rather to know the lasting will of the pope than to show a deference extorted by base motives.

Moreover, I could most truthfully point out what kind of people the authors of this trouble are, but I fear that I should seem abusive, even though I continue to speak the truth. I know many of them intimately; many have revealed themselves in their published books, where their minds and their lives are reflected as clearly as in a mirror. Would that they who arrogate to themselves the censor's rod, whereby they expel from the Christian fold whom they will, would that they had deeply imbibed the teaching and spirit of Christ! This power belongs only to those who have purged themselves of all the filth of this world's lusts. Whether the men I speak of be such he will soon discover who treats with them on any matter which pertains to their profit, glory, or revenge. I wish that I could convince Your Highness of what I have observed and learned about these affairs, but it is fitting that I remember Christian restraint.

I speak of these things more freely because I am not involved in any way in the cause of Reuchlin and Luther. I myself neither wish to write thus, nor do I espouse that teaching so that I wish to defend what has been written by another; but I do not refrain from making this clear, that these troublemakers aim at something quite different than they publicly proclaim. For a long time they have been distressed that learning flourishes, that languages flourish, that the ancient authors, formerly covered with dust and consumed by the moth, are reviving, and that the world is being recalled to the sources themselves. They fear for their own shortcomings, they do not want to seem not to know something, they dread lest anything decrease their majesty. Though they concealed this ulcer a long while, it has, however, recently erupted, the pain of it all surpassing any concealment. Even before Luther's books appeared, they were already at work with great zeal, especially the Dominicans and the Carmelites. Would that many of them were not more villainous than untaught! When Luther's books were published, they grasped them as if they were a handle and used them to link the cause of language and learning, that of Reuchlin and of Luther, and indeed my own, together in the same bundle, presenting their case poorly as well as distinguishing badly between the objects of their attack. For what has literary study to do with a matter of faith? And how am I involved in the cause of Reuchlin and Luther? But by this trick they have mixed these things together so that they may burden all friends of learning with a common reproach.

Further, that this whole matter is not sincerely prosecuted may be surmised from what follows: Although they admit that there are no ancient or modern authors in which errors are not found, even errors that would make them heretical, if anyone should obstinately uphold them, why, with certain exceptions, do they investigate only this one or the other, and with such hatred? They do not deny that Alvarus, the cardinal of San Sisto, and Sylvester Prierias err in many places. No mention is made about them, for these men are Dominicans. The clamor is reserved for Reuchlin, because he has an excellent knowledge of languages, and for Luther, whom they believe endowed with our literary interests, although his attainments in this field are slight. Luther has written much that is more imprudent than impious; and they have taken it very ill that he has little regard for Thomas, that he reduces the profit from indulgences, that he takes small account of the mendicant orders, that he defers more to the Gospels than to scholastic dogma, and that he slights the refined quibbling of the debaters. These undoubtedly are the intolerable heresies. But they have disguised these complaints, and, crafty men united in the desire only to do harm, they conceal their hateful aims from the pope.

At one time the heretic was heard respectfully, and he was absolved if he made amends; but if he persisted in his heresy after his conviction, the extreme penalty was his exclusion from communion with the Church. Now the crime of heresy is a different matter, and yet for any trifling reason the cry is immediately raised, "This is heresy, this is heresy." Formerly he was a heretic who dissented from the Gospels, the articles of faith, or something of comparable authority. Now, if anyone disagrees in any way with Thomas, or even if anyone disagrees with a false theory which some sophist in the schools recently invented, he is called a heretic. Whatever is not pleasing, whatever they do not understand is a heresy. To know Greek is a heresy. To speak in a polished manner is a heresy. Whatever they themselves do not do is a heresy. I admit that the charge of a corrupted faith is grave, but it is not necessary to turn everything into a question of faith. And whoever treats matters of faith should be far removed from every taint of ambition, self-advantage, hatred, or revenge.

Who does not see what these men stand for and in what direction they are heading? Once the restraints on their evil passions are relaxed, they will begin to rage indiscriminately against every good man, and finally they will threaten the bishops themselves and even the Roman pontiff. I will not deny that this charge would seem to be a false one, except that we see certain individuals already doing this. What the Dominicans have dared to do, Savonarola and the villainous affair at Berne, not to mention anything else, should serve as a warning to us.[6] I am not going to reopen the disgraceful story of that order, but I warn what we must be on guard against if these men should succeed in what they rashly attempt.

What I have said thus far is aside from the cause itself of Luther. I am discussing only the manner of dealing with it and the danger therein to us all. The Roman pontiff has reserved Reuchlin's case for his own judgment. The affair of Luther has been transferred to the universities. Whatever verdict they will render will not threaten me. I have always taken care not to write anything offensive or seditious or alien to the teachings of Christ. I shall never knowingly teach error or cause confusion; I would endure anything sooner than provoke dissension. Nevertheless, I wished that Your Eminence be informed about certain matters, not that I presume to give advice or command, but that if the adversaries of learning should attempt to hide behind your dignity, the best course of action on these matters can more surely be determined; but, in my opinion, the more one keeps out of this business, the more directly he preserves his own peace. I have revised the *Methodus* which I dedicated to Your Highness, and I greatly enlarged it. May the All-good and All-powerful Christ ever keep Your Excellency safe and flourishing.

ERASMUS OF ROTTERDAM

Louvain
19 October 1519

---

6. The reference to Savonarola is interesting in this context. Erasmus considers the fiery Dominican preacher of Florence as disobeying and defying the pope. The "villainous affair at Berne" refers to some bogus apparitions which the Dominicans had engineered there in 1507–9 and the attempted poisoning of their dupe. They were exposed and punished. See Allen, IV 106.

VII

The *Axiomata*

This interesting document consists of twenty-two axioms or statements concerning the controversy over Martin Luther.[1] It was drawn up by Erasmus for the guidance of Luther's prince, Elector Frederick of Saxony, following an interview with the Elector at Cologne on 5 November 1520.[2] Both Erasmus and Frederick were in Cologne in the entourage of Emperor Charles V, who had been crowned at Aachen in late October and was now en route to Worms for a meeting of the imperial Diet. Frederick at this moment was again being pressed by the papal representatives to imprison Luther or to turn him over to the higher ecclesiastical authorities. In this situation he sought the advice of the distinguished scholar. Immediately after the interview that advice was drafted in the terse form of the *Axiomata* and given to Spalatin, the Elector's secretary and Luther's friend, for transmission to the Elector. There can be little doubt that Erasmus' counsel, so favorable to Luther, confirmed and encouraged Frederick in his policy of protecting Luther at this critical juncture.

The *Axiomata* are also one of the last expressions of a truly pro-Lutheran stance on the part of Erasmus. After 1520 Erasmus' hope of a peaceful settlement of the controversy and his efforts in that direction seemed a lost cause, or at least a disheartening and forlorn endeavor. Luther had by then assumed a defiant and extreme position beyond the hope of compromise (as witness his *The Babylonian Captivity of the Church* of October 1520 and his burning of the bull *Exsurge Domine* on 10 December 1520), and in 1521 his formal excommunication by the Church and his banning by the Empire were pronounced.

The *Axiomata* were not intended for publication, and Erasmus was quite concerned lest they fall into the hands of Jerome Aleander, the

---

1. The Latin text is in *Erasmi opuscula*, ed. W. K. Ferguson (The Hague, 1933), pp. 336–37. The present translation was made by the editor.
2. See Ferguson's introduction to the *Axiomata*, pp. 329–33 and Allen, IV 370–71. For an appraisal of the *Axiomata* in the general context of the Erasmus–Luther relationship, see C. R. Thompson's introduction to his edition of Erasmus' *Inquisitio de Fide*, pp. 19–23. Erasmus had previously written to Frederick warmly recommending Luther (CWE 6: *Ep.* 939).

papal legate, who also was in Cologne at this time. But, like the letter to Albert of Brandenburg on Luther, they were soon in print—in a pamphlet issuing from Leipzig within a month or so after they were written.

AXIOMS OF ERASMUS OF ROTTERDAM IN BEHALF OF THE CAUSE OF MARTIN LUTHER, THEOLOGIAN

The origin of the case is evil: the hatred of letters and the desire for supremacy.

The way in which it is being conducted corresponds to the origin, with wild cries, plots, bitter hatred, poisonous writing.

Those who are conducting the case are open to suspicion.

Since all the best and closest to the Gospel teaching are said to be the least offended by Luther.

It is well known that certain men take advantage of the good nature of the pope.

All the more should their rash advice on this case be shunned.

The case is tending toward a greater crisis than certain men suppose.

The severity of the bull offends all upright men as unworthy of the most gentle vicar of Christ.[3]

All the more diligently should it be considered by persons who are above suspicion and who are experienced in these matters.

Only two universities out of such a countless number have condemned Luther, and they have merely condemned him, not convicted him of error; nor are they in agreement.[4]

He himself seems to all fair men to seek what is fair, since he offers himself for public debate and submits to judges who are above suspicion.

3. The bull referred to is the *Exsurge Domine*, promulgated by Pope Leo X on 15 June 1520. Forty-one of Luther's statements were condemned and he was given sixty days after the bull was posted in Germany to recant or be excommunicated.
4. The theological faculty at Cologne condemned eight of Luther's statements on 30 August 1519. The theologians at Louvain followed suit in their condemnation of 7 November 1519, though, as Erasmus points out, the opinions condemned at Louvain differed from those condemned at Cologne.

Those who attack Luther introduce that which offends pious ears.

But he who makes himself a judge or censurer should himself be without blame.

Luther is not soliciting anything; therefore he is less suspect.

The interest of others is being pressed.

For the pope the glory of Christ comes before his own, and what is of profit to souls takes precedence over any other advantage.

Although these matters ought especially to be discussed, it was fitting, however, that this be done at another time.

Difficult matters press upon us, and the guidance of Charles should not be defiled by such hateful measures.[5]

It seems to the advantage of the pope that this affair be settled by the mature deliberation of serious and impartial men; in this way will regard best be shown for the dignity of the pope.

Those who up to now have written against Luther are disapproved even by theologians who otherwise are opposed to Luther.

The world thirsts for the Gospel truth, and it seems to be carried in this direction by a longing ordained, as it were, by fate.

Therefore, since it so happens, opposition [to Luther] ought to be without hate.

5. Charles, of course, is Emperor Charles V, who was soon to preside at the Diet of Worms where the question of Luther was to be discussed. Erasmus is obviously asking for calm and impartial judgment.

VIII

Letter to Jodocus Jonas on Luther

10 May 1521

Erasmus wrote this letter to Jodocus Jonas a few weeks after Luther appeared before the imperial Diet of Worms to answer charges of heresy in his writings.[1] Jonas (1493–1555), a professor at the University of Erfurt, had accompanied Luther to Worms and was now more or less his committed disciple. Erasmus, who had met Jonas two years before, was writing to dissuade him from going over wholeheartedly to the Lutheran camp. The tone of this letter is in sharp contrast to that of the earlier letter to Albert of Brandenburg and of the *Axiomata*, and unlike these previous statements, it castigates the immoderation of Luther and warns of the danger he poses to the peace of the Church and the progress of true reform.

In this letter to Jonas and in the one which follows it in this volume, Erasmus "did what he could to hold him back . . . but without avail."[2] Jonas left Erfurt in June 1521 to take up residence at Wittenberg and to become a professor of theology at the university there. He married the following year, wrote a *Defensio pro conjugio sacerdotali*, and, along with Philip Melanchthon, became one of Luther's closest associates. Erasmus wrote in early 1524 that Jonas had defected from "our brotherhood" and that he had warned Jonas and other defectors in vain.[3]

This letter is a companion to the one which appears here as Selection IX, wherein Erasmus continues his argument, though in a different way, against Jonas' adherence to the Lutheran cause. Both letters were published by Froben in 1521 in Erasmus' *Epistolae ad diversos.*

1. The Latin text is in Allen, IV 486–93. The present translation was made by the editor from Allen.
2. Allen, III 413. Heinz Holeczek, "Die Haltung des Erasmus zu Luther nach dem Scheitern seiner Vermittlungspolitik," *Archive for Reformation History*, 64 (1973), 85–112.
3. Letter to Conrad Mutianus (Allen, V 110).

To Jodocus Jonas,
Greetings from Erasmus of Rotterdam:

There is a rumor persistent here for a long time now, dear Jonas, that at Worms you were with Martin Luther continuously; nor do I doubt that your sense of duty prompted this, as I should have urged if it happened that I were present, so that this tragedy might be so settled on reasonable grounds that in the future it could not erupt again with greater evil for the world. For my part I wonder that that was not accomplished, since this achievement would have been very agreeable to the best men, who, as is worthy of souls truly Christian, desired that the tranquillity of the Church be taken into account, the name "church" being lost if concord is not joined to it. For what else is our religion than peace in the Holy Spirit? Furthermore, the orthodox Fathers testify that in former times the Church of Christ was afflicted with great vices, because thus far it embraces good fish and bad in the same net and is forced to endure the cockle mixed with the wheat; and they repeatedly lamented the most corrupt morals of those orders from whom it was proper that examples of an inherent piety proceed. Moreover, when the Roman church in times gone by departed from a devotion to exangelical purity, this was made clear enough either by Jerome, who calls it the Babylon of the Apocalypse, or by St. Bernard in the books which he entitled *De consideratione*—although there have not been wanting also among modern authors, men of celebrated name, who have demanded the public renewal of ecclesiastical discipline.

Yet I do not know whether the princes of the Church have ever coveted the privileges of this world, which Christ taught should be despised, with so much zeal and so openly as we see today. Nor had the study of Sacred Scripture sunk lower than morals themselves. Divine literature was forced to be the servant of human ambition, the credulity of the people was turned to the profit of the few. Pious minds, to whom nothing is more important than the glory of Christ, groaned at the sight of this. And the result was that in the beginning Luther had as much approbation on all sides as, I believe, has come to any mortal for several centuries past. For, as we easily believe what we ardently desire, they thought that a man had arisen who, free from all the attachments of this world, could bring some remedy for such great evils. Nor was I entirely without hope, except that immediately at the first sampling of the tracts which had begun to appear under Luther's name I was quite afraid that the matter might end in tumult and general dissidence throughout the world. And so through my letters I at one time warned Luther himself, then friends of his whose authority I thought would have force with him. I do not know what advice they gave him; in any event the matter was handled in such a way that there is the danger that because of the attempt to apply remedies improperly, the evil for us may be doubled.

And I greatly wonder, my dear Jonas, what god has stirred up the heart of Luther, in so far as he assails with such license of pen the Roman pontiff, all the universities, philosophy, and the mendicant orders. Even if all were true, which those who undertake to judge Luther's writings say is by no means the case, what other outcome could be expected, because of the provocation of so many, than this which we see? Up to now I have not had the time to read Luther's books, but on the basis of those which I have sampled and what in passing I have sometimes gathered from the report of others, although it was not within my competence, perhaps, to pronounce on the truth of the opinions which were advanced, certainly the manner and method of going about the business were by no means approved by me. For when in itself an issue is a matter of bitter truth to very many, and when in itself a turbulent issue usually leads, by long experience, to violent upheaval, it were better to mitigate through courteous treatment an issue sharp by its very nature than to add ill will to ill will.

What purpose did it serve, therefore, to act in a contrary way and to expose certain matters in such a way that at first sight they were even more offensive than when seen at closer and steadier range? For some things even in deliberate obscurity, as it were, are troublesome. What was achieved by raging with such fierce outcries? If it was against those he desired to correct, his method must be attributed to imprudence; but if it was against those he wished to provoke to evil everywhere, his method should be attributed to impiety. Moreover, although it is the part of the experienced steward to dispense the truth, that is, to bring it forth when the occasion demands, and to bring forth enough of it, and to bring forth what is suitable for each, he poured out everything at the same time in so many pamphlets cast forth headlong, divulging everything and making public even to cobblers what is usually treated among the learned as mysterious and secret; and frequently by some unbridled impulse, in my opinion, at least, he is carried beyond what is just. For example, he calls the whole philosophy of Aristotle the death of the soul, when it was sufficient to remind theologians that they too are entangled in Peripatetic, or rather sophist, philosophy.

That evangelical spirit of Christ has its own prudence, it has its own courtesy and gentleness. Thus even Christ accommodated Himself to the temperaments of the Jews. He speaks one thing to the more uncultivated crowds, another to the disciples, and he gradually leads these very men, bearing with them for a long time, to an understanding of heavenly philosophy. With this in mind he bids his disciples that they first preach penance and the imminent kingdom of God, that they not speak of Christ. Thus Peter, in the Acts of the Apostles, with words that are gentle and loving, not abusive, adds so great a multitude as the first fruits to the Church.[4] He does not scream at those who had killed Christ, he does not magnify in dreadful language their wicked madness, although it is probable that there were in that number men who had brought Christ to death. But, as if assuaging them, he says that this was thus accomplished by the divine purpose; then he even casts the impiety of the crime back on the age itself. "Save yourselves," he says, "from this perverse generation." He does not hurl back abuse at those who said the Apostles were drunk with new wine, but he offers reasonable explanations: it is the energy of a new spirit, not of wine. He quotes the testimony of Joel, which he knew would have very much weight among them. And not yet does he proclaim Christ God and Man; he reserved this mystery for its own time. Meanwhile he calls Him the just man, he proclaims Him Lord and Messiah, and he does this on the authority of the God whom these men also piously worshiped, so that from the Father whom they acknowledged he might win favor for the Son. Moreover, when he made known that the statement which they understood about David was said of Christ, not of David, softening the words that would be offensive, he says, "Brothers, let me say to you freely of the patriarch David."

Thus Paul became all things to all men, so he might win all to

4. The reference is to St. Peter's discourse in Acts 2.

Christ, instructing his disciples to teach with all gentleness, not estranging anyone by harshness of manner and speech, but overcoming with gentleness even the ill-tempered and the rude. With what great courtesy he preaches Christ to the Athenians, casting back their faults on the age itself.[5] "The times of this ignorance God has, it is true, overlooked," he says. In an appropriate and pleasing introduction he calls them "men of Athens." Nor does he with fierce words rail at their wicked cult of demons, but with courteous speech he accuses them of excessive observance who have worshiped more than they ought. He turns the inscription on the altar, which he observed by chance, into an argument for the faith, after he had indeed changed and pruned some of the words; nor does he thus far call Christ other than the Man through whom God has chosen to bestow salvation on all mankind; nor does he quote among them the testimony of the Prophets, which would have very little weight, but he speaks to them of the testimony of Aratus. With what great urbanity does he plead his case before Festus and Agrippa![6]

Thus Augustine refutes the frenzied Donatists and the more than mad Manichaeans, so that he both becomes angry within the merits of the case and mingles the sweetness of his charity everywhere, thirsting for their salvation, not their destruction. Gentleness in teaching these doctrines, the prudence of divine discourse in dispensing them captured the world and, what no arms, no philosophical subtlety, no oratorical eloquence, no human power or skill could ever do, brought it under the yoke of Christ. All the more does it behoove us, if we desire to do good, to refrain from all violent reproaches, especially if we take issue with those who are prominent because of their public authority. Paul wished that honor be given magistrates, even those who were heathen; and he recanted, as it were, because he had spoken ill of the openly wicked Mosaic high priest.[7] He wished slaves who had become Christian to submit to their heathen masters even more scrupulously than they had done before; he wished wives by their profession of Christ to be even more obedient to their irreverent husbands, for no other reason than that by the forbearance of their conduct they might entice all to the love of the Gospel teaching. He who has a pious mind

5. Acts 17:22ff.
6. Acts 26.
7. Acts 23:2–5.

desires only to do good, either proceeding in silence if there is no hope, or disclosing and dispensing the truth in such a way that he does not intensify the disease rather than cure it.

Brutus was indignant at Cicero for provoking those in his speeches and writings whom he could not hold in check when provoked. Deceit and dissimulation in the philosopher–prince was not displeasing to Plato, provided that his wiles were employed for the public good. It is proper, I confess, that the Christian be free from every deceit; but nevertheless it happens sometimes that the truth may well be silent, and everywhere it is a matter of great importance when, among whom, and by what means the truth is disclosed. Trustworthy physicians do not immediately have recourse to extreme remedies. They first prescribe gentler drugs for the ill body; and they regulate the dosage in such a way that they may restore it to health, not bury it. Nor do I agree with those who say that the illness of this present time is too serious to be healed with gentle remedies. According to the Greek proverb, it is better for an evil to lie as it is, rather than to be disturbed by improper remedies.

Indeed, I do not deny that God sometimes corrects His flock by war, pestilence, and suffering; it is not for the pious, however, to cause war and wicked torment, if God at times turns the misfortune of others into a good for His own. The cross of Christ brought salvation to the world, and yet we execrate those who brought Him to the cross. The death of the martyrs adorned and at the same time strengthened the Church of God; nevertheless, the wickedness of those through whom this good has come to us has been condemned. Many would be less wicked if they were deprived of their riches. It is not for the upright man, however, to despoil anyone of his possessions in order to make him better. Moreover, since everything new and unusual gives rise to a disturbance, even when there is a call to better things, if anything differs from what is customary, it must be proposed in such a way that it appears to differ as little as possible.

Yet it is said that Luther, although he teaches the same doctrine as others, several times endeavors by the very language he uses, so it would seem, to make it appear that he asserts the most dissimilar views. Moreover, as men's behavior is inclined to the worse, their vices must be so corrected that the occasion for sinning more freely is not offered to others. Paul preaches evangelical liberty as against the ruinous servitude of the law, but he adds, "Only do not use liberty as an occasion for sensuality."[8] He exhorts against the cold works of the law so that he may incessantly encourage to works of charity. Perhaps there were some who out of honest zeal favored calling the orders and princes of the Church to better things. But I do not know if they are those who under this pretext covet the wealth of the churchmen. I judge nothing to be more wicked and destructive of public tranquillity than this. For if they believe it is right to seize the property of priests because some consume their wealth in extravagant living or otherwise spend it for purposes not too honorable, not many citizens or magnates will find the possession of their goods sufficiently secure. This certainly is a fine turn of affairs, if property is wickedly taken away from priests so that soldiers may make use of it in worse fashion; and the latter squander their own wealth, and sometimes that of others, so that no one benefits.

I do not even agree with those men, my dear Jonas, who say that Luther, provoked by the intolerable shamelessness of his adversaries, could not maintain a Christian moderation. Regardless of how others conduct themselves, he who had undertaken such a role ought to be faithful to himself and disregard all other matters. Finally, a way out should have been provided before he descended into that pit, lest there occur what happened to the goat in the fable. Even in pious matters it is foolish to begin what you cannot finish, especially if a not-too-fortunate attempt brings the greatest misfortune instead of the advantages that were desired. We see the affair brought to that point that I reasonably see no good outcome, unless Christ through His own skill turn the rashness of these men into a public good.

Some excuse Luther because, forced by the incitement of others, he first wrote more violently and then did not entrust himself to the judgment of most clement Leo and of Emperor Charles, by far the noblest and most gentle prince of the faith. But why was he more disposed to give ear to these inciters than to other friends, neither unlearned nor inexperienced in affairs, urging him along different paths? With what kind of defense, I ask, did a great many who favored him attempt to protect him? With ridiculous little books and with empty threats. As if, in fact, this type of nonsense either frightens his adversaries or at-

8. Galatians 5:13.

tracts good men, to whose judgment the whole affair should have been made to conform, provided that they wished their stories to mark a fruitful turning point. How great a swarm of evils this foolhardiness now yields! And ill will greatly weighs down the study of letters as well as many good men who in the beginning were not particularly hostile to Luther, either because they hoped he would handle the matter differently or on account of the enemies they had in common. For it happened by some chance that those who at the outset made trouble for Luther were enemies of learning, and on this account the devotees of letters were less hostile to Luther lest by supporting the ranks of his adversaries they strengthen the power of their own enemies. Although, whatever the case may be, the care of religion must take precedence over that of studies.

And here, my dear Jonas, I have been forced at times to wish for evidence of the evangelical spirit when I saw Luther, but especially his supporters, strive with skill, as it were, to involve others in a hateful and dangerous affair. For what did it avail to have Reuchlin, burdened enough thus far, weighed down with heavier ill will? What was the need to make mention, so often invidious, of my name, when the case by no means demanded it? I have advised Luther in a private and sealed letter; it was soon printed at Leipzig.[9] I had advised the Cardinal of Mainz in a sealed letter lest he rashly surrender Luther, whose cause thus far was praiseworthy to most good men, to the wanton pleasure of certain ones.[10] It was published before it was delivered. Pirckheimer complains in his letter to me that certain letters are circulating in printed form which no one ever delivered to him.[11] In these they urge him to continue steadfastly in what he had begun, so that it is clear that they drag him, whether he wishes or not, into the fellowship of that faction.

They extracted certain offensive passages which seemed to have a relationship to some of Luther's tenets from books I wrote before I dreamed that Luther would arise, and they published them in Ger-

---

9. Erasmus' letter to Luther of 30 May 1519 is CWE 6: *Ep.* 980.
10. Selection VI.
11. Willibald Pirckheimer (1470–1530) was a German scholar and humanist whose attitude toward Luther at this time was similar to that of Erasmus. See Allen, IV 491.203*n*, regarding this reference.

man.[12] And those who do this wish to be considered friends, although a mortal enemy could do nothing more hostile. The men who wish me the most ill have not had as much ingenuity in injuring me. They have presented this weapon to my enemies so that now in public sermons they might proclaim where I agree with Luther. As if, indeed, falsehood may not be the neighbor on both sides of truth, if you go beyond the mark! I somewhere warn, perhaps, that vows should not rashly be made, and I disapprove of those who run off to the shrine of St. James or to Jerusalem, where they had no business, and leave at home their wife and children, whose life and virtue should have been their chief concern. I warn that young men should not be enticed into the bonds of the religious life before they know themselves and know what the religious life is. Luther, so they say, totally condemns all vows. I complain somewhere that the burden of confession has been made heavier by the subtleties of certain men. Luther, so they say, teaches that all confession should be rejected as a dangerous institution. I have taught somewhere that the best authors should be read first, adding that as much profit may not be gained from the books of Dionysius as their titles appear to promise.[13] Luther calls the man absurd, I hear, and unworthy of being read at all.

This is indeed a fine state of agreement, if, going beyond the limit of my words, another distorts what I have properly written at a favorable time and with moderation. The laws, however, would be most unjust to me if I should be held responsible lest anyone in the future also abuse my writings. This fate did not even befall the Apostle Paul, if we are to believe his colleague Peter![14] Nevertheless, to speak frankly, if I had foreseen that an age such as this would arise, either I would not have written certain things which I did write, or I would have written them in a different way. For I desire to be of service to all in such a way that no one is injured, if that is possible. Little books composed by conspirators, in which Erasmus also is portrayed, are cir-

---

12. Erasmus may refer here to his letter to Volz (Selection V), which Spalatin translated into German in 1520 and which was published about this time.

13. Dionysius the Areopagite was the supposed author of several theological works highly regarded in the Middle Ages, including *On the Heavenly and Ecclesiastical Hierarchies, On the Divine Names,* and *On Mystical Theology.*

14. 2 Peter 3:16.

culated. However, no name is more hateful to me than that of conspiracy or schism or faction.

This whole affair, whatever the story is, has been started against my advice, or at least with my constant disapproval of the manner employed. My letters have never served any faction other than that of Christ, whom we all have in common. I do not know what influence I have by this mode of thinking and by these letters; certainly I have tried and I desire to be of service not only to the Germans but to the French, the Spanish, the English, the Bohemians, the Russians, and indeed to the Turks and Saracens as well, if possible. So far am I from ever having wished to be involved in a faction as dangerous as this! And in the meantime I also look for prudence among those who believe that by tricks of this kind anyone can be enticed into their camp. If they wish to alienate any judicious man, by what method might they better do this? But they proclaim enough that this is a weak support, as they say, although they put their trust in such aid in so hazardous an affair. Moreover, I am desperately afraid lest among the other nations this affair bring a great disgrace to our Germany, as the great mass of men are accustomed to impute the foolishness of a few to the entire nation.

What else has been accomplished, therefore I ask, by so many harsh little books, by so much foolish talk, by so many formidable threats, and by so much bombast save that what was previously debated in the universities as probable opinion may be hereafter an article of faith, and that then indeed it may be scarcely safe to teach the Gospel, while everything is seized and misrepresented because all have been exasperated? Luther could have taught the evangelical philosophy with great profit to the Christian flock, he could have benefited the world by bringing forth books, if he had restrained from those things which could only end in disturbance. He has also taken away from my works a good part of the profit they contained. Not even the disputations in the universities, which used to be most frank, are free. If it is right to hate anyone because of personal offenses, the Lutherans have injured no one more than me. And yet I would desire, in spite of that, that this discord, by far the most dangerous, be adjusted, and be adjusted in such a way that it does not break out later with more serious peril, as an ulcer often does that has been badly treated.

Will you tell me, dear Jonas, why you have given me the occasion for this now tardy complaint? First, because, although the affair has gone on longer than it should have, yet even now one may watch for the opportunity of quieting so great a disturbance. We have a pontiff who is by his very nature most clement, we have an emperor endowed with a mild and placable disposition. If it cannot be done, I do not wish you to entangle yourself in this trouble. I have always loved in you the splendid gifts of Christ: all the more I wish that you be saved for the work of the Gospel. And the more I loved the inborn ability of Hutten, the more I grieve that it was snatched away from us by these disorders.[15] Who, indeed, would not be distressed in spirit if Philip Melanchthon, a youth provided with so many exceptional gifts, was deprived of the public good will of the learned by this storm?[16] For if certain things offend them with regard to those by whose will human affairs are governed, I am of the opinion that the latter must be left to their Lord. If they prescribe what is right, it is proper to obey; but if what is unjust, it is a holy act to bear it lest anything worse happen. If this age does not bring forth the whole Christ, it is, however, something to preach Him to the extent that one may.

These matters which I now discuss with you, dear Jonas, I would like you to discuss with Philip, or with any others like Philip. Above all, I am of the opinion that discord, ruinous for all, must be avoided. And that thus by what I might call a holy artfulness the needs of the time must be served, that by no means the treasury of the Gospel truth be betrayed, whence can come the reformation of corrupt public morals. Perhaps someone will ask whether I have another mind regarding Luther than I had formerly. No, indeed, I have the same mind. I have always wished that, with changes made of certain things which were displeasing to me, he discuss purely the Gospel philosophy, from which the morals of our age have departed, alas, too far. I have always preferred that he be corrected rather than suppressed. I desired him to carry on the work of Christ in such a way that the leaders of the Church

---

15. Ulrich von Hutten (1488–1523), German knight and scholar, was an enthusiastic supporter of Luther. He and Erasmus had been friends, but the Lutheran issue was now provoking a bitter quarrel between them.

16. Philip Melanchthon (1497–1560) became professor of Greek at Wittenberg in 1518. Though he was one of Luther's closest associates, he and Erasmus remained on good terms.

either approved or certainly not disapproved. I desired that Luther be loved openly and without danger. Nor do I have a different mind about my wrangling critics than about him. If they should preach Christ as piously as they rage against me impiously, I would forget what they accomplish in my case, and I will admire their zeal in Christ. I will not detest those babblers, if they begin to herald Christ. Farewell.

Louvain
10 May 1521

IX

Letter to Jodocus Jonas
on Vitrier and Colet

13 June 1521

This second letter to Jonas is a logical companion to the first one.[1] Written a month later, it continues Erasmus' argument that Jonas should avoid the extravagances of Luther and should work for reform within the framework of the old Church. Whereas the first letter is a direct appeal, the second one approaches its theme in a somewhat oblique but nevertheless most meaningful way. Erasmus presents Jonas with the picture of two reformers—"two men of our age whom I consider to have been true and sincere Christians"—who from within the Church devoted their energies to evangelical renewal and reform. Erasmus' intent is quite obvious, and at the beginning of his letter as well as at its close Erasmus indicates that he is giving Jonas examples that he may well consider and imitate.

The two men who are sketched in this letter are Jehan Vitrier, a Franciscan friar whom Erasmus had met in 1501 at the Franciscan house at St. Omer in Artois, and John Colet, the famous English scholar and dean of St. Paul's in London. Vitrier is known chiefly from this letter to Jonas and from a reference in the Botzheim Catalogue where Erasmus speaks of him as approving his early *Enchiridion*.[2] Colet (ca. 1466–1519), of course, is very well known.[3] Distinguished as a scriptural scholar, he had been a close friend of Erasmus ever since Erasmus' first trip to England in 1499. In 1510 he had founded St. Paul's School, which Erasmus describes in this letter. Erasmus' sketch of Colet is a biographical document

---

1. The Latin text is in Allen, IV 507–27. The English translation presented here with some modification of spelling and punctuation is from Erasmus, *The Lives of Jehan Vitrier and John Colet*, trans. J. H. Lupton (London, 1883), pp. 1–47. The Lupton translation was made from *Erasmi opera omnia*, ed. Johannes Clericus (Leyden, 1703–1706), III No. 435, and is the first of the entire Jonas letter to be published. It is accompanied in its original edition by extensive notes, but these have not been reprinted; those appended here are by the editor.

2. Allen, I 20. See also André Godin, *Spiritualité franciscaine en Flandre au XVIème siècle: L'Homéliaire de Jean Vitrier* (Geneva, 1971).

3. On Colet, see J. H. Lupton, *A Life of John Colet* (London, 1887).

of considerable importance, and it ranks with the famous sketch of Thomas More which Erasmus sent to Ulrich von Hutten in 1519.[4]

To Jodocus Jonas of Erfurt,
greetings from Erasmus of Rotterdam:

With your earnest request, my worthy friend, that I would briefly portray for you, as in miniature, the life of John Colet, I will gladly comply; and the rather, from an impression that you are trying to find some eminent pattern of religion by which to regulate your own course of life. I have been acquainted with many persons, my dear Jonas, whose high principles I greatly esteemed; but I must own that I never yet saw anyone in whose character I did not after all miss some trait of Christian sincerity when compared with the single-mindedness of the two whom I am about to describe.

It was my fortune to become acquainted with the former of them at a town in Artois commonly called St. Omer, at the time when the plague (in this respect, at least, of service to me) had driven me there from Paris. The latter I met within England, to which country I had been drawn by attachment to my patron Mountjoy.

If I give you two portraits instead of one, you will be the gainer; and to that, I know, you have no objection.

The first of the two was named Jehan Vitrier. He was of the Franciscan order, having lighted on this way of life in his youth. And in no other respect, I should say, was he to be deemed inferior to Colet than that from the restrictions of his system his sphere of usefulness was more limited. He was about forty-four years of age when our acquaintance began; and unlike as our dispositions were, he became attached to me at once. With men of worth his influence was always very great, and many people of rank valued him most highly. In person he was tall and well-proportioned, of a happily constituted nature, high-spirited, yet most courteous withal. In his youth he had drunk deeply of the subtleties of Scotus. And without setting any great value on these, he yet did not wholly disparage them, as containing some things well put, though in uncouth phrase. But when he had the fortune to make ac-

4. CWE 7: *Ep.* 999.

quaintance with Ambrose and Cyprian and Jerome, his relish for the other became very small in comparison. There was no writer on theology whose genius he more admired than Origen's. And on my objecting that I was surprised to see him take pleasure in the writings of a heretic, I was struck with the animation with which he replied that a mind from which there had issued so many works fraught with such learning and fervor could not but have been a dwelling place of the Holy Spirit.

He by no means approved of the system of life which he had entered by chance, or had been drawn into in the inexperience of youth. I have repeatedly heard him say that to sleep and wake and return to sleep again by the sound of a bell, to talk and leave off talking, to come and go, to eat and desist from eating, to do everything, in short, by man's injunction instead of by the rule of Christ, was the life of idiots rather than of religious men. Nothing, he would aver, was more unreasonable than equality among men so unequal, especially seeing that, buried beneath the rites and ordinances of man's invention, or even devoured with spleen, were often to be found minds of heavenly temper, minds born for better things. Yet at no time did he either counsel anyone else to change this way of life, or attempt anything of the kind himself, being ready to bear all things sooner than be a stumbling block in anyone's way. In this too he would copy the example of his beloved Paul. There was indeed nothing so unreasonable that he would not cheerfully put up with in his desire for the preservation of peace.

He had so thoroughly learnt by heart the books of Holy Scripture, St. Paul's Epistles more particularly, that he had the words of his favorite, St. Paul, completely at his finger ends. At whatever passage you set him on, he would, after a moment's thought, go on right through the Epistle without a single mistake. He remembered also considerable portions of St. Ambrose. And it is almost past belief how much he recollected of other orthodox writers of antiquity as well. This advantage he owed in part to a naturally good memory and in part to constant practice.

I once asked him in the course of conversation what his way of mental preparation was before going into the pulpit. He answered that it was his custom to take up St. Paul, and to spend the time reading him till he felt his heart grow warm. He would continue thus engaged, with the addition of fervent prayers to God, till warned that it was time for him to begin.

As a rule, he did not divide his sermons under heads. Most preachers, indeed, do this as if no other course were open to them, the result being in many cases a stiff and formal subdivision. And yet all this care about subdivision does but make the discourse cold and stiff and lessen our confidence in the preacher by the artifice it betrays. But Vitrier would so link together the Epistle and Gospel that had been read, in an unbroken flow of eloquence, as to send his hearers home both better instructed and more ardent in the pursuit of religion. With no unbecoming gesticulation, with nothing exciting or declamatory, but perfectly under control, his delivery was yet such that you felt the words to proceed from a fervent and sincere, yet a sober spirit withal. On no occasion did he preach to a wearisome length, nor did he make a parade of citing a variety of names, in the way that some do. For these will tack together formal extracts now from Scotus, Aquinas, and Durandus, now from canon and civil law doctors, or again from the philosophers or the poets, that the people may think they know everything. The discourse he delivered would be all full of Holy Scripture, and his tongue could run on nothing else. His heart was in his subject. He was possessed, good soul, with an enthusiastic desire of drawing men to the pure wisdom of Christ.

It was by labors such as these that he aspired to the glory of martyrdom. Nay more, he had once, as I learnt from his most intimate friends, obtained leave from his superiors to visit countries where Christ is either unknown or worshiped amiss, deeming his end a happy one if in the discharge of his duty he should have earned the martyr's crown. But when already on his way, he was recalled by hearing, as it were, a voice from heaven saying: "Return, John; thou wilt not want for martyrdom among thine own people." He obeyed the admonition, and soon found the truth of what that voice had foretold.

There was in his neighborhood a convent of nuns in which the whole system of religious life had sunk to such a low ebb that it was in truth a house of ill fame rather than a convent. Not but that there were some among them both capable and desirous of amendment. While seeking to recall these to Christ by frequent addresses and exhortations, a plot was laid against him by eight abandoned ones of the number. Having waylaid their victim, they dragged him to a secluded spot and there flung their wimples about him and tried to strangle him. Nor did they desist until some chance passersby interposed and stopped their criminal outrage. The injured man was by this time unconscious, and breathing was with difficulty restored. Yet he made no complaint about the matter in any quarter, not even to his most intimate acquaintances, nor omitted any service in which he was accustomed to minister to the spiritual welfare of those nuns. Nay, even the very looks with which he regarded them never showed any unwonted sternness. He was well acquainted with the instigator of the plot, a Dominican, suffragan bishop of Boulogne, a man of notoriously wicked life. Yet he never troubled him either with any words about the matter, though there was no class of men to whom he was less favourably disposed than to such as, being religious teachers and guides by profession, by their wicked life and doctrine estranged people from Christ.

I have known him preach as many as seven times in one day, nor so long as Christ was to be his theme did a fund of words full of matter ever fail him. In truth, his whole life was nothing else than one continued sermon. At table he was lively and without the least tinge of austerity, yet still in such a way as never to show any signs of frivolity or indecorum, much less of wantonness or excess. He would season the repast with learned conversation, generally on sacred subjects and conducive to religion. Such was his way of talking, if he received or paid a visit. But if on a journey—when some of the influential friends he had would often lend him a horse or mule to ride on, for the sake of having a more convenient chat with him on the road—on such an occasion the good man would brighten up and let fall sayings more precious than any jewels. He let no one ever go away from him disconsolate, no one that was not rather the better for his visit and more encouraged to love religion. There was nothing to make you feel that he studied any private interests of his own. Neither gluttony, nor ambition, nor covetousness, nor love of pleasure, nor enmity, nor jealousy, nor any other bad passions held him under their sway. He thanked God all the same, whatever befell him. His only joy lay in inspiring men to follow after the religion of the Gospel. And his efforts to this end were not in vain. Numbers of both men and women had he won to Christ, whose deathbeds showed how far they differed from the common run of Christians in these days. For you might have seen his disciples meet death with the greatest cheerfulness of spirit, singing a truly swanlike song at its approach and testifying by their utterances to a heart moved with a holy inspiration; while the rest, after performing the due rites and making the customary professions, would breathe their last—in assurance or doubt, as the case might be.

A witness of this fact was a distinguished physician of St. Omer named Ghisbert, a steady practicer of true religion and one who was present at the deathbeds of many persons of each party.

He had also won over some of the members of his own fraternity, though few by comparison, even as Christ could not do many mighty works among His own people. For men of his order are commonly best pleased with those who, by their teaching, bring most provisions to the kitchen, rather than with those who win most souls to Christ.

Averse from all vices as was that purest of souls, that temple truly dedicated to Christ, he recoiled most of all from licentiousness. The very atmosphere of such things was utterly repulsive to him: much less could he listen patiently to indecent language. Without ever indulging in bitter invectives, or disclosing anything gathered from private confessions, he would yet draw such a picture of virtue that every hearer tacitly recognized himself by the contrast. In giving counsel he showed singular prudence, integrity, and tact. While he would listen to private confessions—not, indeed, with any particular good will but following, in this respect also, the dictates of Christian charity—he openly expressed his dislike of oversolicitous and oft-repeated confessions. To superstitious rites and ceremonies he attached very little importance. He would eat of any kind of food that there might be, though soberly and with giving of thanks; and his dress was in no respect different from that of others. It was his wont to take a journey occasionally for the sake of his health at times when he felt overcharged with bodily humors. So one day, while completing along with his companion the allotted task of morning prayers, feeling his stomach squeamish—by reason, perhaps, of his having fasted the day before—he went into the nearest house, and after taking something to eat there, resumed his journey and was proceeding with his prayers. Thereupon his companion thought that all would have to be begun again from the beginning, seeing that he had taken food before the prayers for Prime had been said. But he maintained with spirit that no fault had been committed, nay, that God would rather be the gainer. "For while before," said he, "we were slow and listless at our prayers, we shall now utter spiritual songs to Him with ready minds; and with such sacrifices— such as are offered by a cheerful giver—God is well pleased."

At that time I was staying with Antonius à Bergis, the abbot of St. Bertin.[5] Dinner was not served there till afternoon; and as my stomach could not bear so long an abstinence (especially as it was Lent, and I was studying hard), I was in the habit of staying my appetite before dinner with a basin of warm soup in order to hold out till dinnertime. On my asking Vitrier what he thought about the lawfulness of my plan, he first gave a glance at the companion he then had, who chanced to be a layman, for fear he should be at all scandalized, and said: "Why, truly it would be a sin if you did not act so, if for the sake of a morsel of food you were to interrupt those sacred studies of yours and injure your frail constitution."

When Pope Alexander, to gain ampler revenues, had made two jubilees instead of one, and the bishop of Tournai had bought as a speculation, for ready money, the privilege of granting dispensations from it, his commissaries began to use every effort that the bishop might not lose his investment but rather be the receiver of a handsome profit. Hereupon, such preachers as were acceptable to the people in their sermons were invited to be the first to play their part. Vitrier, observing that the money which had previously gone to the relief of the poor was now being put into the commissaries' boxes, did not approve of it, while yet not finding fault with what was offered by the pope. But this he did find fault with, namely, that people of scanty means should be defrauded of their accustomed support. He condemned also the foolish confidence of those who thought that by merely dropping a coin into the boxes they were freed from their sins. At length the commissaries offered him a hundred florins toward the building of the chapel in his convent, then in course of erection, on condition that if he were not willing to recommend the papal indul-

5. Antonius à Bergis, or Anthony of Bergen, was the brother of Henry of Bergen, bishop of Cambrai, Erasmus' early patron. He had been forcibly installed as abbot of the monastery of St. Bertin, in St. Omer, by his brother in 1493.

gences, he would at least say nothing against them. Hereupon, as if prompted by some inspiration from above, he bade them begone with their simoniacal money. "Think you," he cried, "that I am one to keep back the truth of the Gospel for money? What if that does hinder your profits? I am bound to have a greater care for souls than for your gain."

For the moment they quailed, conscience-stricken, before the energy of this evangelic spirit. But in the interval, by early dawn next day, there was unexpectedly posted upon the church door a notice of excommunication against him—only to be torn down again by one of the townspeople, before any great number came to know about it. He, however, nothing daunted by these threats, went on teaching the people and sacrificing to Christ with the utmost composure of mind; nor did he show any fear of anathema, aimed at him for preaching Christ. Presently he was cited before the bishop of Boulogne. He obeyed his diocesan and, having no uneasiness about his own safety, went attended by only a single companion. But the townspeople, without his knowing it, had posted guards of horsemen on the road for fear that he might be waylaid and thrown into some den or other; for there is nothing on which the "accursed lust for gold" will not venture. When the bishop brought against him certain articles, gathered by his opponents from his sermons, he defended himself with spirit and satisfied his superior. Some time afterward he was summoned afresh, and more articles were brought up against him. After replying to these in like manner, he asked why his accusers were not present to prefer their charges at their own risk as well as his. He had now come twice, he said, to show respect to him as his bishop, but he would not come a third time if similarly cited, for he had something better to occupy him at home. And so he was left to his own devices, either because his enemies had no pretext for injuring him or because they feared an uproar of the people. For, without his courting any such favor, his integrity had made all the most respectable men among them his devoted adherents.[6]

I know you will long have had the question on your lips, what the

---

6. The comparison—and contrast—between this whole episode and Luther's indulgence controversy is most striking and is quite obviously stressed by Erasmus as a lesson for Jonas.

end of this man was. He offended not only the commissaries but also many of his own fraternity—not that they had any fault to find with his way of life, but because it was in fact too good to suit their interests. His heart was wholly set on winning souls. As to replenishing the larder, or erecting buildings, or inveigling young men of property— he was not so active for this as they could have desired. Not that he was inattentive, good man, to these duties either, provided that they tended in any way to relief of pressing want. But he did not, as so often happens, give them a disproportionate share of his attention. He had even gone so far as to estrange one supporter of the convent named Thynne.[7] This person was a courtier, and of decidedly courtierlike morals—a common invader of the marriage chamber, a promiscuous violator of wedded sanctities, one who had deserted his own wife, though a lady of high family and the mother of several children. By chance it fell out that she too went astray; on which he divorced the poor woman at the very first false step—he who had pardoned so many false steps in himself. She, sinking to lower and lower depths, came at last to the extremity of misfortune; for besides her degraded state, she fell victim to a loathsome disease. Vitrier tried every means to reconcile the husband and wife, but without success. The hardened reprobate was moved neither by respect for his wife's family, nor by affection for their common children, nor by any twinges of conscience at having caused the mischief by his own frequent adulteries and neglect. And so Vitrier gave the man up as hopeless. Not long afterward the latter sent, as he was accustomed to do, a ham or flitch of bacon to the convent. Now Vitrier, who was then filling the office of warden, had given orders to the porter to take nothing in without first calling him. Accordingly, on the arrival of the contribution, he was sent for. But on the servants presenting it with their master's compliments, he exclaimed: "Take back your load to the place you brought it from! We receive no devil's offerings here."

And so, though not ignorant that his life and teaching were a prolific nursery, so to speak, of Christian piety, yet, as he was not of equal service for provisioning the kitchen, they called upon him to resign the

7. Allen (IV 513.205n) points out that the word *thynnum* should not be understood as a proper name, as it is here, but that it means in this context "a fish caught in their net."

warden's office. This he did with as much good will as ever he did anything. In his stead there was appointed a man well known to me, whom they sent for from another neighborhood. Of what character he was, and what a contrast to his predecessor, I will not say; only that in my opinion he was one to whom no person of sense would have liked to entrust even his kitchen garden. Whether it was that he was thrust upon them by those who wished to get rid of him, or that they really thought him better suited for the office, I know not. But when still further, as the result of associating with Vitrier, there began to spring up a few other like-minded ones, whose absorbing passion was for serving the cause of Christianity and not for increasing the commissariat, they sent him away to a little convent of nuns at Courtrai. There, with character unchanged, still, so far as was allowed him, teaching, consoling, exhorting, he peacefully ended his days. He left behind him some treatises in French, in the way of extracts made from sacred writers; and these, I doubt not, are of a piece with the life and conversation of the author. Yet I hear that they are now condemned by some, who think it very dangerous for the people to read aught but the silly tales of histories or the dreams of monks.

There are many in whose breasts some sparks of his teaching still keep alive, and compared to these you would call other people rather Jews than Christians. Though held in such light esteem by his own community, I doubt not that, had this eminent man been allotted to the Apostle Paul for a colleague, he would have preferred him even to his own Barnabas or Timothy.

I have given you my jewel of a Vitrier, as he may truly be called, a man unknown to the world but famous and renowned in the kingdom of Christ. Now take his exact counterpart, Colet.

I had described each of them to the other, and they were both ardently desirous of seeing each other. In fact, Vitrier had crossed over to England with this object; and Colet related to me afterward that he had had a visit from a Franciscan, with whose sensible and religious conversation he had been beyond measure delighted. But he added that he had brought with him a stoical companion of the same order, who seemed to take their Christian conversation amiss, and so cut short the interview.

It may indeed be that Colet deserves the greater praise of the two on this account, namely, that neither the smiles of fortune nor the impulse of a far different natural bent could divert him from the pursuit of a Gospel life. For he was the son of wealthy and distinguished parents; born, too, in London, where his father had twice filled the highest municipal office in his city, called by them the mayoralty. His mother, who still survives, is a most worthy woman. She bore her husband eleven sons and as many daughters; of whom John, as the eldest, would have been heir to the entire estate, according to the English law, even had the others been alive. But at the time when my acquaintance with him began, he was the sole survivor of the band. To these advantages of fortune was added that of a tall and graceful figure.

During his younger days in England he diligently mastered all the philosophy of the schools and gained the title expressive of a knowledge of the seven liberal arts. Of these arts there was not one in which he had not been industriously and successfully trained. For he had both eagerly devoured the works of Cicero and diligently searched into those of Plato and Plotinus, while there was no branch of mathematics that he left untouched.

After this, like a merchant seeking goodly wares, he visited France and then Italy. While there, he devoted himself entirely to the study of the sacred writers. He had previously, however, roamed with great zest through literature of every kind, finding most pleasure in the early writers, Dionysius, Origen, Cyprian, Ambrose, and Jerome. I should add that among the old authors there was none to whom he was more unfavorable than Augustine. At the same time he did not omit to read Scotus and Thomas and others of that stamp, if the occasion ever required it. He was also carefully versed in treatises of civil and canon law. In a word, there was no work containing either the chronicles or enactments of our forefathers which he had not perused. The English nation has poets who have done among their own countrymen what Dante and Petrarch have done in Italy. And by the study of their writings he perfected his style, preparing himself even at this date for preaching the Gospel.

Soon after his return from Italy he left his father's house, as he preferred to reside at Oxford, and there he publicly and gratuitously expounded all St. Paul's Epistles. It was at Oxford that my acquaintance with him began, some kind providence having brought me at that time to the same spot. He was then about thirty years old, some two or three months younger than myself. Though he had neither obtained nor sought for any degree in divinity, yet there was no doctor there, of either divinity or law, no abbot or other dignitary but came to hear him and brought his textbooks with him as well. The credit of this may have been due to Colet's personal influence, or it may have been due to their own good will in not being ashamed to learn, the old from the young, doctors from one who was no doctor. However, the title of doctor was spontaneously offered him some time later and accepted by him, though rather to oblige the offerers than because he sought it.

From these sacred occupations he was called back to London by the favor of Henry VII and made dean of St. Paul's, so as to preside over the cathedral of that Apostle whose Epistles he loved so much. This takes precedence over all the deaneries in England, though there are others with richer incomes. Hereupon our good Colet, feeling his call to be for the work and not for the empty honor, restored the decayed discipline of the cathedral body and—what was a novelty there—commenced preaching at every festival in his cathedral, over and above the special sermons he had to deliver now at court, now in various other places. In his own cathedral, moreover, he would not take isolated texts from the Gospels or Apostolic Epistles but would start with some connected subject and pursue it right to the end in a course of sermons: for example, St. Matthew's Gospel, the Creed, or the Lord's Prayer. He used to have a crowded congregation, including most of the leading men of both the city and the court.

The dean's table, which in former days had ministered to luxury under the guise of hospitality, he brought within the bounds of moderation. For having done without suppers entirely for some years before, he was thus free from company in the evening. Moreover, as he dined rather late, he had fewer guests on those occasions as well, and all the fewer because the repast, though neat, was frugal, and the sitting at table short, and lastly, the conversation such as to have no charms but for the good and learned. When grace had been said, a servant would read aloud in a clear, distinct voice a chapter from St. Paul's Epistles or the Proverbs of Solomon. He would then usually repeat some passage selected from the part read and draw a topic of conversation from it, inquiring of any scholars present, or even of intelligent laymen, what this or that expression meant. And he would so season the discourse that, though both serious and religious, it had nothing tedious or affected about it. Again, toward the end of the meal, when the requirements of nature, at any rate, if not of pleasure had been satisfied, he started some other topic; and thus bade farewell to his guests, refreshed in mind as well as in body and better men at leaving than they came, though with no overloaded stomachs. The pleasure he took in conversing with friends was extreme, and he would often prolong the talk till late at night. But still it was all either about literature or about Christ. If there was no agreeable person at hand to chat with—and it was not every sort that suited him—a servant would read aloud some passage from Holy Scripture. Occasionally he took me with him for company on a journey, and then nothing could be more pleasant than he was. But a book was ever his companion on the road, and his talk was always of Christ.

He could not endure any slovenliness, so much so as not to tolerate even an ungrammatical or illiterate mode of expression. All his household furniture, his service at table, his dress, his books he would have neat; as for splendor, he did not trouble himself. He used to wear only dark-colored robes, though priests and divines in England are usually robed in scarlet. His outer garment was always of woollen cloth, not lined; but if the cold required it, he would protect himself with an inner lining of fur.

All the revenue that came in from his preferments he left in his steward's hands, to be laid out in household expenses. His private fortune, a very large one, he would himself dispose of for charitable purposes. At his father's death he had inherited a large sum of money; and fearing lest, if he hoarded it up, it might breed some distemper of mind in him, he built with it in St. Paul's Churchyard a new school of splendid structure, dedicated to the Child Jesus. He attached to it also a handsome residence for the two masters to dwell in and assigned them a liberal stipend to teach free of charge, but on condition that the school should only admit a fixed number. The school was divided by him into four partitions. The one first entered contains those whom we may call the catechumens, none being admitted but such as can already both read and write. The second contains those under the sur-master's teaching, and the third those who are instructed by the high master. Each of these partitions is separated from the others by a curtain, drawn to or drawn aside at pleasure. Over the high master's chair is a beautifully wrought figure of the Child Jesus seated in the attitude of one teaching, and all the young flock as they enter and leave school salute it with a hymn. Over it is the countenance of God the Father, saying: HEAR YE HIM (an inscription added at my suggestion). At the far end is a chapel in which divine service may be held. The whole school has no bays or recesses, so much so that there is neither any dining room nor dormitory. Every boy has his own proper seat on regularly ascending tiers with gangways left between. Each class contains sixteen, and the head boy in each class has a stall somewhat higher than the rest. Boys of all kinds are not admitted promiscuously, but a selection is made according to natural capacity and ability.

A most farsighted man, Colet saw that a nation's chief hope lay in having the rising generation trained in good principles. But though the undertaking cost him a very large sum of money, he allowed no one to share it. Some person had left a legacy of a hundred pounds sterling toward the building. But when Colet perceived that on the strength of this outsiders were claiming some rights or other, he obtained his bishop's sanction to apply the sum toward providing sacred vestments for the cathedral. Over the revenues and the entire management of his school he placed neither priests, nor the bishop, nor the chapter (as they call it), nor noblemen, but some married citizens of established reputation. And when asked the reason, he said that, while there was nothing certain in human affairs, he yet found the least corruption in these.

This was a work that no one failed to approve. But many were surprised at his building a magnificent dwelling within the precincts of the Carthusian monastery, not far from what is called Richmond Palace. He said that he was preparing an abode for his old age, when he should be no longer equal to his work or be enfeebled by sickness and so compelled to retire from society. There he was minded to philosophize with two or three chosen old friends, among whom he was accustomed to reckon myself. But death forestalled him. For having been seized a few years before with the sweating sickness (a disease that is the special scourge of England), he was now for the third time attacked by it; and though he recovered from it to some degree, an internal disorder ensued from what the disease left behind it, of which he died. One physician pronounced him dropsical. Nothing fresh was discovered by the post-mortem examination except that the liver was found to have the extremities of the lobes rough with tuft-like excrescences. He was buried at the south side of the choir in his cathedral, in a modest grave chosen by himself some years before for the purpose, with the inscription placed over it: IOAN. COL.

Before I conclude, my friend Jonas, I will mention a few particulars, first of his natural disposition, then of his peculiar opinions, and lastly of the stormy scenes in which his sincere religion was put to the test. It was but a very small portion of this religious spirit that he owed to nature. For he was gifted with a temper singularly high and impatient of affront; he was, as he himself confessed to me, naturally prone to incontinence, luxuriousness, and indulgence in sleep; overmuch disposed to jests and raillery; and he was besides not wholly exempt from the taint of covetousness. But these tendencies he combated so successfully by philosophy and sacred studies, by watching, fasting, and prayer that he led the whole course of his life free from the pollutions of the world. As far as I could gather from my intimate acquaintance and conversations with him, he kept the flower of chastity even unto death. His fortune he spent on charitable uses. Against his high temper he contended with the help of reason, so as to brook admonition even from a servant. Incontinence, love of sleep, and luxuriousness he vanquished by a uniform abstinence from supper, by constant sobriety, by unwearied exertions in study, and by religious conversation. Yet if an occasion had ever presented itself of either conversing with ladies or being a guest at sumptuous repasts, you might have seen some traces of the old nature in him. And on that account he kept away, as a rule, from laymen's society, and especially from banquets. If forced at times to attend them, he would take me or some similar companion with him in order, by talking Latin, to avoid worldly conversation. Meanwhile he would partake sparingly of one dish only and be satisfied with a single draught or two of ale. He was abstemious in respect of wine, appreciating it if choice, but most temperate in the use of it. Thus keeping a constant watch upon himself, he carefully avoided everything by which he might cause anyone to stumble, not forgetting that the eyes of all were upon him.

I never saw a more highly gifted intellect. But though he felt a peculiar pleasure on this account in kindred intellects, he liked better to bend his mind to such things as fitted it for the immortality of the life to come. If at times he sought relaxation in sprightlier talk, he would still philosophize on every topic. He took a delight in the purity and simplicity of nature that is in children, a nature that Christ bids His disciples imitate, and he was wont to compare them to angels.

To complete, now, the second part of my promised account, his opinions differed widely from those commonly received. But in this matter he showed a remarkable discretion in adapting himself to others, so as to avoid giving offence to any persons or bringing any slur on his good name. For he knew well how unfair men's judgments are, how ready they are to believe evil, and how much easier a thing it is for slanderous tongues to tarnish a man's good name than for kind-spoken ones to repair it. Among friends and scholars, however, he would express his sentiments with the utmost freedom. As to the Scotists, for example, to whom the common run of men ascribe a subtlety peculiarly their own, he said that he considered them dull and stupid and anything but intellectual. For it was the sign of a poor and barren intellect, he would say, to be quibbling about the words and opinions of others, carping first at one thing and then at another, and analysing everything so minutely. Yet for some reason he was even harder on Aquinas than on Scotus. For when I once praised Aquinas to him as a writer not to be despised among the moderns, since he appeared to me to have studied both the scriptures and the early Fathers—such being the impression I had formed from his *Catena aurea*—and had also a certain unction in his writings, he checked himself more than once from replying and did not betray his dislike. But when in another conversation I was reiterating the same opinions more strongly, he looked hard at me, as if watching whether I were saying this in seriousness or in irony. And on perceiving that I was serious in what I said, he broke out like one possessed: "Why do you preach up that writer to me? For without a full share of presumption, he never would have defined everything in that rash and overweening manner; and without something of a worldly spirit, he would not have so tainted the whole doctrine of Christ with his profane philosophy." Struck with his impetuous manner, I began a more careful study of this author's writing, and, to be brief, my estimate of him was undoubtedly diminished.[8]

Though no one approved of Christian devotion more warmly than he, he had yet but very little liking for monasteries—undeserving of the name as many of them now are. The gifts he bestowed upon them were either none or the smallest possible, and he left them no share of his property even at his death. The reason was not that he disliked religious orders but that those who took them did not come up to their profession. It was in fact his own wish to disconnect himself entirely from the world, if he could only have found a fraternity anywhere really bound together for a Gospel life. And he had even commissioned me to seek for such a one when I was about to visit Italy, telling me that among the Italians he had discovered some monks of true wisdom and piety. Moreover, he did not consider what is popularly deemed religion to be really such, being as it often is mere poverty of intellect. He was accustomed also to praise certain Germans, among whom there even yet lingered, as he said, some traces of primitive religion. He was in the habit of declaring that he nowhere found more unblemished characters than among married people, on whom such restraints were laid by natural affection and family and household cares that they were withheld, as by so many barriers, from rushing into all kinds of wickedness. Though himself living in perfect chastity, yet of all in the list of offenders he was less hard on those—were they priests or even monks—whose only offense was incontinence. It was not that he failed to abhor the vice of unchastity but that he found such persons not nearly so bad, in comparison, as some others who thought no small things of themselves—though overweening, envious, slanderous, backbiters, hypocrites, empty-headed, ignorant, given up heart and soul to money-making and ambition—while their acknowl-

---

8. Regarding Erasmus' view of Thomas Aquinas, see Jean-Pierre Massaut, "Erasme et Saint Thomas," *Colloquia Erasmiana Turonensia*, ed. J.-C. Margolin, 2 vols. (Toronto, 1972), II 581–611.

edged infirmity rendered the former more humble and unassuming. Covetousness and pride, he would say, were more detestable in a priest than keeping a hundred concubines.

I would not have anyone strain these opinions to such a degree as to suppose incontinence in a priest or monk to be a slight offense, but only to infer from them that those of the other kind are still further removed from true religion.

There was no class of persons to whom he was more opposed or for whom he had a greater abhorrence than those bishops who acted the part of wolves instead of shepherds, showing themselves off before the people with their guise of sanctity, their ceremonies, benedictions, and paltry indulgences, while at heart they were slaves to the world, that is, to ostentation and gain. He had a leaning to some opinions derived from Dionysius and the other early divines, though not to such a degree as to make him contravene in any points the decisions of the Church. Still, they made him less hard on such as disapproved of the universal adoration of images in churches, whether painted or of wood, or stone, or bronze, or silver; or again, on those who doubted whether a priest, openly and notoriously wicked, had any efficacy in the administration of the sacraments. Not that he in any way leaned to this error of theirs, but he was indignant against such as, by a life of open and unmixed depravity, gave occasion to surmises of this kind.

The colleges established in England at a great and imposing cost he used to say were a hindrance to profitable studies and merely centers of attraction for the lazy. And in like manner he did not attach much value to the public schools, on the ground that the race for professorships and fees spoilt everything and adulterated the purity of all branches of learning.

While strongly approving of auricular confession, saying that there was nothing from which he derived so much comfort and spiritual advantage, he yet as strongly condemned its too solicitous and frequent repetition. It is the custom in England for priests to celebrate the Holy Eucharist every day. But Colet was content to do so on Sundays and festivals, or at the most on some few days in addition, either because it kept him away from the sacred studies by which he used to prepare for preaching and from the necessary business of the cathedral, or because he found that he sacrificed with devouter feelings if he let an interval elapse. At the same time he was far from disapproving of the principles of those who liked to come every day to the Table of the Lord.

Himself a most learned man, he did not approve of that painful and laborious erudition which is made complete at all points, so to speak, by an acquaintance with all branches of learning and the perusal of every author. It was his constant remark that the natural soundness and simplicity of men's intellects were impaired by it, and they were rendered less healthy-minded and less fitted for Christian innocence and for pure and simple charity. He set a very high value on the Apostolic Epistles; but he had such a reverence for the wonderful majesty of Christ that the writings of the Apostles seemed to grow poor by the side of it. He had with great ability reduced almost all the sayings of Christ to triplets, intending to make a book of them. The rule that priests, even though busily occupied, must say long prayers right through every day, no matter whether at home or on a journey, was a thing that he greatly wondered at. As to the public service of the Church, he was quite of the opinion that that should be performed with proper dignity.

From numbers of the tenets most generally received in the public schools at the present day he widely dissented and would at times discuss them among his private friends. When with others, he would keep his opinions to himself for fear of coming to harm in two ways: that is to say, only making matters worse by his efforts, and sacrificing his own reputation. There was no book so heretical but he read it with attention. For from such, he said, he many a time received more benefit than from the books of those who so define everything as often to flatter their party leaders, and not seldom their own selves as well.

He could not endure that the faculty of speaking correctly should be sought from the trivial rules of grammarians. For he insisted that these were a hindrance to expressing oneself well and that result was obtained only by the study of the best authors. But he paid the penalty for this notion himself. For though eloquent by both nature and training, and though he had at his command a singularly copious flow of words while speaking, yet when writing, he would now and then trip on such points as critics are given to mark. And it was on this account, if I mistake not, that he refrained from writing books, though I wish he had not so refrained, for I should have been glad of the thoughts of such a man, no matter in what language expressed.

And now, that nothing may be thought wanting to the finished religious character of Colet, listen to the storms by which he was harassed. He had never been on good terms with his bishop, who was, to say nothing about his principles, a superstitious and impracticable Scotist, and thinking himself on that account something more than mortal.[9] I may say that, whilst I have known many of this school whom I should not like to call bad men, I have yet never to this day seen one who, in my opinion at least, could be termed a real and sincere Christian. Colet was no great favorite either with many of his own college, being too strict about canonical discipline; and these were every now and then complaining of being treated as monks, though in fact this college was formerly what in ancient deeds it is styled, the Eastern Monastery. However, when the animosity of the old bishop (who was, I should have said, full eighty years of age) was too virulent to be suppressed, he took as his coadjutors two other bishops, as wise and as acrimonious as himself, and began to give Colet trouble. His weapons were just what such persons resort to when plotting anyone's destruction, that is to say, he laid an information against him before the archbishop of Canterbury, specifying certain articles taken from his sermons. One was that he had taught that images ought not to be worshiped. Another, that he had done away with the hospitality commended by St. Paul, seeing that in expounding the passage from the Gospel with its thrice repeated "feed my sheep," while he was in accordance with other expositors on the first two heads (feed by example of life; feed by the word of doctrine), he had disagreed with them on the third, saying that it was not meet that the Apostles, poor as they then were, should be bidden to feed their sheep in the way of any temporal support; and he had substituted some other interpretation in lieu of it. A third article was that having said in the pulpit that there were some who preached written sermons—the stiff and formal way of many in England—he had indirectly reflected on his bishop,

---

9. The bishop referred to is Richard Fitzjames (ca. 1440–1522), who had become bishop of London in 1506. Allen (IV 518.365n) indicates his theological orientation was other than that described by Erasmus. He possessed manuscripts of Origen, Jerome, Augustine, Seneca, et al.

who, from his old age, was in the habit of so doing. The archbishop, to whom Colet's high qualities were perfectly well known, undertook the protection of the innocent, and as Colet himself disdained any reply to these and still more frivolous charges, he became a protector instead of a judge. Still the old bishop's animosity was not allayed. He tried to excite the court, with the king at its head, against Colet, having now got hold of another weapon against him. This was that he had openly declared in a sermon "an unjust peace was to be preferred to the justest war,"[10] a war being at that very time in preparation against the French. A leading part in this play was being taken by two Franciscan friars, of whom one, a very firebrand of war, earned a miter while the other used to declaim like a Stentor in his sermons against poets— meaning Colet, who had not the least taste for poetry, though in other respects not unskilled in music. At this juncture the noble young king gave a conspicuous token of his kingly disposition, for he privately encouraged Colet to go on without restraint, and improve by his teaching the corrupt morals of the age, and not to withdraw his light from those dark times. He was not unaware, he said, of the motive that incited those bishops against him, nor unconscious of the benefits he had conferred on the English nation by his life and doctrine. He added, that he would put such a check on their attempts that others should clearly see that whoever assailed Colet would not go unpunished. On this, Colet expressed his gratitude for such kind feeling on the king's part but prayed leave to decline the offer. He would have no one, he said, worse off on his account: sooner than that, he would resign the office which he bore.

Some time afterward, however, the faction had an occasion given them for hoping that now at last Colet might be crushed. An expedition was being got ready against the French, to start after Easter. On Good Friday, Colet preached a noble sermon before the king and his court on the victory of Christ, exhorting all Christians to war and conquer under the banner of Him their proper King.[11] For they, he said, who through hatred or ambition were fighting, the bad with the

10. Cicero, *Ad Familiares* 6.6.5.

11. This forthright sermon was preached before the court on Good Friday 1513. Erasmus' summary is all that remains of it. The only one of Colet's sermons that is extant is his Convocation Sermon of 1512 on the reformation of the Church, the English translation of which is John C. Olin, *The Catholic Reformation: Savonarola to Ignatius Loyola* (New York, 1969), chap. III.

bad, and slaughtering one another by turns, were warring under the banner not of Christ but of the Devil. At the same time, he pointed out to them how hard a thing it is to die a Christian death, how few entered on a war unsullied by hatred or love of gain, how incompatible a thing it was that a man should have that brotherly love without which no one would see God and yet bury his sword in his brother's heart. Let them follow, he added, the example of Christ as their Prince, not that of a Julius Caesar or an Alexander.[12] Much more to the same effect he gave utterance to on that occasion, so that the king was in some apprehension lest the soldiers whom he was on the point of leading abroad should feel their courage gone through this discourse. On this, all the mischief-makers flocked together like birds setting upon an owl, in the hope that now at last the mind of the king might be exasperated against him. By the king's order Colet was sent for. He came and had luncheon in the Franciscan convent adjoining Greenwich Palace. When the king was apprised of his arrival, he went down into the convent garden, dismissing his attendants as Colet came out to meet him. As soon as they were alone, the courteous young prince bade him be covered and converse with him without ceremony, himself beginning in these terms: "To spare you any groundless alarm, Mr. Dean, we have not sent for you hither to disturb your sacred labors, which have our entire approval, but that we may unburden our conscience of some scruples, and with the help of your counsel may better discharge the duties of our office." (I will not, however, repeat the whole conversation, which lasted nearly an hour.) Meanwhile Bricot, who from a Franciscan friar had now become a bishop, was in high spirits in the palace, supposing Colet to be in danger; whereas the king and he were at one upon all points, save only that the king wished him to say at some other time, with clearer explanation, what he had already said with perfect truth, namely, that for Christians no war was a just one. And this was for the sake of the rough soldiers, who might put a different construction on his words from that which he had intended. Colet, as became his good sense and remarkable moderation of temper, not only set the king's mind at rest but even increased the favor in which he stood before. On returning to the palace, the king

12. A clear and pointed reference by Colet to Pope Julius II, who had died just the month before (February 1513), and to his predecessor, Alexander VI.

had a wine cup brought to him and pledged Colet in it before he would let him depart. Then embracing him most courteously and promising all that could be expected from the most gracious of sovereigns, he let him go. And as the throng of courtiers was now standing round, eager to hear the result of this conference, the king, in the hearing of all, said, "Let every man have his own doctor, and every one follow his liking; but this is the doctor for me." Thus they departed, like the baffled wolves in the adage, Bricot more than all; nor did anyone from that day forward venture to molest Colet.

I have now given you, Jonas, not finished portraits but outline sketches only—all that the scanty limits of a letter allowed—of two men of our age whom I consider to have been true and sincere Christians. It will be for you to select from each what you think most conducive to true religion. And if you ask which of the two I prefer, I deem them worthy of equal praise, considering that they were in circumstances so unlike. On the one hand, it was a great thing for Colet, in worldly circumstances such as his, to have steadily followed the call not of natural inclination but of Christ. On the other hand, the merit of Vitrier makes yet a fairer show in having attained, amid such conditions of life, to so much of the Gospel spirit as he displayed. It is as though a fish were to contract no marshy flavor, though ever living in a marsh. In Colet were some traits which showed him to be but man. In Vitrier I never saw anything that savored at all of human weakness. And if you take my word for it, Jonas, you will not hesitate to enroll these two in the calendar of saints though no pope should ever canonize them.

Happy spirits! to whom I owe much, aid by your prayers Erasmus, still struggling in the miseries of this life, that so I may rejoin your society, never to be parted from you more.

Adieu, Jonas! If I have done justice to your wishes, it is well. I have been far, I know, from doing justice to my subject.

Anderlecht
13 June 1521

X

Letter to Carondelet
Erasmus' Preface to His Edition of
St. Hilary of Poitiers
5 January 1523

This preface is in the form of a dedicatory letter to Jean de Carondelet, a high official at the Hapsburg court in the Low Countries. It first appeared in the large folio edition of the works of St. Hilary of Poitiers which Erasmus edited and Johann Froben published in Basel in February 1523. Carondelet belonged to a prominent Burgundian family whose members had long served the Hapsburgs in many posts. He had been a secretary to the young Charles V, and at the time of Erasmus' dedication he was chief counselor to Margaret of Austria, Charles's aunt and his regent in the Low Countries. He had also been appointed Archbishop of Palermo in 1519, although the appointment was contested and he never resided in that primatial see.

The patristic edition which the essay introduces contains the work of the fourth-century Father and bishop of Poitiers who had led the fight against the Arian heresy in the West. His years are ca. 315 to 367, and he was one of the earliest and most important western Fathers. Most of his works were composed in the context of the Arian struggle, and Erasmus in his preface uses the example of St. Hilary or at least the occasion of his role in that widespread controversy to draw certain lessons about doctrinal controversy in general and the recently arisen Lutheran controversy in particular. It is this aspect of the essay which gave it a special thrust in its own day and which continues to render it of considerable interest and importance. Indeed it contains some of Erasmus' most pungent comments on the nature of theology and on the baleful consequences of theological argument and contention. "The sum and substance of our religion is peace and concord," he tells us in a frequently quoted sentence from the preface, and his recurrent theme is that excessive theologizing destroys the unanimity that should exist among Christians whose faith ought to be manifested in their lives rather than in their debates and quarrels. "Once faith was more a matter of a way of life than of a profession of articles," he declares in another memorable passage. The significance of this familiar Erasmian message restated so forcefully in the midst of the religious crisis which had now developed can easily be grasped. And it seems quite evident too that Erasmus has taken this opportunity to expound and defend his point of view before Carondelet and other influential friends.

The preface, however, gave Erasmus' critics additional cause for anger and complaint. The Sorbonne censured several passages from it in 1526. These were passages generally in which Erasmus impugned scholastic theology and excessive dogmatic definition, and the *censurae* corrected his "errors" and accused him of following the heretics.[1] The following year at a conference of theologians at Valladolid in Spain which had been called specifically to examine certain writings of Erasmus several other passages were vehemently attacked.[2] These dealt chiefly with statements about the Holy Spirit or contained Erasmus' comments on St. Hilary's references to the Holy Spirit in his *De Trinitate*. He was accused of questioning the divinity of the Holy Spirit and of denying the Trinity. The Valladolid conference did not condemn Erasmus, but some very serious charges were hurled against him. The essay thus became one of Erasmus' more controversial writings, and the great Maurist edition of Hilary's works in 1693 still warned of Erasmus' preface and of his misrepresentation of the words and role of St. Hilary.[3]

Erasmus' edition of St. Hilary was one of the dozen or more patristic editions which the great scholar prepared, beginning with the edition of St. Jerome published by Froben in 1516.[4]

His Hilary edition replaces an earlier volume of the *Opera* of the Father edited by Robert Fortuné and published by Josse Badius Ascensius in Paris in 1511. It appears that Erasmus based his edition on this earlier one, collating it with certain manuscripts and either correcting it or more frequently noting in the margin the variant readings and additions to the text which he had found. The only manuscript we have any specific reference to is one which had been sent to Froben by Maternus Hatten, vicar of the cathedral of Speyer, in May 1522.[5] A revised edition was brought out by the Froben firm in 1535, and subsequent revisions were published in Paris in 1544 and in Basel in 1550. Erasmus considered his

---

1. *Collectio judiciorum de novis erroribus*, ed. Charles du Plessis d'Argentré, 3 vols. (Paris, 1728–36), II 73, 76–77. The censured passages are indicated in the text.
2. Marcel Bataillon, *Erasme et l'Espagne* (Paris, 1937), Chap. V, and Allen, VI 471. The passages criticized at Valladolid are also indicated in the text.
3. See Migne, *PL*, IX 14–15.
4. Olin, *Six Essays*, essay 3.
5. Allen, V 73.

dedicatory letter to Carondelet an important one and asked to have it included among the *epistolae* in his own *Opera omnia.*[6]

To the most reverend Father in Christ and Lord, Jean Carondelet, Archbishop of Palermo, Highest Counselor of the Imperial Court in Brabant, greetings from Erasmus of Rotterdam:

Unless the word Destiny is entirely meaningless, most illustrious Prelate, indeed I think I am destined to return again and again into labyrinths of the kind from which comes a great deal of vexation and weariness but the least possible measure of glory. In fact, without actual experience no one will believe, unless he personally has made the test, what effort he must expend who tries to emend the text of ancient authors which have been corrupted in various ways through fault of the times and copyists but above all because of the rashness of half-learned and foolhardy men. But it seems to me to be a mark of a great and lofty spirit publicly to serve all well even without the exception of receiving thanks for such service. Further, it is the mark of even a loftier spirit and one which is wholly regal, as the saying goes, to be ill spoken of when one has done something worthwhile. And I would be more vexed that this has happened so often to me if I did not observe that the same thing has happened not only to all who have tried by their own industry to do something notably useful in the affairs of men, but even to St. Jerome himself whose learning or holiness is unsurpassed in the Latin world.

I had found the editing of Jerome's works a very arduous task, but editing Hilary's text entailed even greater labor. The latter's style, even where the subject matter itself is clear, is difficult to understand and susceptible to corruption. What, then, do you think was the nature of the task, when in that peculiar style of his he discusses rather than explains matters which are not only very difficult but even inexplicable? Yet scarcely in the case of another author has the rashness of the

6. The following English translation of this letter was made by James F. Brady and John C. Olin from the Latin text in Allen, V 173–92. For an analysis of this letter, see John C. Olin, "Erasmus and His Edition of St. Hilary," *Erasmus in English*, 9 (1978), 8–11.

half-learned allowed itself greater liberty, and that especially with regard to *De Trinitate* and *De Synodis*. Because theological problems fraught with danger are treated in these works the greatest care must be taken, nor must the slightest change be made. If we discover after comparing different copies that in some places prefatory remarks have been added to the beginning of chapters and also flourishes at the end and that in the middle patches have been sewn on, we are discovering that in some places someone with little learning has tried to explain more completely and clearly what Hilary in his own fashion had said. On some pages twenty or thirty lines had been added.[7]

How often they excise passages which seemed at variance with the opinions accepted among the orthodox. Indeed in more than twenty places they had compounded a remedy, especially where he debates about the pains and torments which affected the body and soul of our Lord Jesus Christ. He does this in several places but chiefly in the tenth book of *De Trinitate*, though so confusedly that sometimes he clearly seems to attribute to Christ a body and soul subject to no troublesome conditions. When, to illustrate this, he used the comparison of a weapon penetrating water or fire by a violent thrust without the sign of a wound because the body attacked is not susceptible of a wound, although it is the nature of a weapon to inflict a wound, someone took it upon himself to add the qualification "if however this comparison can aptly be made." Again when a little later he added that "that body of the Lord may indeed have had pain similar in nature to ours, if our body is so constituted that it treads upon the waves and walks upon the waters," etc., concluding from this difference undoubtedly that the body of Jesus even in the sensation of pain was unlike our bodies, they had corrected the text to read as follows: "That body of the Lord may indeed have had (because of sin) pain similar in nature to ours, if our body is so constituted that it treads upon the waves (by its own nature or by the extraordinary help of God) and walks upon the waters," etc.[8]

A little later when St. Hilary had written, "And that man is from God, having indeed a body to suffer, and He did suffer, but not having

---

7. Erasmus' complaints about the liberty of copyists and the corruption of Hilary's text are echoed in P. Smulders, S.J., "Remarks on the Manuscript Tradition of the *De Trinitate* of Saint Hilary of Poitiers," *Studia Patristica*, III Part 1 (Berlin, 1961), 133–34.

8. *De Trinitate* 10.23.

a nature to feel pain," the passage was corrected, that is, corrupted, in this way: "And He did suffer, but not having a nature (weak because of sin like ours) to feel pain." Further on where Hilary had written, "The opinion based on human judgment therefore that He feels pain because He suffers is mistaken," they emended the wording thus: "That He (as if in the flesh of sin) feels pain because He suffers."[9] Likewise at the end of the second book when it was written as follows: "Therefore we must seek this Holy Spirit, we must deserve Him, and then we must hold Him by that faithfulness to and observance of the commandments," they had woven in, "we must deserve Him, we must adore Him." They feared undoubtedly that someone might suspect that he thought the Holy Spirit should not be adored when he teaches in many ways that the Father and the Son should be adored but makes no such pronouncement about the Spirit. Evidently this was because it did not come to his mind or because at that time this had not yet been precisely defined.

It is amazing, however, that the same individuals did not also corrupt the end of this work where consistently it is written: "May I adore you, our Father, and your Son together with you, and may I be deserving of your Holy Spirit who is from you through the only begotten Son." For here also when he declares that the Father and the Son "should be adored," he says only that the Holy Spirit "should be deserved." We have discovered such additions in more than thirty places in Hilary, although we have cited no more than one or two passages as examples to avoid irritating the reader. Again I am amazed that when he writes that the Holy Spirit is from the Father through the Son and that He does not proceed from both, it was not also corrected. Indeed in one particular text I discovered this correction: *through Him* was changed to *with Him.*

Now what is this rashness shown toward the writings of others, especially those of ancient authors whose memory, as it should be, is sacred to us, I mean the readiness to erase, expunge, add to, delete, change, forge—when there is no personal risk—any author at will? Is

---

9. *De Trinitate* 10.47. The reference to this theme in Hilary's *De Trinitate* recalls Erasmus' dispute with John Colet in 1499 on the nature of Christ's agony in the garden of Gethsemane. He upheld the traditional view that Christ in His human nature feared death. He subsequently published a printed version of their exchange under the title of the *Disputatiuncula de tedio, pavore, tristicia Iesu.*

the object of this to prevent anyone from thinking that there are any errors in the works of the ancients? Indeed whoever should try that would wash a brick, as they say.[10] God has willed that the happy state of freedom from error be reserved for the sacred books alone. Everyone else, however learned and keen sighted he may be, on occasion stumbles and gropes blindly. Obviously therefore all remember that they are human and as humans they are read by us, with discrimination, with judgment, and at the same time with indulgence. But if anything occurs in these writings which has the appearance of error, when the author has a different opinion, the work must not be contaminated, but scruples should be allayed by adding explanatory notes. Peter Lombard attempts this in very many places, at the same time citing and explaining several passages concerning the pain and fear of Christ in the third book of the *Sentences*.[11]

That famous epigrammatic poet does not tolerate him who wishes to show his cleverness in another's book.[12] But who would tolerate those who arrogate so much to themselves that they sew on their own patches in place of the genuine text wherever they please? It is a mark of courtesy to interpret a work properly. To change arbitrarily the actual words in the works of the ancients, however, is an act of rashness, not to say irreverence. And yet we discover that this has been done even in the books of St. Ambrose and in more than one place. If the risk to the writer must be taken into account when a text is changed, it would be more fitting to do this in the books of modern authors whom time has not yet placed outside the uncertainty of judgment, nor death thus far delivered from envy. Now almost too scrupulously fair toward the ancient writers, we distort certain passages which have nothing wrong with them in the authors of our own age and we interpret everything improperly, just as if such an exegete would not be likely to find even in the Pauline epistles something which he would be able to misrepresent as erroneous, as suspect of heresy, as scandalous, as irreverent.

But let us drop this subject. It is better that I briefly express my opinion about each of Hilary's works individually. He wrote the twelve

10. Terence, *Phormio*, 186. See also Erasmus' *Adagiorum chiliades*, No. 347.
11. *Sentences* 3.15.5. In the part Erasmus refers to, Peter Lombard discusses certain passages from Hilary.
12. Martial 1, preface.

books of *De Trinitate* when an exile in Phrygia where he had been banished by the faction of a certain Saturninus, bishop of Arles, which had circumvented the Emperor. Indeed the Arian faction had sunk its roots so widely, had become so strong, that the world for a long time wavered in doubt as to which cause it would espouse, especially when the Emperor Constantius by the use of exile, plundering, threats, and alarms forced men to go over to the side of the Arians. Wherefore Hilary complained to Caesar that it was shameful that men in an unprecedented fashion were being forced rather than persuaded to accept the faith, granting that the faith of the Arians was sincere. And indeed he himself testifies in several places that for a long time he was silent. He observed this silence either because the soul even of that great man felt some doubt amid such widespread discord in the world or because when there was no hope that the better side could win he thought it preferable to look to a calm silence rather than to exacerbate, not remove, the world's general depravity by untimely boldness. He seems to have exerted all his energy, however, to manifest and put forth in this work whatever he could by his natural ability, by his eloquence, and by his knowledge of Holy Scripture. For we see that it was usually the ambition of distinguished writers as well as of outstanding painters and sculptors to leave in some one work a finished and complete example of their art by which posterity might be able to evaluate what they would have been able to do, if they had wished to exert their fullest powers. Virgil seems to have attempted this in the *Georgics*, Ovid in his *Medea*, Cicero in *De Oratore*, Augustine in *The City of God*, Jerome in the *Commentaries on the Prophets*, Thomas Aquinas on the subject of the Eucharist, Bernard on the Canticle.

We are stimulated more to this effort if there should come to hand a theme which is not only lofty and important but also new and accordingly not hackneyed. Indeed the grandeur of a work besides permitting a lofty treatment also lends dignity of itself, and the newness adds to the charm. Moreover, the ancient authors philosophized very rarely about theological questions, and they did not dare to make any pronouncement about such matters which was not clearly set forth in those writings whose authority is inviolable to us. But the irreverent rashness of the Cerinthians and the Ebionites first drove John the

Evangelist to commit to writing certain mysteries concerning the divine nature of Christ.[13] Later the elaborate subtlety of the Arians drove the orthodox to a greater necessity—namely, to discuss which great controversy the question of the extension of the divine nature, of the creation of the Son, of the adoption into the name of God, and then the matter of ὁμοούσιον and ὁμοιούσιον, and finally to formulate definitions about these matters.[14] Repeatedly the most saintly Hilary deplores this necessity, knowing full well how fraught with danger and how inimical to devotion it is to speak out on matters which are beyond discussion, to examine matters beyond understanding, to make pronouncements on matters beyond the grasp of the intelligence.[15] But St. Augustine was carried still farther on this sea, evidently because the joy of inquiry like a favorable breeze lured the rich talent of the man from one realm of thought to another. More restraint is exercised by Peter Lombard, who when he cites another's views does not lightly add anything of his own, or if he adds anything, he offers it with diffidence. At length the matter advanced to the point of irreverent audacity.

But may the ancients gain the pardon besought by those whom necessity has driven to this pass. On what pretext will we ask pardon for ourselves, we who raise so many meddlesome, not to say irreverent, questions concerning matters very far removed from our nature, and who formulate so many definitions about matters which could have been either ignored without loss of salvation or left in doubt?[16] Or is he not destined to have fellowship with the Father, Son, and Holy Spirit who cannot disentangle according to the method of philosophy what distinguishes the Father from the Son or the Holy Spirit from both or what the difference is between the generation of the Son from the Father and the procession of the Spirit? If I believe, as has been handed down, that the three are of one nature, what is the need of

13. The Cerinthians and Ebionites were early heretical sects, both of which held that Jesus was born as a mere man. Irenaeus asserted that St. John wrote his Gospel to refute the heretic Cerinthus.

14. ὁμοούσιον and ὁμοιούσιον mean "of the same substance" and "of similar substance," respectively, and were terms used in the controversy in the fourth century over the divinity of Christ.

15. This passage is one which was censured by the Sorbonne in 1526. The *censura* declared that St. Hilary did *not* think it dangerous to make pronouncements which were in conformity with an ecumenical council.

16. Also censured by the Sorbonne as being "contumelious" toward General Councils and the study of the Doctors of the Church.

labored disputation? If I do not believe, no human reasons will convince me. And such a dangerous inquisitiveness has generally arisen in us from the study of philosophy, a fact which the illustrious Tertullian, the most learned by far of all the Latin theologians, has asserted in several places, although he himself was a philosopher of the first rank.

Socrates of Athens, to whom is attributed this famous axiom, "What is above us is of no concern to us," brought down philosophy from the contemplation of natural phenomena into the midst of human life and frequently quoted that line from Homer:

What evil and what good have been wrought in thy halls.[17]

Nevertheless, many things are apprehended with certainty concerning the nature of the stars, the motion of the celestial spheres, lightning, the winds, the rainbow, and similar phenomena, because either the bodily senses themselves or the observation of effects provide the beginnings of knowledge for matters of this nature, and the knowledge is especially pleasing and moves one at the same time to wonder and to love of the Maker. But yet because the wise man perceived that men sat idle all their lifetime in such study and neglected meanwhile what has greater relevance for us, he called down all study from the contemplation of natural phenomena to the consideration of morals.[18] But those questions which we investigate and which we define sometimes have not been recorded in Holy Scripture, so that even if they cannot be understood they must at least be believed; nor can they, as they stand, be proved by any satisfactory arguments or grasped by the intellect or even vaguely conceived of by like means. And after the richest talents have applied all their energy for a long time to the investigation of them, this at last is the final result of their effort: they realize they know nothing; and what is more they contribute nothing to the devout life. Thus nowhere more does that well-known passage of Paul apply, "Knowledge puffs up, charity builds up."[19]

What arrogance, what contentions, what tumult, what discord in

17. *Odyssey* 4.392.
18. The wise man is Socrates, and Erasmus here and above is echoing what Cicero said of Socrates in *Tusculanae disputationes* 5.4.10.
19. 1 Cor. 8:1. The passage beginning "But those questions" was censured by the Sorbonne which defended the definition of doctrine about the Trinity and denied that this was "knowledge that puffs up."

the world do we see gush forth from this kind of absurd learning! Although our life is so fleeting, we neglect meanwhile those things without which no one has any hope of attaining salvation. Unless I pardon my brother's sins against me, God will not pardon my transgressions against Him. Unless I have a pure heart, I shall not see God. Therefore with all my energy I must aim, I must practice, I must strive to cleanse my soul of malice, envy, hatred, pride, avarice, and lust. You will not be damned if you should not know whether the Spirit proceeding from the Father and the Son has a single or a double principle, but you will not escape perdition unless you see to it in the meantime that you have the fruits of the Spirit, which are charity, joy, peace, patience, kindness, goodness, forbearance, gentleness, faith, moderation, self-control, and chastity.[20] Toward this end the chief concern of our study therefore must be focused and directed. Not that I think either that inquiry in the three divisions of philosophy or that the investigation of phenomena beyond this world should be entirely condemned, provided that the inquirer is endowed with rich talent and is purged of rashness in defining, of obstinacy, and of the bane of harmony, the stubborn passion to get the upper hand.

The sum and substance of our religion is peace and concord. This can hardly remain the case unless we define as few matters as possible and leave each individual's judgment free on many questions. This is because the obscurity of most questions is great and the malady is for the most part intrinsic to our human nature: we do not know how to yield once a question has been made a subject of contention. And after the debate has warmed up each one thinks that the side he has undertaken rashly to defend is absolute truth. In this regard certain men were so lacking in moderation that after defining everything in theology they contrived for those who are no more than men a new status of divinity,[21] and this has aroused more questions and greater commotion in the world than the Arians in their foolishness once did. But certain pundits on some occasions are ashamed to have no rejoinder to make. On the contrary this is indeed the mark of theological learning: to define nothing beyond what is recorded in Holy Scripture, but to dis-

---

20. Gal. 5:22. This sentence was censured by the Sorbonne.

21. This sentence was censured by the Sorbonne. The *censura* defended the value of scholastic theology.

pense in good faith what is there recorded.[22] Many puzzling questions are now referred to an Ecumenical Council. It would be much more fitting to defer such questions to that time when we shall see God face to face without the mirror and without the mystery.[23]

But these matters will be discussed perhaps more appropriately elsewhere. I now return to our main theme. The subject of Hilary's *De Trinitate* was especially magnificent and worthy of his lofty style, and it was new because, unless I am mistaken, Hilary was the first of the Latins to draw the sword of his eloquence against the Arians. That engagement also brought a great deal of fame to him chiefly because the issue was joined with a renowned foe. I do not doubt that several among the Greeks besides Athanasius did the same. But it was a practice of that age to cite no one by name with the exception of Holy Scripture, especially if the material was drawn from Greek sources, for these they claimed for themselves as if they had a right to them. In any case it seems to me to be the part of candor not to conceal the names of those whom you have used to your advantage. Hilary governs his expression throughout his work, however, as if he personally had dug each of his ideas out of the sacred books. And although I might have wished that such a talent, such an eloquence, such a mind might have richer and more fruitful material, nevertheless the profit to the reader from this work will also be not insignificant because he explains with no less felicity than accuracy, in my opinion, very many passages in John and Paul which are quite obscure.

Furthermore Jerome in a certain letter to Paulinus as he passes judgment on the learned writes that Hilary is distinguished by a lofty Gallic style although in other respects his manner is marked by the embellishments of the Greeks; he further says that he is read in vain by the more ignorant because he sometimes uses long involved periods.[24] Although everywhere Hilary has his own characteristic style, it is especially present in this work. For to the subject matter which, as is probable, he bor-

22. In his *Ratio verae theologiae* (1518) Erasmus declares that "the chief aim of theologians is to interpret wisely Holy Scripture." LB, V 83.

23. Cf. 1 Cor. 13:12. The above paragraph was a particularly controversial part of the preface. Five separate statements or propositions from it were censured by the Sorbonne, the sentence beginning "But certain pundits" being one of these. The "pundits" (Erasmus actually uses the term "rabbis") were understood to be scholastic doctors, and the *censura* states that they are ashamed when they see Councils contemned and Holy Scripture twisted *ad haereticum sensum.*

24. Epistle 58.10.

rowed from the Greeks he has added Gallic grandiloquence; for a learned simplicity is characteristic of the Greeks, and a graceful and clear style is more to their liking than a lofty and labored one. And he often plays with standard themes [*loci communes*] such as the following: it is very risky to discuss theological questions; it is deplorable for a man to incur the shame of defending stubbornly in debate even an acknowledged error; Holy Scripture should not be twisted to our inclinations, but our way of thinking should be corrected in accordance with the norm of Scripture.[25] Moreover he frequently rises to what I might call the grandeur of theatrical embellishment, especially in those parts which easily lend themselves to brilliant expression, as for instance parts dealing with the structure of the universe, the nature of the heavenly bodies, the harmonious discord of the elements, the gush of springs, the course of rivers, the ebb and flow of the tides, and the various fruits of the earth. And not infrequently he rises to the grandeur of tragic figures, personification and apostrophe, by means of which he addresses either heretics or God Himself.

Perhaps this grandiloquence is a characteristic of the Gallic genius. Sulpicius Severus possesses something of this sort, and Eucherius also has it; the latter's is a grandiloquence which is even more elaborate but marked by a more felicitous care, if I am any judge.[26] Nor does Guillaume Budé, most renowned of the writers of this age, fail to reach the level of this style. His style is so elevated that one imagines one hears a trumpet sounding, not a man, and so felicitously finished that he never cloys the learned reader and keeps at a distance those who have only a rudimentary education. Furthermore obscurity of expression results, albeit only in part, from the fact that Hilary often barely rounds off in a long circuitous way a sentence composed of various clauses. Clarity, however, is also hindered by the fact that in handling a subject in itself involved and subtle he has also sought applause for his acumen and sometimes for his richness of style—a mannerism which likewise marks the writing of Budé in his *De asse*. But this disadvantage becomes easier to handle once you have become accustomed

25. See *De Trinitate* 1.18. This last sentence recalls the dictum of Egidio da Viterbo in his opening address to the Fifth Lateran Council in May 1512: "Men must be changed by religion, not religion by men."
26. Both Sulpicius Severus and St. Eucherius were early Christian authors, and both were Gauls, Eucherius being a bishop of Lyons in the first half of the fifth century.

to it. For as you may have difficulty understanding certain speakers unless you hear them with some frequency, and as a type of music is less enjoyable for the very reason that it is new and unusual, so because each author has his own style that style becomes more familiar and therefore more pleasing by our becoming accustomed to it. Indeed even Titus Livy, the most pleasing of writers, is at first taste somewhat bitter. This happens, however, chiefly in the case of those authors who, aside from what I might call their individual flavor, bring to their work a capacity for taking pains and a striving for subtlety. Among orators of this kind Quintilian especially ought to be classed, and among poets Horace.

It appears that St. Jerome perceived this. He writes as follows in a letter to a Roman orator: "Hilary, a confessor of my times and a bishop, imitated the twelve books of Quintilian both in style and in number."[27] It is most difficult, however, for the man who either teaches the rules of an art or offers arguments on matters naturally subtle to combine a concern for polished style with clear expression. In addition to these difficulties Quintilian also strove for brevity. When I consider the varied diction of the ancient writers it seems that hardly any provincials successfully reproduce the simplicity of Roman speech except the few who were educated at Rome from boyhood. For both Tertullian and Apuleius have a style of their own, and in the decrees of the Africans, many of which Augustine refers to against Petilianus and Cresconius, you may observe an anxious striving for eloquence, but such is their style that you recognize their African origin. Augustine also sometimes is rather obscure and labored, nor is Cyprian entirely without African traits, although he is clearer than the others. Nor is it strange if a Gaul reflects something Gallic or a Carthaginian something Carthaginian when traces of Paduan idiom in Livy's Latin is offensive to some. Generally, however, the striving is greater in one whose command of a language is characteristic of provincials rather than citizens and who is a foreigner rather than native-born. Undoubtedly this is why that old woman, as the story goes, called Theophrastus a "foreigner" because his language was too Attic.[28]

27. Epistle 70.5. Quintilian's great work was *Institutiones oratoriae*, which like Hilary's *De Trinitate* consisted of twelve books.
28. This story is told in Cicero's *Brutus* 172 and in Quintilian 8.1.2.

Nevertheless, it seems to me indeed that St. Jerome is misusing the term "imitated" for one who is like or resembles another. For the child is like or resembles the parent rather than imitates him. But it is nature which in the production of offspring more truly imitates now the father, now the mother, now the grandfather or grandmother, now the aunt or uncle. Accordingly, imitation is a matter of effort, likeness is a result. Nor do we always resemble that which we imitate, and sometimes resemblance is unwitting. Moreover, though perhaps it may not be improper to emulate Quintilian's style, yet it would rightly seem characteristic of what I might call an over-anxious scrupulosity to have aimed at even the same number of books especially when the subject was different. For the rest, as Hilary is unlike Quintilian in the fullness of style (for he continually repeats and hammers home the same idea in different words), so he is almost in distress in imitating a concern for order, spending no little time in promising what he is going to say and in repeating what he has said (in this indeed he is more like Aristotle than Quintilian), and spending much time in devising transitions to make neat connections between the various parts and much time apologizing when, as the occasion arises, he touched on a topic which according to the division of contents he promised should have been treated in another place. In two respects he recalls Pliny who wrote a history of the world, first because of a preface which is too elaborate, secondly because he intended the first book, which, it appears, he wrote last, to be a catalogue of the entire work.

And so much for the work bearing the title *De Trinitate*. The *De Synodis* follows it and treats the same subject in another way. For it reports on those assemblies of bishops in which the heresy of the Arians was condemned. He wrote this work for the bishops of Gaul, congratulating them for holding back from the Arian faction amid such great confusion in the world. He translates it, as he himself testifies, from the Greek; he takes the liberty, however, of avoiding everywhere a word-for-word translation and only renders the thought, and where the opportunity presents itself he mixes in his own ingredients. He allows himself this liberty also in discussing the Psalms, as we shall soon explain in its proper place. Furthermore, although this book restates the synodal decisions, he nevertheless seeks to avoid the risk of defending them, not so much, I think, because he lacked confidence in those for whom he was writing *De Synodis* or because there were certain propositions of which he did not fully approve, but because of what I might call a scrupulous concern to avoid strong assertions, a concern which little by little we have so forgotten that nothing causes shame. For thus generally in the affairs of men a situation from modest beginnings gains greater significance until it proliferates into something evil. St. Hilary at the end of the twelfth book of *De Trinitate* does not dare to make any pronouncement about the Holy Spirit except that He is the Spirit of God—and it was unlikely that he would have dared to say this unless he had read it in Paul: he does not dare to use the word "creature" because he has not read it anywhere in Holy Scripture.[29]

This kind of profession would not be sufficient in this age because the needful diligence of the ancient Fathers has been very instructive for us, but we are carried far beyond what is needful. Once faith was more a matter of a way of life than of a profession of articles. Soon necessity inspired the imposition of articles, but these were few and apostolic in their moderation. Then the wickedness of the heretics made for a more precise examination of the sacred books, and intransigence necessitated the definition of certain matters by the authority of synods. Finally faith began to reside in the written word rather than in the soul, and there were almost as many faiths as men.[30] Articles increased, but sincerity decreased: contention boiled over, charity grew cold. The teachings of Christ, which in former times were not touched by the clash of words, began to depend on the support of philosophy: this was the first step of the Church on the downward path. There was an increase of wealth and an accretion of power. Furthermore, the intervention of imperial authority in this situation did not improve much the purity of faith. At length the consequence of all this was sophistical controversy and the eruption of thousands of articles. And then it became a matter of intimidation and threats. Although life may abandon us, although faith may be more on our lips than in our hearts, although that genuine understanding of Holy

---

29. This last sentence was one of the passages criticized at the Valladolid conference in 1527.

30. Erasmus is echoing Terence's *Quot homines, tot sententiae* (*Phormio* 454).

Scripture may fail us, yet we force men by intimidation to believe what they do not believe, to love what they do not love, and to understand what they do not understand. Compulsion is incompatible with sincerity, and nothing is pleasing to Christ unless it is voluntary.[31] St. Jerome calls to mind this work in a letter to Florentius, in these words: "I ask that you send me the very comprehensive book *De Synodis* of St. Hilary which I had copied with my own hand at Trier."[32]

Coupled with this is the book he wrote against the Emperor Constantius who favored the Arian faction, but he wrote this book against him, unless I am mistaken, after the Emperor had died. For he is reproached in strong terms, whereas two other books addressed to the same man—one written when he was alive; the other, it is believed, he also presented to him—are milder in tone. St. Jerome recalls this in the *Catalogus* [*scriptorum ecclesiasticorum*]: "Also there is that essay of his addressed to Constantius which he had presented to him when he was living in Constantinople. There is another one against Constantius which he wrote after his death." So much for Jerome. The harsher tone of the work against the deceased was due to religious devotion, the milder tone of his plea to the living was inspired by Christian prudence which prefers to cure an evil, should the opportunity be offered, rather than to aggravate it. But none of these books in my opinion should be considered finished. For although they promise a piece of work complete and developed in detail they do not fulfill their promise, but suddenly as it were they fall silent. Because of the similarity of subject matter there is joined to these an epistle written against Auxentius whom he prosecuted for his involvement in the Arian heresy at Milan.[33] The epistle of Auxentius in which he offers a defense of himself to the Emperors Valentinian and Valens accompanies it.

During my discussion of the foregoing the thought struck me in passing that perhaps some will be astonished that Hilary has scarcely

31. These last sentiments regarding imperial intervention and the use of force are most interesting to consider in view of the times and the person Erasmus is addressing. The entire passage beginning with the words "The teachings of Christ" had at one time been obliterated in the actual copy of the Hilary edition Erasmus sent to Jean de Carondelet: Houghton Library, Harvard University, *fNC5/Er153/523h/(A).

32. Epistle 5.2.

33. Auxentius was appointed to the see of Milan by Constantius in 355 and was a major supporter of Arianism in the West.

anything to say about the Holy Spirit, although the thrust of so many books and so much zeal and effort and so many arguments, decisions, and anathemas is to make us believe that the Son is true God and of the same essence, or, as Hilary several times says, of the same genus and nature as the Father—the Greeks use the term ὁμοούσιον (that is, equal in power, wisdom, goodness, eternity, immortality, and all other attributes)—and although the entire controversy about the name of true God, about the term ὁμοούσιον, and about equality has no less a bearing on the Spirit than on the Son. Indeed nowhere does he write that the Holy Spirit must be adored and nowhere does he assign the word God to Him, save that in one or two passages in *De Synodis* he refers to those who dared to call the Father, Son, and Holy Spirit three Gods as condemned.[34] The reason was either that he thought at that time it was more important to defend the Son whose human nature made it more difficult to win assent to the divinity of Him who was also human—and the Arians were trying to rob Him of divinity, whereas the question about the Holy Spirit had not yet been raised— or that it was the scrupulous concern of the ancients that, although they worshiped God devoutly, they nevertheless did not dare to make any pronouncements about Him which were not explicitly set forth in the sacred books. Though in Scripture the name of God is several times assigned to the Son, yet nowhere is it explicitly assigned to the Holy Spirit.[35] It should be acknowledged, however, that the devout probing of the orthodox later ascertained with sufficient proof from Holy Scripture that whatever was attributed to the Son was appropriate to the Holy Spirit, except for the individuality of the Person. But because of the impenetrable obscurity of theological questions there existed reverential reluctance in assigning names: they thought it was wrong in theology to use words other than Holy Scripture used and the general authority of the Church handed down. They had read Holy Spirit, they had read the Spirit of God, they had read the Spirit of Christ. They had learned from the Gospel that the Holy Spirit is not separated from the Father and the Son. For the Apostles are taught to baptize in the name of the Father and of the Son and of the Holy Spirit. The fellowship of the three Persons is preserved in those short

34. This sentence also came under attack at the Valladolid conference.
35. This sentence too was criticized at Valladolid.

customary prayers left to us from the most ancient usage of the Church, at once brief and learned, in which the Father is addressed in prayer through the Son in the unity of the Holy Spirit. The Father is most frequently called God, the Son several times, the Holy Spirit explicitly never.

And these remarks of mine are not meant to call into question what has been handed down to us from Holy Scripture by the authority of the orthodox Fathers, but to show how much reverential reluctance the ancients had in making pronouncements in theology, although they had a greater devotion to theology than even we have—we who have rushed to such extremes of boldness that we have no scruples about dictating to the Son the way in which His mother should be honored. We dare to call the Holy Spirit true God, proceeding from the Father and the Son, which the ancients did not dare to do, but on the other hand we have no scruples about driving Him repeatedly out of the temple of our soul by our evil deeds, just as if it were our belief that the Holy Spirit is nothing more than a meaningless name.[36] By the same token the majority of the ancients who revered the Son with the greatest devotion nevertheless feared to use the term ὁμοούσιον because that term is nowhere used in Holy Scripture. Indeed the progress of the Church at first depended on purity of life rather than on an exact knowledge of the divine nature, and it has never sustained a greater loss than when it seemed to make the greatest possible advances in philosophical knowledge, yes, and in the things of this world, not because they are evil in themselves but because they frequently involve man in the cares of this world.

Nor is learning evil in itself, but it often begets factions and dissension. The defense of the Catholic faith is put forward as a pretext, and in the meantime personal feelings become involved and the devil's business is pursued in the name of Christ. I do not say this because I suspect anything of the sort about Hilary, which we certainly have found in the case of certain men of this age. Nevertheless, when he was alive he was a man; he did not lack human feelings; he could make mistakes, he could be misled. He had been banished and condemned by Saturninus; he spent several years in exile among the

36. The first part of this sentence and the last portion of the preceding one evoked considerable objection at Valladolid.

Phrygians, notorious for their uncivilized manners; he was hard-pressed in every way by the Arian faction. These influences and very many others could have played upon the feelings of even a good man under the guise of piety.

I do not deny that heretical intransigence must be abhorred, if incurable. But meanwhile because of our hatred of one error we must beware of falling into another. Let us preserve that self-control, to prevent controversy from convincing us that the straight is crooked and the bitter sweet and vice versa. If this has happened to nearly all the ancients to some extent, indeed I shall not be expressing disapproval of the character of a learned man in the remarks I am going to make. Tertullian while he fought too aggressively against those who set a higher value on marriage than was reasonable fell into another pitfall in condemning what Christ approved, and demanding what He did not demand but only recommended. Jerome fights with such excessive zeal against those who extolled marriage to the detriment of virginity that he himself with difficulty could defend his case in an unfriendly court, if he should be charged with treating wedlock and a second marriage without enough respect. Montanus in opposing rather vigorously those who opened the doors of the Church indiscriminately to the worthy and the unworthy at a time when there was an inordinate relaxation of Church discipline fell into the opposite error. St. Augustine in combating Pelagius with all his energy somewhere attributes less to free will than those who now reign in the theological schools think ought to be attributed.[37]

I could mention very many examples to illustrate this point even from modern authors, but it is better, I believe, not to be too wordy in dealing with an unpleasant subject. We now turn to the subject of Hilary who because of the sanctity of his life, because of his extraordinary learning, and because of his admirable eloquence was the light of his age. How great is the anger with which he attacks the Arians, again and again calling them impious, diabolic, blasphemous, devils, plagues, Antichrists! For already the label heretic is of little importance. And yet it is probable that there were men in the Arian

---

37. One of the basic issues in the Lutheran controversy was the question of free will. The next year—in 1524—Erasmus was to write and publish his treatise *De libero arbitrio* defending the freedom of the will against Luther's doctrine. He will uphold a very moderate position, neither Pelagian nor Lutheran.

faction who were convinced that their preaching about Christ was true and devout. Their doctrine rested on many and important authorities. Some passages in Holy Scripture gave the appearance of supporting it, and rational arguments were not lacking which displayed some semblance of truth. In addition there was the authority of Caesar and beyond that the huge number of adherents, which by right should have been added, if the majority were always the better side. Finally it was a controversy about matters far beyond human comprehension. I would have recommended that anyone in agreement with Arius be admonished and instructed, but I would not immediately have called him Satan or Antichrist.

Indeed if these accusations must be hurled against anyone who errs on some point, what shall we do with our Hilary himself, not to mention so many outstanding doctors of the Church—Hilary who in so many passages seems to think that Christ had a body which was not susceptible to pain, that hunger, thirst, weariness, and other states of this kind were not natural to it but were assumed? For he plainly wrote this in his exposition of Psalm 68, while in a council he pronounces an anathema against the man who would deny that the Father alone is called unborn God, as if the Holy Spirit either is not God or is also born Himself of the Father. No one may plead that in councils Hilary is simply repeating decisions already made and is not their author as well. For he makes the same statement in his own name in the twelfth book of *De Trinitate*, asserting that the Father alone is unborn God, that the Son alone is begotten, not created, that the Holy Spirit proceeds from both in such a way that He can neither be said to be born nor yet be admitted to share the name of creature, which some assign to the Son, calling Him a creature, for we utterly condemn the term creature no less in the case of the Holy Spirit than in that of the Father and the Son. And both elsewhere and in the eighth book of *De Trinitate* he maintains with great vehemence that we also are one with the Father and the Son by nature and not by adoption or by consensus only. Again in the third book of his work, but more in the tenth book, he speaks in such a way about the body of Christ that apparently he thinks that the Virgin Mary contributed nothing of her own except the service of conception, pregnancy, and parturition, although the orthodox believe that Christ was conceived by the agency of the Spirit, it is true, but from the substance of the Virgin's body. And indeed there are other passages which demand a courteous and proper interpreter. But what law does he establish in his own case who becomes so furious with others?[38]

We say this by no means to dim the glory and damage the reputation of a very holy and learned man, but to warn the bishops and theologians of our day against allowing themselves to be caught unawares by the kind of thing we see happen to so great a man. First, it is the part of evangelical honesty to interpret fairly the deeds and writings of brothers. Then, if anyone has erred whom we cannot ignore, he should not at once be subjected to our wrath, since everyone errs, but an effort should be made to eliminate the error without hurting the person concerned. Finally, a neighbor should be admonished as we would wish to be admonished, if we had fallen into human error. Today we see some who falsely censure everything in the books of others, who vent what I might call their rage against the good name of a neighbor, although in their own books one finds clear blasphemies against Christ. This would be an idle comment, if I should not point out in reality that in the books of certain men, which in great numbers now for the past several years have rushed forth from every quarter as champions of the majesty of the pope, there are notions openly insulting to Christ which at the same time give strong support to the dignity of a human being. If the actual facts should not provide conclusive confirmation for this, I would be an unreliable witness.

I do not condemn the zeal of those who with moderation defend the authority of the pope against the seditious impudence of certain men; nevertheless I would prefer that the glory of Christ so flourish that it eclipse the glory of all the world, even of Peter and Paul, should it be possible, not only of the Roman pontiff. For thus eclipsed we would truly be glorious, if we of ourselves were nothing, but Christ were all in all. However, I speak about a few who while they strive intemperately to claim for man his proper dignity have not been sufficiently mindful of the dignity of Christ to whom alone all dignity is owed. In matters like this, although a Maevius may excuse himself, toward

38. A passage which now follows in the 1523 edition (lines 530–69 in Allen) has been omitted in this translation. Erasmus himself omitted it in the revised edition of Hilary's *Opera* in 1535 because in it he had erroneously discussed a reference in St. Jerome to another Hilary than the one he was concerned with.

others he is so fierce, so pitiless, and so unjust.[39] What judgment can there be in a matter in which hate is so unbridled? The sword of the Gospel's word must always indeed be brandished against all wicked errors, and one should make every effort to combat heresies as they spring up. But this must be our first concern that what we rail at in others is not found in ourselves, and this must be our second that we not be corrupted by our own personal feelings and call what is good evil, what is sweet bitter, what is clear obscure. For this is the mark of stubbornness implanted in the temperaments of the majority of men that they never stop defending a statement they have once made on some occasion or other, even if they discover that they have been wrong. First, shame stands in the way. Through contention it leads to stubbornness, and at length stubbornness develops into a madness. As a consequence, while the dispute becomes violent on both sides, on both sides the truth is lost.[40] The error is called a schism if anyone diminishes the authority of the Roman pontiff. But why is no one disturbed when some men, extraordinarily impudent and basely servile, attribute too much to that authority? If falsehood causes displeasure, why does it not cause displeasure everywhere? Finally, why is the assertion that the Virgin Mother is free from original sin heretical among the Dominicans, orthodox among the Scotists? Is this not tantamount to openly declaring that judgment has been corrupted? Is this "cutting a straight furrow" for the Word of God? We gladly use this Pauline word.[41] Therefore, let the eye of him who is ready to take the mote out of his brother's eye be clear and unclouded. Let us always keep before our eyes the gentleness of Him who, although He alone was free from all error, nevertheless did not extinguish the smoking flax, nor crush the bruised reed.[42] But these matters also will be discussed more appropriately elsewhere.

The *Commentaries on Matthew*, as Jerome calls them, come next. Others have preferred to call them a catalogue because, I believe, he ex-

---

39. Maevius was an inferior Latin poet who had attacked Virgil.

40. An interesting observation (together with the example he gives regarding papal authority) in view of the then very serious Lutheran controversy! Erasmus felt himself caught in the middle between two warring factions.

41. The Pauline word is the Greek verb "to cut straight," which St. Paul uses in 2 Timothy 2:15.

42. Erasmus refers to the prophecy in Is. 42:3 which is also quoted in Matt. 12:20. He has on several occasions used this example in discussing the approach which one should take to Luther at this time.

pounds some headings separately. I do not doubt that he translated this work from Origen; in fact it savors of both the genius and the style of Origen throughout. For although Hilary's work imparts much excellent instruction clearly revealing the author's expert knowledge of Holy Scripture, nevertheless his allegories are rather far-fetched in several instances and sometimes rather harsh, and his excessive preoccupation with allegorizing results in the loss of the historical sense. It is as if there is no place for allegorizing without impairing the historical sense. Sometimes in joining the two (for he also gives his attention to this) he has amused himself, it seems, with his cleverness rather than treated a serious subject. We see, however, that among his innumerable gifts this failing is peculiar to Origen in nearly all his writings. I wish that the man had many imitators of his other qualities as he had some followers even among Latin authors in this aspect of his work. Furthermore Jerome declares that the commentaries which he published on the Psalms were more truly imitations of Origen's commentaries than translations, especially since he himself had made some contributions of his own. What these are the experienced reader will have no difficulty perceiving, for they are by and large the ideas which he had advanced in so many books against the Arians. He himself does not indicate anywhere whom he has followed; however, I think he did this not to conceal his benefactor but to avoid the odium attaching to Origen's name. Ambrose does the same thing everywhere.

Jerome mentions this work in the preface of the second book on Micah. He cites Hilary as having paraphrased nearly forty thousand lines from Origen on the Psalms. One wonders, however, what Hilary's plan was in selecting certain Psalms for translation and passing over the rest, unless by chance it was because he did not happen to come upon the complete work of Origen. He wrote, as Jerome recounts, on the first and second Psalm, then on the fifty-first to the sixty-second, and again on the hundred and eighteenth to the last. But we have more than the number Jerome gives—namely, besides the first two we have commentaries from the fifty-first Psalm to the sixty-ninth and again from the hundred and eighteenth Psalm to the end, except that the last part appears to be missing in the copies. This happened, I suspect, because the final page of the manuscript codices had been either torn off or had worn out. That page as a rule is lost like the last bean plant in the proverb.[43] It is inferred from this that Hilary's work on the Psalms did not reach Jerome in its entirety. For he published the *Catalogus* of famous writers after the death of Hilary, so no one can claim that Hilary made certain additions to his work after Jerome published his *Catalogus*. And he testifies in this connection that he heard from some persons that Hilary had written commentaries on the Song of Songs, but he denies that he had seen this work.

Many works indeed have been lost to us, namely, letters which he wrote to various persons and also a book of hymns. For an extant letter to his daughter Apra has nothing of Hilary and a hymn has far less and not even the character of verse, although Jerome testifies somewhere that he wrote verse. Nevertheless, we have included both to provide a sample for anyone who by chance might wish to make a judgment on these matters. The literary style and composition of Hilary show that he was not infelicitous in writing verse, and perhaps several hymns which the Church sings today, not without art but of uncertain authorship, are his, as for example the hymn *De ligno crucis* which begins "Crux fidelis" and the hymn *De Ioanne Baptista* which begins "Ut queant laxis."[44] We also lack the commentaries on Job which, as Jerome in the same work declares, he paraphrased from Origen. And indeed there is extant among the remains of Origen a commentary on Job, the style of which has no affinity with Hilary's. In fact the preface testifies that this same work had been translated by some others but with neither accuracy nor learning. They made bad Latin out of good Greek. The author of the preface himself in reality makes clear that he was a man who neither knew Latin nor had talent or learning but whose presumptuousness matched his ignorance. We are also lacking that book which he wrote against the prefect Sallustius or against Dioscorus the physician. In it he displayed, it seems, all the powers of his talent and eloquence. St. Jerome makes this point in a letter to the orator Magnus: "In a brief essay which he wrote against Dioscorus the physician he has shown his literary power."[45] Also missing is a book against Valens and Ursacius which contains a history of

43. Erasmus refers to the proverb "Tam perit quam extrema faba" which he found in Festus Pompeius and which he included in his *Adagiorum chiliades* (No. 3372).

44. These two hymns are not by Hilary. The first is the Good Friday *Pange, lingua* by Venantius Fortunatus; the second is by Paulus Diaconus.

45. Epistle 70.5.

the Council of Rimini and the acts of the Council of Seleucia, unless by chance this work was added to *De Synodis.*[46]

So much for the discussion of the individual works of our author. Now we shall offer a few remarks in general about the gifts of this most praiseworthy man. But first what point is there in speaking about the sanctity of his life when ecclesiastical authority has long since inscribed his name in the catalogue of saints? In any event, however, all his books breathe what I might call a wonderful fervor of holiness. How great the authority attaching to his name was may be surmised even from the fact that St. Jerome who came close to belittling Augustine and who did not regard Ambrose too highly often cites Hilary with great veneration, calling him in one place "the Deucalion of the world,"[47] in another "a trumpet of the Latin language," and in another "the Rhône of Latin eloquence." And in more than one passage Jerome made use of the example of that man like a shield against those who falsely charged him with consorting with the Origenists, and he accorded him the fullest testimonial in a letter to Marcella, when he says: "I do not dare criticize so great a man, the most eloquent of his day, who is praised for his meritorious service as a witness as well as for the industry which marked his life and the clarity which characterized his eloquence wherever the name of Rome has reached."[48] What statement covers more ground than this? And Jerome mentions him with no less respect in his Commentary on Isaiah, when he says: "Do not Cyprian, a holy and most eloquent martyr, and Hilary, a confessor of our time, seem to you to be like lofty trees, the kind we find once in a lifetime, in the building of the Church of God?" Indeed St. Augustine also by way of introduction cites not without praise the authority of Hilary in his *De Trinitate.*

On the other hand Hilary was entirely untrained in Hebrew. Hence if he dealt with anything in this language either he used Origen as a source or he handled it with little success. Indeed in explaining a

---

46. Valens and Ursacius were Arian leaders in the West. The Councils of Rimini and Seleucia of 359 were dominated by the Arians. Parts of the book Erasmus refers to came to light later and were published in Paris in 1598.

47. This reference in Jerome to Deucalion (a figure in Greek mythology comparable to Noah) actually applies to another Hilary, and Erasmus should have omitted it in his revised edition as he did the passage mentioned in n. 38.

48. Epistle 34.3. Erasmus will quote this letter again below and will continue to discuss its reference to Hilary.

Psalm he suggests that *Bresith* is more correctly rendered by *in filio* than by *in principio*—so Jerome reports in his notes on *The Traditions of the Hebrews on Genesis*—yet the authority of the Septuagint stands in clear opposition to this, as do Symmachus and Theodotion who fully concur in the translation ἐν ἀρχῇ.[49] It is also at odds with the Hebrew text itself which has *Bresith* and which Aquila takes to mean ἐν κεφαλίδι—that is, *in capitulo*. It does not have *Babem* which is the translation of *in filio*. The word "head," however, is also used for the beginning of anything. In this instance one may rightly ask for consistency in Hilary who, although he highly praises in more than one passage the authority of the Septuagint from which he thinks it wrong to depart a hair's breadth, as it were, has not hesitated to disagree on this word. I suspect that the passage which Jerome alludes to is in the commentary which Hilary wrote on the second Psalm, for there he notes in passing that *Bresith* in Hebrew has three meanings: *in principio*, *in capite*, and *in filio*. Although this word has been rendered in different ways by translators Jerome thinks that there must be no deviation from the authority of the Septuagint. But Hilary made an even more extraordinary mistake with the term *Hosanna*. In his commentary on Matthew he states that the word in Hebrew means *sanctificatio domus David*, although there is nothing in this term which has any affinity with such an interpretation. Indeed in Hebrew *redemptio* is *Pheduth*, and *domus* is *Beth*. Moreover, it is self-evident to all that *David*, since it is the same word in Latin, Greek, and Hebrew, was not inserted here, as Jerome somewhere informs us.

Furthermore he had studied Greek literature superficially, if indeed we believe Jerome whose comment on this I quote from the letter to Marcella wherein he explains the one hundred and twenty-sixth Psalm.

> However, he should not be blamed [he writes], ignorant of Hebrew as he was and with only a smattering of Greek, but the priest Heliodorus with whom he was intimately associated should be blamed. He used to ask him what Origen meant by those words he could not understand.

49. The Septuagint is the Greek version of the Old Testament produced by seventy (*septuaginta*) translators in the third and second centuries B.C. Symmachus and Theodotion as well as Aquila who is mentioned in the next sentence all made Greek translations of the Old Testament in the second century of the Christian era. Origen's *Hexapla* sets forth all of these translations in parallel columns. *Bresith* is the Hebrew word which begins Genesis and is rendered *In principio* in Latin or *In the beginning* in English. The Greek ἐν ἀρχῇ is the equivalent of *in principio*.

Heliodorus, since he could not find Origen's commentary on this Psalm, was not reluctant to insinuate his own opinion rather than to admit his ignorance, and Hilary adopted it and discussed it in clear language and with some eloquence set forth the error of another.[50]

So far we have reviewed the words of Jerome in which while he zealously defends Hilary he treats Heliodorus with repugnance, especially since his explanation is only conjectural. But at this point to defend Hilary in passing, it is not likely, I think, that such a great man was so credulous that in expounding Holy Scripture he placed his total reliance on the judgment of another or that he was so deficient in his knowledge of Greek literature that he could not of himself grasp the meaning of the original, especially in the case of Origen whose language is admirably clear. This we can easily infer from those works surviving in a Latin translation. Yet I do not quite see what caused the displeasure of St. Jerome here. For the fact that he gives various translations from the Hebrew by ancient scholars has no bearing on Hilary who admittedly always follows the Septuagint version which in this passage has the translation ἐκτετιναϲμένων.[51]

Moreover, St. Jerome asserts that Hilary interpreted the phrase "the sons of those shaken off" to mean the Apostles because they were ordered to shake the dust off their feet with reference to those who had not accepted the Gospel.[52] But if anyone should read with some attention Hilary's commentary on the Psalm *Unless the Lord build the house* he will find that the case is somewhat different. For in my opinion Hilary calls those who through their own fault have been rejected by God and have been "shaken off" as accursed because of their stubborn disbelief "the apostles and prophets of those shaken off"—that is, "the sons of the wicked." But his passing mention in two

50. Epistle 34.3. This passage continues the quotation concerning Hilary which Erasmus quoted above. Jerome's letter to Marcella is devoted to explaining certain terms or phrases in Psalm 126, *Nisi Dominus aedificaverit domum* (Unless the Lord build the house), and Jerome refers, as will Erasmus, to Hilary's commentary on it.

51. The passage Erasmus refers to and which Jerome sought to explain in his letter to Marcella is Ps. 126:4, which contains the phrase in the Latin of Hilary's text (as well as of Marcella's) *filii excussorum*. Literally it means "the sons of those shaken off." In the Septuagint the word for *excussorum* is ἐκτετιναϲμένων. Jerome criticizes Hilary's explanation of this enigmatic phrase and indicates how other Greek translators have rendered the original Hebrew expression. Erasmus will discuss this question at some length.

52. Matt. 10:14: "If anyone will not receive you or listen to what you say, then as you leave that house or that town shake the dust of it off your feet."

words of the dust shaken from the feet means not that the Apostles are said to be "shaken off" but that the dust shaken off in the case of the disbelieving Jews signifies that because of their stubborn rejection of the grace of the Gospel they themselves have been "shaken off" for the falsity of their understanding. This he also explains more clearly in his Commentary on Matthew in the words: "And by the sign of the dust shaken off the feet let an everlasting curse be left behind." I might also refer to the words of Hilary himself from the Psalms except that it would be tedious and irksome for the reader, especially in a preface. The fact is, then, that here Jerome either had a lapse of memory or had not read Hilary's commentary with enough attention. Now when Jerome approves the comment of Marcella who wrote that the Apostles were "the sons of those shaking off" rather than "of those shaken off," I for my part do not see what he means, unless perhaps as the Greeks speak of "sons of doctors" for "doctors" so the Apostles were called "the sons of those shaken off" for "the shaken off." Otherwise the successors of the Apostles ought rather to have been called "the sons of those shaken off," if the Apostles are correctly known by the name of "the shaken off." Yet it is not absurd for those who have shaken themselves off to be called "the shaken off," just as those who have washed themselves are called washed and those who have dined are called the dined. For so it is that both the dust has been shaken off and the man or his foot shaken off, as we say something that stains has been spattered on a man and a man has been spattered by something that stains.

It seemed appropriate to touch on these matters in passing not only to defend Hilary, but also to show that at one time the holiest men had no scruples about disagreeing with authors however great, and further that even the greatest men sometimes nod, as did Jerome in this instance in criticizing Hilary. Each man is a friend, but the truth ought to be the greater friend for everyone.[53]

Let us now return to the original point. I would readily believe all the same that Hilary did not have a complete knowledge of Greek literature. For as far as elegance of style is concerned he is more exu-

---

53. This dictum is drawn from Aristotle's *Nicomachean Ethics* 1.6.1096 and was given a wording and usage similar to Erasmus' by Petrarch in *On His Own Ignorance*. See *The Renaissance Philosophy of Man*, edd. Ernst Cassirer et al. (Chicago, 1948), p. 111.

berant in what he writes of and by himself than in what he translates, for his translations are more concise and restrained in thought. I suspect that the cause of this was his practice not to undertake to translate anything unless he was free to use his own discretion in rendering the meaning and to omit or add what he thought proper. This is the safer course for anyone who does not have full command of the language he is translating. Poggio availed himself of the same privilege in translating Diodorus Siculus, Rufinus did the same in almost everything he translated especially in the case of the books of Origen and the history of Eusebius of Caesarea. Even so this is not the liberty of the translator but rather the license which contaminates the writings of another. Hilary, however, never professed to be a translator save in *De Synodis*, any more than did Ambrose who for the most part drew upon the works of Origen in his writings. It is my opinion that as the Greek text presented itself to him he erred when in assigning attributes to each Person of the Trinity he ascribes Eternity to the Father, Image to the Son, and Use to the Holy Spirit.[54] Perhaps he read in Greek τὸ χρῆστον or χρηστότητα which is derived from the Greek ἀπὸ τοῦ χρῆσθαι—that is, "from using." From this εὔχρηστος means friendly and suitable to everyday life, and ἄχρηστος means useless. But χρῆστον or χρηστότης in Greek has to do not with use or utility so much as with goodness, friendliness, agreeableness, or, a frequent translation, kindness. Power is attributed to the Father, Wisdom to the Son, and Goodness to the Holy Spirit. Augustine cites this passage in his *De Trinitate*, going to some trouble in explaining what the term "Use" means.[55]

However this may be, although St. Hilary did not have full command of Greek, it is nevertheless worthwhile to see how carefully he philosophizes about the usage of Greek words in his Commentary on the Psalms, now diligently pointing out their aptness and significance, now seeking the meaning of the Greek not rendered with requisite propriety by the Latin translator, now removing the ambiguity from Latin words with the help of the Greek. And where meanwhile are those who say that Greek literature is of no value in the study of Holy Scripture? Where are those individuals—camels rather than men—

---

54. Erasmus refers here to Hilary's *De Trinitate* 2.1.
55. St. Augustine's *De Trinitate* 6.10.

who bleat that nothing comes out of Greek literature except heresies? And though they keep shouting out these thoughts in public sermons, they are amazed if some persons think that they are in need of a dose of hellebore. Indeed the translation he uses is different from the one which has now been commonly accepted![56] Moreover, since Cyprian has his own translation, as do Augustine and Ambrose, and Hilary, and Tertullian (his is different from all others), it is quite clear that at one time there was no translation which everyone used.[57]

But indeed I am remarkably shameless in keeping the eager reader from perusing the inspired work by so wordy a preface. I shall come to a close, therefore, after I have made this one request of you, most gracious Prelate. I ask that you accept this work of mine, such as it is, dedicated to your name, as a pledge and memorial of my devotion to you. Let others judge what we have done. At least we have made a great effort to place Hilary, that unique light of Gaul, into the hands of men in a considerably more correct and refined form. The publication of his work will have even greater appeal with the addition of your approval, since your influence is foremost in the opinion of all and your sound and sincere judgments are well known to everyone. Your outstanding abilities are one with the abilities of the Carondelet family which in its abundant fruitfulness has given us many besides the distinguished Chancellor of Burgundy.[58] I have known five of them, men of no less cultivation than integrity, loaded with every kind of honor.

You understand therefore what I am seeking. I am of course seeking to gain from the luster of the Carondelet name some favor for Hilary who ought to be held in the highest esteem by all students of theology. For I see that some in view of the new books which are now springing forth from every quarter are disdainful of the ancient authors, and to such an extent that they think that both Origen and Jerome like

56. Erasmus refers somewhat abruptly to the fact that Hilary's Latin text of Scripture differs in its translation of some Greek and Hebrew words from the later Vulgate. The phrase *filii excussorum*, discussed above, is a good example. In the Vulgate text of Psalm 126 the Hebrew in this instance is rendered *filii juventutis*.

57. A passage which now follows in the Latin text (lines 842–88 in Allen) has been omitted. In it Erasmus points out that Hilary used certain Latin words and grammatical forms oddly or incorrectly, and he gives several examples. Since these involve Latin terms, case endings, etc., their translation is not feasible.

58. The Chancellor of Burgundy was Jean de Carondelet's father. He had several sons, five of whom Erasmus knew, as he tells us in the next sentence.

sexagenarians in the proverb must be driven from the bridge.[59] Just
as men of genius in these times who either invent something new or
restore something old should, I think, be above contempt, so it is
characteristic of an inferior mind not to accord to old age the honor
due it and characteristic also of an ungrateful mind to reject those to
whose persevering efforts the Christian world owes so much. For what
could we accomplish now in scriptural studies without the aid of the
works left us by Origen, Tertullian, Chrysostom, Jerome, Hilary, and
Augustine? I do not think that the works of either Thomas or Scotus
should be rejected in their entirety. They wrote for their own age,
and they passed on to us much that was drawn from the books of the
ancient Fathers and examined with some discrimination. But I do not
approve of the rudeness of those who ascribe so much to this kind of
author that they believe they have the obligation to clamor against
good literature happily springing up again everywhere. Diverse are
the gifts of men of genius, and many are the different kinds of ages.
Let each one reveal the scope of his competence, and let no one be
envious of another who in keeping with his own ability and style tries
to make a useful contribution to the education of all. Reverence is the
due of ancient authors, especially those authors who are recommended
by the sanctity of their lives in addition to their learning and eloquence; but this reverence does not exclude a critical reading of them.
Fairness is the due of modern authors so that they may be read without
ill-will, though not without discrimination. Let the absence of furious
contention, the bane of peace and concord, prevail everywhere. And
let the Graces whom the ancients not without good reason conceived
as the companions of the Muses attend upon our studies.

May He without whom there can be no salvation preserve your
Excellency safe for us for a long time, most illustrious Prelate.

Basel
5 January 1523

---

59. The sexagenarians in the proverb are those who because of their age were no
longer permitted to vote in ancient Rome. They were driven back from the bridge
which led to the voting place. Erasmus includes this proverb in his *Adagiorum
chiliades* (No. 437).

BIBLIOGRAPHY

The following list is selective and contains (1) the main source collections of Erasmus' writings, (2) selected works of Erasmus in English translation, (3) recent and/or important books and articles about Erasmus and his times. It is intended both as a guide for further study and as a reference for the notes in this volume. Additional bibliographical information can be found in Vander Haeghen's *Bibliotheca Erasmiana* (Nieuwkoop, 1961; a reprint of the original Ghent edition of 1893). This work is particularly valuable for its listing of all editions of Erasmus' own works and editions. More recent bibliograpies have been compiled by Jean-Claude Margolin: *Douze années de bibliographie érasmienne (1950–1961)* (Paris, 1963), *Quatorze années de bibliographie érasmienne (1936–1949)* (Paris, 1969), and *Neuf années de bibliographie érasmienne (1962–1970)* (Toronto, 1977).

1. SOURCE COLLECTIONS

Erasmi Opera omnia. Ed. Johannes Clericus. 10 vols. Leyden, 1703–1706.
Erasmi Opera omnia. Amsterdam, 1969———. This new edition now in progress will run approximately 30 volumes.
Opus epistolarum Des. Erasmi Roterodami. Edd. P. S. Allen, H. M. Allen, and H. Garrod. 12 vols. Oxford, 1906–1958.
Erasmi opuscula. Ed. W. K. Ferguson. The Hague, 1933.
The Poems of Desiderius Erasmus. Ed. C. Reedijk. Leyden, 1956.
Desiderius Erasmus Roterodamus: Ausgewählte Werke. Ed. Hajo Holborn. Munich, 1933.
Douze lettres d'Erasme. Edd. Roland Crahay and Marie Delcourt. Paris, 1938.

2. ERASMUS IN ENGLISH

The correspondence and major writings of Erasmus are now being translated into English and published in a scholarly edition, *Collected Works of Erasmus*, by the University of Toronto Press. Approximately 80 volumes are planned, the first volume of which appeared in 1974: *The Correspondence of Erasmus. Letters 1 to 141 (1484 to 1500).* Trans. R. A. B. Mynors and D. F. S. Thomson, annotated by Wallace K. Ferguson.

A. *Adagia* (1500 and after):

Phillips, Margaret Mann. *The "Adages" of Erasmus*. Cambridge, 1964. (A study with translations of many of the important adages.)

B. *Enchiridion militis Christiani* (1501):

A Book called in Latin Enchiridion Militis Christiani and in English the Manual of the Christian Knight. London, 1905. (Edition of a 1533 English text attributed to William Tyndale.)
Enchiridion militis Christiani: An English Version. Ed. Anne M. O'Donnell, S.N.D. Oxford, 1981.
The Enchiridion. Trans. and ed. Ford Lewis Battles, in *Advocates of Reform from Wyclif to Erasmus*, ed. Matthew Spinka. (The Library of Christian Classics, Vol. XIV) London, 1953. Pp. 295–379. (Abridged.)
Erasmus, Handbook of the Militant Christian. Trans. John P. Dolan. Notre Dame, 1962. (Abridged.)
The Enchiridion of Erasmus. Trans. Raymond Himelick. Bloomington, 1963.

C. *Moriae encomium* (1509):

The Praise of Folly. Trans. John Wilson (1668), ed. Mrs. P. S. Allen. Oxford, 1913.
The Praise of Folly. Trans. Hoyt Hudson. Princeton, 1941.
The Praise of Folly. Trans. Leonard F. Dean. Chicago, 1946.
The Praise of Folly. Trans. Betty Radice, introd. A. H. T. Levi. Baltimore, 1971.
The Praise of Folly. Trans. Clarence H. Miller. New Haven, 1979.

D. *De utraque verborum ac rerum copia* (1512):

On Copia of Words and Ideas. Trans. D. B. King and H. D. Rix. Milwaukee, 1963.
Also in CWE 24.

E. *Julius exclusus* (1513):

Julius exclusus. Trans. Paul Pascal. Bloomington, 1968.

F. *Institutio principis Christiani* (1516):

The Education of a Christian Prince. Trans. Lester K. Born. New York, 1936.

G. *Querela pacis* (1517):

The Complaint of Peace. Introd. William J. Hirten. New York, 1946. (Facsimile edition of a 1559 English text.)

H. *De libero arbitrio* (1524):

Erasmus–Luther. *Discourse on Free Will.* Trans. and ed. Ernst F. Winter. New York, 1961.
Luther and Erasmus: Free Will and Salvation. Trans. and edd. E. Gordon Rupp et al. (The Library of Christian Classics, Vol. XVII) Philadelphia, 1969.

I. *Ciceronianus* (1528):

Ciceronianus. Trans. Izora Scott. New York, 1908.

J. *De sarcienda ecclesiae concordia* (1533):

Erasmus and the Seamless Coat of Jesus. Trans. Raymond Himelick. Lafayette, 1971.

K. *Familiarium colloquiorum formulae:*

The Colloquies. Trans. Nathan Bailey (1725), ed. E. Johnson. 3 vols. London, 1900.
The Colloquies. Trans. Craig R. Thompson. Chicago, 1965.
Inquisitio de fide, a Colloquy by Desiderius Erasmus Roterodamus. Ed. Craig R. Thompson. (Yale Studies in Religion, No. XV) New Haven, 1950; repr. 1975.

L. Writings on education:

Woodward, W. H. *Desiderius Erasmus concerning the Aim and Method of Education.* Cambridge, 1904; repr. 1964.
Also in CWE 24, 25, and 26.

M. Letters:

The Epistles of Erasmus. Trans. and ed. Francis Morgan Nichols. 3 vols. London, 1901–1918; repr. 1962. (Letters through 1518.)
Erasmus and Cambridge: The Cambridge Letters of Erasmus. Trans. D. F. S. Thomson. Toronto, 1963.
Erasmus and Fisher. Their Correspondence, 1511–1524. Trans. Jean Rouschausse. Paris, 1968.

The Lives of Jehan Vitrier and John Colet. Trans. J. H. Lupton. London,
1883. (Translation of Erasmus' letter to Jodocus Jonas, 13 June 1521.)
"Selection from the Letters of Erasmus." Trans. Barbara Flower, appended
to J. Huizinga, *Erasmus of Rotterdam.* New York, 1952.
Erasmus and His Age: Selected Letters of Desiderius Erasmus. Ed. Hans J.
Hillerbrand, trans. Marcus A. Haworth, S.J. New York, 1970.
And in CWE 1–22.

3. Books and Articles about Erasmus and His Times

Several conferences were held to commemorate the five-hundredth anniversary
of Erasmus' birth, and the papers delivered on these occasions have been published. These volumes afford a comprehensive introduction to recent Erasmus
scholarship and contain a great variety of material:

Colloquium Erasmianum. Mons, 1968.
Scrinium Erasmianum. Ed Joseph Coppens. 2 vols. Leyden, 1969.
Erasmus of Rotterdam. A Quincentennial Symposium. Ed. R. L. DeMolen.
New York, 1971.
Colloquia Erasmiana Turonensia. Ed. J.-C. Margolin. 2 vols. Toronto, 1972.

Attention is also called to the *Erasmus of Rotterdam Society Yearbook,* ed.
Richard L. DeMolen, the first volume of which appeared in 1981.

Adams, R. P. *The Better Part of Valor.* Seattle, 1962.
Allen, P. S. *The Age of Erasmus.* Oxford, 1914.
——. *Erasmus: Lectures and Wayfaring Sketches.* Oxford, 1934.
Bainton, Roland H. *Erasmus of Christendom.* New York, 1969.
Bataillon, M. *Erasme et l'Espagne.* Paris, 1937.
Béné, Charles. *Erasme et Saint Augustin.* Geneva, 1969.
Bentley, Jerry H. *Humanists and Holy Writ.* Princeton, 1983.
Bietenholz, P. G. *History and Biography in the Work of Erasmus of Rotter-
dam.* Geneva, 1966.
Bouyer, Louis. *Erasmus and His Times,* trans. F. X. Murphy. Westminster,
1959.
Boyle, Marjorie O'Rourke. *Erasmus on Language and Method in Theology.*
Toronto, 1977.
——. *Rhetoric and Reform: Erasmus' Civil Dispute with Luther.* Cam-
bridge, 1983.
Chambers, R. W. *Thomas More.* London, 1938.
Chantraine, Georges. *"Mystère" et "Philosophie du Christ" selon Erasme.*
Namur, 1971.
Chomarat, Jacques. *Grammaire et rhétorique chez Erasme.* 2 vols. Paris, 1981.

Coppens, Joseph. *Les Idées réformistes d'Erasme dans les préfaces aux paraphrases du Nouveau Testament.* Louvain, 1961.

Crahay, Roland. "Recherches sur le *Compendium Vitae* attribué à Erasme." *Humanisme et Renaissance,* 6 (1939), 7–19, 135–53.

Drummond, R. B. *Erasmus: His Life and Character.* 2 vols. London, 1873.

Etienne, Jacques. *Spiritualisme érasmien et théologiens louvanistes.* Louvain, 1956.

Febvre, Lucien. *Au Coeur religieux du XVIe siècle.* Paris, 1957.

———. *Le Problème de l'incroyance au XVIe siècle: La religion de Rabelais.* Paris, 1942.

Froude, J. A. *Life and Letters of Erasmus.* New York, 1894.

Gerlo, Alois. *Erasme et ses portraitistes.* Brussels, 1950.

Gilmore, Myron. *Humanists and Jurists.* Cambridge, 1963.

Godin, André. *Erasme lecteur d'Origène.* Geneva, 1982.

Gorce, Denys. "La Patristique dans la réforme d'Erasme," *Festgabe Joseph Lortz.* Baden-Baden, 1958. I 233–76.

Harbison, E. H. *The Christian Scholar in the Age of the Reformation.* New York, 1956.

Hayum, Andrée. "Dürer's Portrait of Erasmus and the *Ars Typographorum.*" *Renaissance Quarterly,* 38 No. 4 (Winter 1985), 650–87.

Holeczek, Heinz. "Die Haltung des Erasmus zu Luther nach dem Scheitern seiner Vermittlungspolitik 1520/21." *Archive for Reformation History,* 64 (1973), 85–112.

Huizinga, J. *Erasmus of Rotterdam,* trans. F. Hopman. New York, 1952.

Hyma, Albert. *The Youth of Erasmus.* Ann Arbor, 1930.

Jarrott, C. A. L. "Erasmus' Biblical Humanism." *Studies in the Renaissance,* 17 (1970), 119–52.

Kaiser, Walter. *Praisers of Folly: Erasmus, Rabelais, Shakespeare.* Cambridge, 1963.

Kohls, E.-W. *Die Theologie des Erasmus.* Basel, 1966.

Kristeller, P. O. "Erasmus from an Italian Perspective." *Renaissance Quarterly,* 23 (1970), 1–14.

Lubac, Henri de. *Exégèse médiévale.* Second Part, II. Paris, 1964.

Mansfield, Bruce. *Phoenix of His Age.* Toronto, 1979.

Margolin, J.-C. *Erasme par lui-même.* Paris, 1965.

———. *Recherches érasmiennes.* Geneva, 1969.

Massaut, J.-P. "Humanisme et spiritualité chez Erasme." *Dictionnaire de spiritualité,* fasc. XLVI–XLVII, 1006–28.

McConica, J. K. *English Humanists and Reformation Politics under Henry VIII and Edward VI.* Oxford, 1965.

Mesnard, Pierre. *L'Essor de la philosophie politique au XVIe siècle.* Paris, 1936.

Oelrich, Karl Heinz. *Der späte Erasmus und die Reformation.* Münster, 1961.

Olin, John C. *Six Essays on Erasmus and a Translation of Erasmus' Letter to Carondelet, 1523*. New York, 1979.

O'Malley, John W. "Erasmus and Luther, Continuity and Discontinuity as Key to Their Conflict." *The Sixteenth Century Journal*, 5 No. 2 (October 1974), 47–65.

Payne, John P. *Erasmus: His Theology of the Sacraments*. Atlanta, 1970.

Phillips, Margaret Mann. *Erasmus and the Northern Renaissance*. London, 1949.

———. "Some Last Words of Erasmus." *Luther, Erasmus, and the Reformation*. New York, 1969.

Rabil, Albert, Jr. *Erasmus and the New Testament: The Mind of a Christian Humanist*. San Antonio, 1972.

Renaudet, A. *Erasme: Sa pensée religieuse, d'après sa correspondance (1518–1521)*. Paris, 1926.

———. *Etudes érasmiennes (1521–1529)*. Paris, 1939.

———. *Erasme et l'Italie*. Geneva, 1954.

———. *Humanisme et Renaissance*. Geneva, 1958.

Reynolds, E. E. *Thomas More and Erasmus*. New York, 1965.

Rogers, Elizabeth Frances (ed.). *St. Thomas More: Selected Letters*. New Haven, 1961.

Rummel, Erika. *Erasmus as a Translator of the Classics*. Toronto, 1985.

Schenk, Wilhelm. "The Erasmian Idea." *The Hibbert Journal*, 48 (1950), 257–65.

Screech, M. A. *Ecstasy and the Praise of Folly*. London, 1980.

Seebohm, Frederic. *The Oxford Reformers*. London, 1869.

Smith, Preserved. *Erasmus*. New York, 1923.

Sowards, J. K. "The Two Lost Years of Erasmus," *Studies in the Renaissance*, 9 (1962), 161–86.

———. *Desiderius Erasmus*. Boston, 1975.

Spitz, Lewis W. *The Religious Renaissance of the German Humanists*. Cambridge, 1963.

Thompson, C. R. "Erasmus and Tudor England." *Actes du Congrès Erasme*. Amsterdam, 1971.

Thompson, Sister Geraldine. *Under Pretext of Praise*. Toronto, 1973.

Tracy, James D. *Erasmus: The Growth of a Mind*. Geneva, 1972.

———. *The Politics of Erasmus*. Toronto, 1977.

Vocht, Henry de. *Monumenta humanistica lovaniensia: Texts and Studies about Louvain Humanists of the First Half of the XVIth Century*. Louvain, 1934.

INDEX NOMINUM